LAST
GREAT
WILDERNESS

LAST
GREAT
WILDERNESS

THE CAMPAIGN TO ESTABLISH
THE ARCTIC NATIONAL
WILDLIFE REFUGE

Roger Kaye

UNIVERSITY OF ALASKA PRESS
FAIRBANKS

© 2006 University of Alaska Press
P.O. Box 756240
Fairbanks, AK 99775-6240
www.uaf.edu/uapress

Publication of *Last Great Wilderness* was supported by a generous grant
from the Alaska Conservation Foundation, Anchorage, Alaska.

Publication of this book was also supported in part by a fund established to honor Thomas
Saunders English in gratitude and respect for his scientific acumen, instructional skills, and
capacity to inspire research and researchers.

Printed in the United States

This publication was printed on paper that meets the minimum
requirements for ANSI/NISO Z39.48–1992 (Permanence of Paper).

This book was printed on paper that was made with 30%
post-consumer content.

Library of Congress Cataloging-in-Publication Data

Kaye, Roger, 1950 Dec. 31–
    Last great wilderness : the campaign to establish the Arctic National
Wildlife Refuge / Roger Kaye.
        p. cm.
    Includes bibliographical references and index.
    ISBN-13: 978-1-889963-83-9 (hardcover : alk. paper)
    ISBN-10: 1-889963-83-6 (hardcover : alk. paper)
            1. Arctic National Wildlife Refuge (Alaska)—History. I. Title.
    QH76.5.A4K39 2006
    333.95'16097987—dc22   2005032845

Text and cover design by Dixon J. Jones, Rasmuson Library Graphics

Cover image by Subhankar Banerjee, *Autumn on the southern taiga, east fork of the Chandalar
River Valley.* All photographs by Subhankar Banerjee are from his book *Arctic National
Wildlife Refuge: Seasons of Life and Land* (Mountaineers Books, 2003).

Photographs by Wilbur Mills are from *Earth and the Great Weather: The Brooks Range*
(Friends of the Earth, 1971), from *Vanishing Arctic: Alaska's National Wildlife Refuge*
(Aperture, 1988), and from his personal collection.

Artwork by Olaus Murie on pages 25 and 226 is from *Two in the Far North*, by Margaret
Murie © 1978; used with the permission of Alaska Northwest Books,® an imprint of Graphic
Arts Center Publishing Company.

Contents

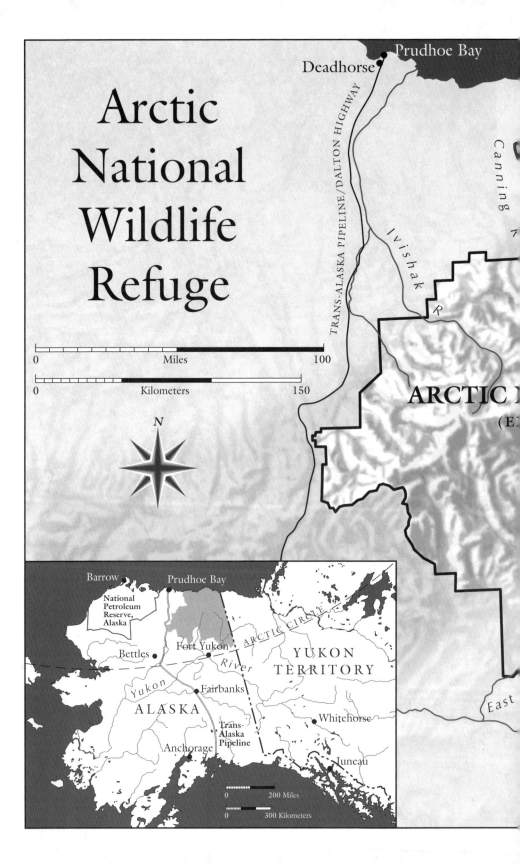

Arctic
National
Wildlife
Refuge

0   Miles   100

0   Kilometers   150

N

Prudhoe Bay

Deadhorse

TRANS-ALASKA PIPELINE/DALTON HIGHWAY

Canning R

Ivishak

R

ARCTIC

(E

East

Barrow

Prudhoe Bay

National Petroleum Reserve, Alaska

Bettles

Fort Yukon

ARCTIC CIRCLE

YUKON TERRITORY

River

Yukon

Fairbanks

ALASKA

Trans-Alaska Pipeline

Whitehorse

Anchorage

Juneau

0   200 Miles

0   300 Kilometers

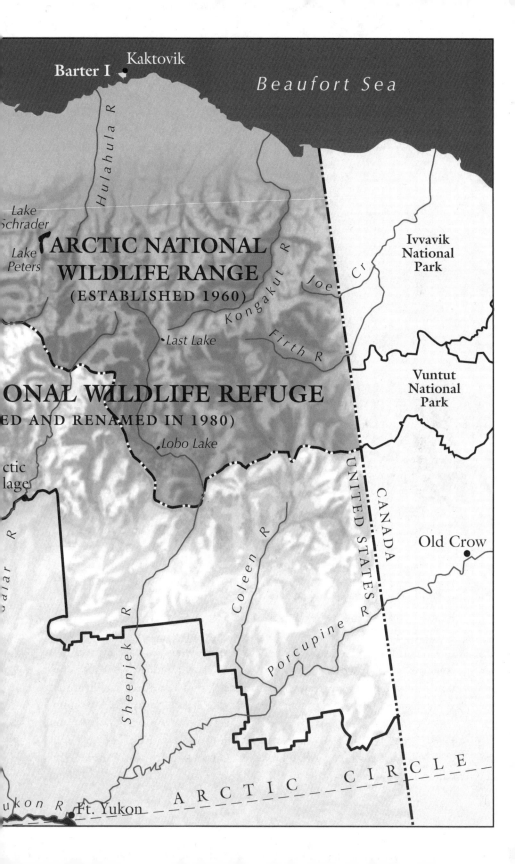

Barter I   Kaktovik

Beaufort Sea

Hulahula R

Lake
Schrader

Lake
Peters

ARCTIC NATIONAL
WILDLIFE RANGE
(ESTABLISHED 1960)

Kongakut R

Joe   *Cr*

Ivvavik
National
Park

Last Lake

Firth R

ONAL WILDLIFE REFUGE
ED AND RENAMED IN 1980)

Vuntut
National
Park

Lobo Lake

ctic
lage

UNITED STATES   CANADA

Old Crow

Coleen R

dar R

Sheenjek R

Porcupine R

A R C T I C   C I R C L E

ukon R Ft. Yukon

Acknowledgments

This story owes much to many people. My greatest debt is to the campaign participants who shared their remembrances. Most granted multiple interviews, reaching back a half-century to recount things thought, said, and done. They include Stewart Brandborg, George Collins, Mercedes Eicholz, Charles Gray, Keith Herrington, Celia Hunter, Anore Jones, Brina Kessel, Jim King, David Klein, Robert Krear, Margaret Murie, William Pruitt, Wenzel Raith, Robert and Reggie Rausch, George Schaller, John Thomson, Ivan Thorall, Margaret Tritt, Peter Tritt, and Virginia Wood.

Other informants who provided valuable insights were William Bacon III, Michael Carey, Richard Carroll, Joshua Collins, Chuck Clusen, Cathy Stone Douglas, Keith Echelmeyer, Simon Francis, Morva Hoover, Sandy Jamieson, Frank Keim, Luna Leopold, Fran Mauer, Michael McCloskey, Debbie Miller, Donald Murie, Martin Murie, Robert R. Olson, Sigurd Olson Jr., Jim Rearden, Bill Reffalt, Moses Sam, Donald Seaton, Ted Swem, Averill Thayer, Ray Trembly, and Joe Vogler.

I am indebted to scholars of various disciplines for their critical and constructive reviews of the manuscript, especially political scientists James Gladden and Tom Morehouse; psychologist Judith Kleinfled; oral historian William Schneider; environmental historians Roderick Nash, Dan Philippon, and Kevin Marsh; natural resource management professors Susan Todd and Harry Bader; wildlife refuge system historian Bill Reffalt; arctic biologist Fran Mauer; wilderness writers Kevin Proescholdt and Terry Tempest Williams; and editor and wilderness historian Ed Zahniser. Other authorities who helped with various sections include historians Claus-M. Naske and Richard West Sellars, and reporter Michael Carey.

For invaluable assistance in helping unearth historical materials and track down elusive documents, I am indebted to the skilled archivists at the Archives at the University of Alaska Fairbanks; the National Archives; the Bancroft Library, Berkeley; the Denver Public Library; the Minnesota Historical Society; the Dwight D. Eisenhower Library; and the Wildlife Conservation Society Archives. And I would be remiss to not mention the countless people, many unknown, who, foreseeing the importance of the story, saved the notes, memos, and personal correspondence that contributed so much to it.

Many contributed photos and I am especially grateful to the professional landscape photographers Wilbur Mills, Subhankar Banerjee, Roy Corral, and Douglas Yates for generously contributing their images. Thanks also to the Murie Center in Moose, Wyoming, for providing historic photos and documents.

A special thanks to my patient editor, Erica Hill, at the University of Alaska Press whose eye for detail and skill in cutting extraneous material and smoothing out the text's rough spots is reflected in each page. Thanks also to Dixon Jones who drafted the map and designed the cover and interior text.

Thanks to daughters Lolly, Polly, and Alice and wife Masako for their usually patient acceptance of "dad's obsession." Finally, this book is dedicated to the modest gentleman who launched the Arctic campaign, and stimulated, informed, and encouraged this documentation of it: George L. Collins.

Introduction

It is inevitable, if we are to progress as people in the highest sense, that we shall become ever more concerned with the saving of the intangible resources, as embodied in this move to establish the Arctic Wildlife Range.

—Olaus Murie[1]

In 1953 a feature article appeared in the journal of the Sierra Club extolling wilderness qualities and experiences that two scientists found in a remote corner of the territory of Alaska. "Northeast Arctic: The Last Great Wilderness" began the transformation of this little-known expanse of mountains, forest, and tundra into a symbolic landscape internationally recognized as one of the finest examples of wilderness—the Arctic National Wildlife Refuge.[2]

The authors, National Park Service senior planner George Collins and biologist Lowell Sumner, were soon joined by Wilderness Society president Olaus Murie and his wife, Margaret, in an effort to secure the area's permanent

◄ FIGURE 1. Mancha Creek near its confluence with the Firth River. *Photo by Subhankar Banerjee.*

xi

preservation. This core group engaged the national conservation organizations and recruited many of the era's leading conservationists, including biologists Starker Leopold, Frank F. Darling, Sigurd Olson, and Stewart Brandborg; Wilderness Act author Howard Zahniser; Conservation Foundation president Fairfield Osborn; and Supreme Court Justice William O. Douglas. The activism of these and the thousands who joined them in the long and hard-fought campaign resulted in the initial establishment of the Arctic Refuge (as a wildlife range) in 1960.

While looking through the early records several years ago, it struck me that few of those who wrote, spoke, and testified for the area's preservation had any notion of journeying to its remote expanses. Then, as now, only a small number of its defenders planned to backpack, camp, hunt, or raft within it, or even catch a firsthand glimpse of its scenery and wildlife.

What, then, was their motivation? What ideas expressed in the early proponents' writings and images connected so many people to this northeast corner of Alaska? What possibilities for its future captured their imagination and galvanized the support necessary to overcome powerful opposition and establish what is now the Arctic National Wildlife Refuge? For a nation engrossed in the postwar boom of the 1950s, what could preservation of this faraway place have represented?

These questions led to a more focused examination of the many articles, reports, news clippings, and press releases documenting the controversial campaign, and then to the 572 pages of Senate and House hearing transcripts it generated. Interest grew as the materials revealed the hope and idealism that pervaded the struggle. The search widened, and as confidential memos, yellowed letters, and personal journals were uncovered, a story of vision, dedication, strategy, angst, and compromise began to unfold. Interviews with dozens who had been involved in the preservation effort, both for and against, others who had watched from the sidelines, and children of proponents and opponents who had since died added to what became a voluminous collection of source material describing the seven-year conflict.[3] These sources revealed that for proponents, this area embodied a diverse range of values. Ultimately, it was an interwoven set of tangible and intangible values—cultural, spiritual, and symbolic as well as wildlife, ecological, and recreational values—that underpinned the campaign to protect the area, with some designation, as an archetypal wilderness.

Like the "once-upon-a-time land" one science writer compared it to, this distant, little-known expanse evoked varied images, imaginings, and possibilities among its enthusiasts.[4] Initially, a wildlife range was not among them.

Protecting wildlife was important to all proponents, but not a singular motivation. In the mind's eye of most, this was to be some kind of gigantic wilderness park. Campaign writings and testimonies reveal the influence of the transcendental and romantic literature associated with national parks, and a park, many felt, would be best suited to provide the historic, adventurous, and inspirational experiences that this literature described. Proponents often pointed to Yellowstone as a precedent, though in citing its developments and domestication they also used the park as an example of what should be avoided. A few of the more scientifically oriented proponents conceived of the area as a repository of uninterrupted ecological and evolutionary processes, a vast natural laboratory where scientists could come to learn how nature works when left alone.

Partisans on both sides of the controversy shared an image of the area as the edge of America's last frontier, though they disagreed on which aspects of the rapidly developing nation's heritage ought to be perpetuated in the region. For opponents of preservation, it was the freedom to pioneer new lands and develop their resources to feed the march of progress that had recently made America the world's industrial and economic leader. Proponents were more concerned that perpetuating the nation's distinctive cultural heritage was dependent upon maintaining its eroding natural heritage. They thought that this corner of northeast Alaska might become something of a living museum, preserving the rugged frontier that had shaped America's character and identity.

Although the wilderness preservation movement had a small following in the early and mid-1950s, the wilderness concept had expanded to encompass the spectrum of values proponents saw in this area. Although legislation that would codify the concept and enable it to become the statutory purpose of federal lands was barely on the horizon, those who initiated the campaign and most who participated in it envisioned northeast Alaska as a potential "wilderness area."

But for many proponents the campaign had a significance that went beyond securing a designation that would preserve this particular place and its wildness. To varying degrees, they saw the Arctic question as one manifestation of a broader, more pressing issue—how to respond to the postwar march of progress that was transforming the nation and, some feared, changing the planet, jeopardizing the right of future generations to inherit healthy land and clean air and water.

Thus, to understand proponents' motives and actions we need to keep in mind that they occurred in the context of the postwar boom, the most rapid economic, industrial, and technological expansion in history. The dominant political institutions were firmly committed to developing resources to fuel the rapidly rising standard of living, and Americans were excited by the commodities, conveniences, and opportunities brought by the new order. But many were growing concerned, some even fearful, of the environmental ramifications. In response, the conservation movement gained momentum, became more broadly based, and, of particular consequence to the Arctic campaign, began undergoing a gradual change in focus.

Many advocates of the reserve, particularly hunters, were more traditional conservationists, motivated by a narrower range of benefits they thought it would provide. They were less concerned with the broader implications of the conflict's outcome. But clearly, for the campaign leaders who rallied them, the issue transcended the boundary lines drawn around this corner of northeast Alaska. For them, the struggle over this distant place was emblematic of the larger contest between competing views of the appropriate relationship between postwar American society and its changing environment. Which notion of progress should this landscape represent—that underlying the prevailing rush toward attaining an ever-higher standard of living, or that underpinning the emerging ecology-based perspective that emphasized sustainability and called for restraint?

I began to realize the campaign's symbolic significance when I found a desperate letter Olaus Murie had written to Alaska U.S. Senator Bob Bartlett in the fall of 1959, the year that the territory of Alaska was admitted to the union. Bartlett, the effort's most powerful opponent, kept establishing legislation locked up in his committee and prevented consideration of it by the full Senate. Time was running out, and with little to lose Murie disclosed to Bartlett an ulterior motive of campaign leaders. "This is a bigger question than some have assumed," he admitted to the new state's champion of unfettered growth and development. "It involves the real problem of what the human species is to do with this earth."[5]

The controversy over preserving this area was multifaceted and not, as suggested by many popular accounts, simply a clash between development and conservation interests or a conflict between potential uses and users of the area. Unlike the concurrent fight against a dam proposed within the Dinosaur National Monument along the Utah-Colorado border, there was no specific, catalyzing threat to this area of northeast Alaska. The "enemy" here was not a developer, a construction project, or an exploitative agency, but a more pervasive force. Those who fought the Arctic proposal were not "bad guys"; I came to realize that they too were compelled by a positive vision for Alaska's future. Though less sustainable, their hope was rooted in the popular, patriotic American dream of unbounded prosperity. Further complicating this history is the fact that debate as to what the area should represent, what uses should be allowed, and how it should be titled played out among proponents as well as between them and opponents.

Last Great Wilderness is the story of the beliefs and values, the ideas and idealism, and the hopes and concerns for the future that inspired the leaders of the campaign and many of their followers. It is also an account of how, by focusing on the pragmatic and most widely accepted benefits of protecting natural areas, the leaders were able to attract an increasing number of con-servationists and galvanize the broad public support necessary to overcome powerful opposition. But readers should not anticipate an unclouded account of victorious conservationists and the triumph of wilderness values. I found ambiguity, manipulation, and veiled motives on both sides, and a final com-promise that even today neither side cares to acknowledge.

As a political history, this study examines the actions of key proponents and opponents and the sequence of events that finally brought the Secretary of the Interior to issue the controversial order establishing the Arctic National Wildlife Range. But its focus is not on who was instrumental or what they said and did, but rather on why. As important as the content of the partisans' philosophies is the context of their time. As it explores the refuge's intellectual and cultural origins, this book examines the varied motives of key players, the social milieu in which they acted, and the historical forces that shaped their perspectives.

But there is much more to be learned from the conflict than how the Arctic National Wildlife Refuge came to be. As it traces the beginnings of a landmark conservation unit of unprecedented size and purpose, the story that unfolds chronicles the evolution of the wilderness concept during a pivotal period of American environmental history. In fact, many of those who drafted, pro-moted, and lobbied for legislation that would enshrine that concept in federal law were, at the same time, leading the Arctic campaign. While a wildlife range was something less than they originally had hoped for, its hard-won establishment in 1960 was a victory that encouraged them and thousands of others who were working to secure passage of what became the Wilderness Act of 1964.

Although its subject is the past, this history, like any history, is written to serve the future. Through providing a contextual understanding of why and how those of the previous generation came to establish what is now the Arctic Refuge, I hope this book will enhance appreciation of the tangible and intangible functions that this unique landscape continues to serve, for the benefit of those who will visit, and for the millions more whom the proponents knew would find satisfaction and inspiration in just knowing that it exists.[6]

The Arctic controversy also has relevance far beyond its location and time. The debate transformed this obscure place into a point of reference for environmental issues that transcend its boundaries and continue today. The story of those who gave this landscape definition helps illustrate how and why people set places apart to embody their ideals. It serves as a case study of the human propensity, found across cultures and throughout history, to imbue places with ideological significance. The story of the Arctic Refuge's origin lends insight into a unique characteristic of our symbol-making species, the capacity to become deeply attached to a place with which we have no direct experience.

A Note on Perspective

I suspect the seed for this project was planted in 1974 when I came to Alaska to work at Camp Denali, a wilderness lodge located at the western edge of Mount McKinley National Park and run by early conservation leaders and Arctic Range advocates Virginia Wood and Celia Hunter. Soon thereafter, I discovered Robert Marshall's wilderness books and these led me to the writings of Aldo Leopold and Olaus and Margaret Murie. Looking back, I can see how their ideas influenced my first experience of the Arctic Refuge during a sheep-hunting trip three years later. Shortly after, I began a career with the U.S. Fish and Wildlife Service and in 1985 transferred to the Arctic Refuge, where I now work as a wilderness specialist and pilot. Over the years, interaction with visiting recreationists, hunters, and resident subsistence users, as well as reading the comments and testimonies of many concerned nonvisitors, expanded my thinking about the varied purposes and publics that this area serves. Involvement in innumerable management issues, planning processes, and the controversy over oil development versus wilderness led me to believe that the history of the refuge's creation offers perspectives that should be considered in making decisions for its future.

However, I need to make clear that although I am employed by the U.S. Fish and Wildlife Service, writing this book was an independent, late-night endeavor; it was not supported, reviewed, or approved by the agency. In light of the current administration's positions on the Arctic Refuge and wilderness, I must emphasize that nothing in this book has official sanction and nothing herein should be construed as representing agency policy.

Interpreting and finding meaning in the past necessarily involves a degree of subjectivity. The process of searching for and then weighing the significance of various sources and secondary materials, interviewing people, synthesizing recurring expressions of meaning into a coherent set of values, placing them in historical context, and selecting representative statements to paraphrase or quote is unavoidably influenced by one's perspective. Like anyone inclined to undertake such an investigation, I have a strong interest in the matters it concerns, in this case the Arctic Refuge and wilderness. So I will state at the outset that my sympathies began and remain with the perspectives of those who led the campaign. That said, I have striven to write an environmental history that correctly reports what proponents and opponents said and did, fairly represents their perspectives, and accurately places their motives and actions in the context of their time.[7] Only to the extent that this study meets these standards of historiography will it serve its purposes.

Founding Versus Statutory Purposes

So as to not disappoint some readers in the final chapter, I'll state now that only three of the values that motivated those who initiated and supported the effort to preserve the Arctic Range and that are detailed herein came to be explicitly stated in the range's establishing order and formalized in ensuing regulations and policy.

As the campaign to establish a Last Great Wilderness progressed, mounting opposition by the mining industry, territorial politicians, and other interests necessitated changes in the advocates' approach. Political realities required that greater emphasis be placed on protecting tangible resources and less on the effort's initial idealism. Advocacy shifted from creating a wilderness area to establishing a less restrictive wildlife range. This change in strategy is reflected in then–Interior Department solicitor Theodore (Ted) Stevens's acknowledgment to a Senate subcommittee that

> when we originally started talking about this area, we were not talking about a range. We were not talking about a refuge. We were talking about a wilderness area, which would have been absolutely sacrosanct.[8]

Despite the compromise, Alaska's senators blocked proposed legislation. An Arctic National Wildlife Range was later established by a secretarial order that gave the area this brief statutory purpose: "For the purpose of preserving unique wildlife, wilderness, and recreational values."[9] But in spite of the shift, the order mandated "preserving . . . values"—wording at variance with the "conservation of resources" purpose found in the legislation and executive orders establishing previous wildlife ranges and refuges.

Nevertheless, most of the cultural, spiritual, ecological, and symbolic values that proponents forwarded as purposes for establishing the range are not its official purposes, except to the extent that they interpret and clarify the secretarial order's three broad values of wildlife, wilderness, and recreation. Since the area was not established legislatively, it lacks any formal legislative history that might have identified the importance of the other values.

The management approach adopted by the agency finally selected to administer the area, the U.S. Fish and Wildlife Service,[10] reflects this shift in emphasis from ideals to more utilitarian resource conservation. Prior to establishment, acting Alaska regional director Urban Nelson described the campaign as "fighting for ideals." He hoped the effort would "preserve a wilderness area with the showing of only God's workings, free from the blemish of man."[11] But a year after establishment, he told a gathering of scientists, including Olaus Murie, that the agency's management approach would diverge from the campaign's original focus on wilderness values. Poignantly, his speech concluded:

> I'm sorry Olaus, the Bureau can't take care of your interests completely since there are other interests. . . . [T]hat's why the Range is established as it is today. It is not purely wilderness area, it is not a game sanctuary, it is a composite of the interests that are involved.[12]

Although perpetuation of all those recurrent founding values was not specifically mandated by the establishing order, all are consistent with, if not inherent in, the area's purposes of preserving wildlife, wilderness, and recreational values. Historic insight provides a contextual interpretation of these broad statutory purposes. It supports the proposition that administration of the area in a way that will perpetuate all the founding values is, where not mandated, at least within the agency's discretionary authority. The full set of meanings that inspired the establishment of the Arctic Refuge, properly understood, could continue to serve in its stewardship. Whether or not they should, I leave to the reader.

Chronological description of the effort to establish what became the Arctic Wildlife Range, expanded and redesignated as the Arctic National Wildlife Refuge in 1980,[13] is complicated by the fact that throughout the campaign, the various proponents referred to the area using a variety of potential titles and classifications. Indeed, the question of what designation (in this pre–Wilderness Act era) might both protect proponents' various focal values and be politically feasible was a recurring issue among supporters throughout most of the effort. All the early proposals referred to some form of Arctic wilderness—either a wilderness "preserve," "reserve," "research area," "sanctuary," "park," "international park," or the original "Last Great Wilderness." Common to all but the last referent was the word "Arctic." To avoid confusion, references to the area or the effort that were not specific to a particular proposal or endorsement will be referred to as the "Arctic proposal" and the "Arctic campaign," respectively.

1

Genesis of the Campaign

Perhaps we should give thought to our ancestors and feel

humbly grateful for the beginnings of thoughtful regard

and enjoyment for our land.

—Olaus Murie[1]

If there is a single event that could be considered the genesis of the Arctic Refuge, it is the publication of Bob Marshall's audacious proposal for a permanent wilderness frontier encompassing nearly all of Arctic Alaska. In 1937, the Forest Service had assigned Marshall, a forester, writer, and wilderness movement leader, to a multiagency committee directed by Congress to formulate a plan for developing the territory's resources. His responsibility for *Alaska: Its Resources and Development* (1938) was limited to making recommendations regarding recreation and tourism. But three trips to the Central Brooks Range in northern Alaska inspired the crusader to go far beyond his charge. After arguing that "in Alaska alone can the emotional

---

◄ FIGURE 2. Field of cottongrass, East Fork Chandalar River, July 1956. *Photo by George B. Schaller.*

values of the frontier be preserved," Marshall proposed that the nation "keep northern Alaska largely a wilderness."[2]

As environmental historian Roderick Nash has noted, Marshall's proposal was "the first direct and specific call for preserving wilderness in Alaska."[3] In fact, never before had wilderness—or any conservation designation—been seriously proposed on such a vast scale. Predictably, Marshall's idea stimulated angry charges of "federal lockup" and "stranglehold on progress"—rhetoric that would be aimed at the proponents of preserving northeast Alaska and subsequent wilderness initiatives for decades to come.[4] Olaus Murie, who would later come to lead the campaign to preserve northeast Alaska, was probably not the only wilderness advocate who, at the time, felt his idealist friend's proposal was politically unwise. He believed that such a grandiose goal would be impossible to attain; the controversy it generated, he felt, would only provoke needless criticism of more realistic preservation efforts.

But years later, during the campaign to establish what became the Arctic National Wildlife Range, Murie came to realize that Marshall's stimulating idea had served to precondition conservationists to imagine landscape preservation in Alaska on a vast, ecosystem-wide scale. Perhaps it was supporters' reference to Marshall's proposal that brought Murie to understand that it had opened minds and expanded thinking about the unique opportunity that Arctic Alaska offered.[5] Regardless of how improbable, Marshall's idea of a huge wilderness preserve was in the air when, in the early 1950s, two visionary Park Service employees launched a campaign for a Last Great Wilderness.

An Archetypal Wilderness

George L. Collins and Lowell Sumner's vision is now the 19.3-million-acre Arctic Refuge. The size of South Carolina, nearly nine Yellowstone parks could fit within its boundaries. It is located in, or more precisely, it *is* the northeast corner of Alaska. And it is remote. Fairbanks, the nearest city and jump-off point for most refuge trips, is 150 miles south. No roads penetrate the refuge boundaries, nor are there trails, save those of wildlife. Access is by small aircraft, by river, or, for the more adventurous, by foot. The refuge is bounded and protected to the south by the expansive boreal forest and wetlands of the Yukon Flats National Wildlife Refuge. Two hundred miles north of its southernmost point, the refuge meets the Arctic Ocean. Canada's Yukon Territory forms the eastern boundary; its Ivvavik and Vuntut National Parks are adjacent to the refuge and assure that the international boundary does not also function as an ecological boundary. Two hundred forty miles to the west, the refuge extends to within a half mile of the Dalton Highway, which leads to the Prudhoe Bay oil fields.

The Arctic Refuge spans five subarctic and arctic ecological zones, encompassing a range of physiographic and ecological diversity unparalleled by any other protected circumpolar area. The southernmost boreal forest zone is a mosaic of spruce, broadleaf forest, and riverine communities dotted with lakes. The boreal forest merges into rolling taiga uplands where spruce becomes increasingly sparse and old with elevation. This foothill zone rises to the Brooks Range, a rugged extension of the Rocky Mountains and a continuation of the Continental Divide. Peaks from six thousand to nine thousand feet in elevation, scattered with ice caps and alpine glaciers and cut by broad valleys and narrow gorges, compose this seventy-mile-wide core of the refuge.

The north face of the Brooks Range drops abruptly onto the rolling plains of the arctic foothills zone, then transitions into the coastal plain. A level expanse of low shrubs, sedges, grasses, and mosses, this "arctic prairie," as proponents called it, is interspersed with shallow lakes and ponds. At the Beaufort Sea, the plain becomes a varied and irregular 140-mile boundary of bluffs, salt marshes, estuaries, lagoons, barrier island beaches, and the wide deltas of several rivers.

The diverse fauna of these ecological zones includes forty-five species of land and marine mammals, ranging from the pigmy shrew to the bowhead whale. The best-known species include polar, grizzly, and black bears, the wolf, wolverine, Dall sheep, moose, musk ox, and the animal that came to symbolize the area's wildness and ecological integrity: the caribou. Thirty-six species of fish occur in refuge waters, and more than 150 species of birds inhabit the refuge for at least some portion of their life cycles.

Slightly more than seven million acres of the refuge are designated "wilderness," and three rivers, the Sheenjek, Wind, and Ivishak, are designated "wild rivers." Because of distinctive geologic, paleontological, and scenic features, several rivers, valleys, canyons, lakes, and a rock mesa have been recommended as national natural landmarks. In recognition of their unique scientific value, two areas have been designated as research natural areas.

The distinguishing ecological aspect of the Arctic Refuge—and a major reason for its establishment—is that this single protected area encompasses an unbroken continuum of arctic and subarctic ecosystems, their unaltered landforms, and the full complement of their native life forms, with the exception of one bird, the extirpated Eskimo curlew. But the most unique feature of the refuge is an unseen presence. Natural processes—large-scale ecological and evolutionary processes—continue here, free of the human intention to control or manipulate. Perhaps more than anywhere else on U.S. soil, this area is sufficiently large, intact, and protected to exemplify the condition that, soon after its establishment, became the statutory definition of wilderness: an area "where the earth and its community of life are untrammeled by man."[6]

The Postwar Context, 1945–1960

One August afternoon a few years ago, I sat on the floor of the mountain-lined Jago River valley and listened to geophysicist Keith Echelmeyer explain the interacting processes that formed the Brooks Range. As the refuge pilot, I had flown the professor and his two research assistants in to resume studies on McCall Glacier, a benchmark site for the study of global climate change. Before beginning the arduous climb to their study area, Echelmeyer sat down to give his associates a short lecture on the natural processes that formed our surroundings. The dynamic processes that shaped the environment he was studying provide a metaphor for understanding how historical, cultural, and social forces shaped the perceptual landscape I was exploring.

Beginning in antiquity, Echelmeyer described the sedimentation processes that formed the Paleozoic seabed that lay beneath us. His geologic history progressed through dramatic collisions of tectonic plates; a series of upthrusts and subsidences; the bending, folding, faulting, and fracturing of rock layers; the glacial carvings of five ice ages; the freeze-thaw cycles of millions of seasons; and the erosion and deposition caused by the forces of wind, water, and pioneering plants.[7]

Just as those ancient and continuing processes interact to shape *what* is seen here, continuing historical and cultural forces interact to shape *how* it is seen. Just as dramatic as those physical forces were the revolutions in thinking that unfolded, merged, and sometimes collided, resulting in layers of thought about nature and humans' relationship to it that a group of Americans in the 1950s drew upon to interpret the value of this place and give it meaning.

Indeed, as Murie's introductory statement reminds us, the evolution in thinking that underpins the Arctic campaign began over ten thousand years ago with the Neolithic Revolution, when the emerging distinction between areas humans were beginning to dominate through agriculture, and those governed by natural processes, gave rise to the campaign's underlying concept: wildness.

The concept passed through Samarian, Egyptian, Greek, and Roman philosophy; Jewish and Christian theology; the Renaissance; the Reformation; the Enlightenment; romanticism; and the Scientific and Industrial Revolutions.

For this fascinating background of the wilderness concept's old-world roots, the treatments of historians Clarence Glacken, Max Oelschlaeger, and Roderick Nash provide great detail.[8] Here we shall simply list the main developments in America that contributed to the wilderness movement, the wellspring of the Arctic campaign:

- a growing body of reflective writings exploring the connection between human nature and wild nature;
- a demographic shift from country to urban living, the development of scenic tourism, and a rising awareness of deforestation and other impacts on the environment;
- a concern for the vanishing frontier associated with American identity and character;
- the rapid expansion of scientific findings and technological developments;
- an increased antimodernist sentiment;
- a growing concern among hunters about decreasing game populations and the changing hunting tradition;
- an interest in natural areas as settings for adventure and catharsis, brought to Alaska by Bob Marshall;
- the formation of organizations to promote recreational interests and conservation;
- the emergence of conservation as an element of national policy and the consequent establishment of national forest, park, and wildlife refuge systems;
- and, in the development of management philosophies for those systems, an emerging conflict between utilitarian conservation and nature preservation.

The immediate social context of the 1951–1960 Arctic campaign was what historian of this era Samuel Hayes describes as the post–World War II transformation of American society. More than in any previous period of history, postwar America was receptive to the idea of setting an area aside for a unique combination of tangible purposes and intangible values.

The prosperous postwar period brought unprecedented social, economic, and technological change and, consequently, environmental alteration. Natural areas were rapidly being converted to residential, commercial, industrial, and resource-extractive uses. A booming economy and rising income brought the world's highest standard of living, and its highest rate of consumption. A baby boom stimulated concern among some that the expanding population might outstrip the nation's supply of natural resources. Higher educational levels and a growing public health movement heightened awareness of worsening air and water pollution, as well as other environmental degradations. The awful power and after-effects of the atomic bomb contributed to doubts about the nation's technological imperative—its tendency to adopt new technologies with insufficient consideration of their potential consequences. Such factors led many to question previous assumptions about what constituted a better life. "Quality of life" became a significant social and political issue during this era, and many people were coming to realize that a quality life depended in large part on a quality environment.[9]

At the same time, concerns similar to those underlying the growing historic preservation movement were being expressed, specifically about the need to preserve remnants of the nation's natural heritage before they were lost to "progress." Although reaction to these concerns probably never represented more than a countercurrent within mainstream society, among educated Americans there was a clear trend toward greater consideration of the environmental ramifications of the era's virtually unbridled progress.

Concurrently, a growing desire to escape the city—made possible by increasing income, leisure time, and automobile ownership—brought record numbers of vacationers along the expanding interstate highway system to parks and forests. As Alaskan economist Richard Cooley would testify at an Arctic Range Senate hearing, "Since World War II the demands of the American people for outdoor recreation have multiplied at an astonishing rate."[10] This trend heightened public support for natural areas as sources of recreation, relief, and inspiration.

Predictions about future needs for recreation lands furthered support for preservation efforts. Cooley and other proponents cited findings of the national study "The Crisis in Outdoor Recreation" (1959), which suggested that by the year 2000 demand for recreation lands would increase by a factor of ten. Moreover, demand for lands of high scenic, wildlife, and wilderness value—which, Cooley noted, included the Arctic proposal—were predicted to increase by a factor of forty.

Concern about the impacts associated with the observed and projected escalation of recreational use increased public receptivity to the idea of preserving some of the remaining wildlands in their natural state. Cooley touched on a growing concern among postwar preservationists when he cited the study's suggestion that overuse could ruin the landscape's vulnerable "capacity to provide intellectual and emotional experience."[11]

In response to growing concern about environmental degradation and the increased demand for outdoor recreation, membership in the leading conservation organizations—all of which would support the Arctic campaign—increased dramatically in the fifteen years following the end of World War II. Further, the range of issues that concerned them expanded in proportion to their growth.

Dominating the conservation movement prior to the campaign were the Izaak Walton League of America and the National Wildlife Federation. Their primary interests were in protecting opportunities for hunting and fishing and they came to support wilderness largely as a means of assuring opportunities for enjoying these activities in a primitive setting. The Audubon Society began to broaden its conservation interests in the late 1940s, and by the early 1950s its advocacy for bird protection was drawing upon the ecological values being incorporated into the fledgling wilderness movement.

Among the most influential organizations to fight for the Arctic proposal was the California-based Sierra Club. In 1945 it had just four thousand members largely concerned with protecting and facilitating backcountry recreation in their region. By 1960, its more widespread sixteen thousand members were defending wild areas across the nation, taking on issues such as pollution and population and, increasingly, arguing for the maintenance of ecological integrity. The Club's biennial wilderness conferences, begun in 1949, became primary venues for publicizing preservation efforts, including the Arctic campaign. Conference agendas serve as an index of how the wilderness concept evolved and grew in importance through the 1950s.

Soon to lead the effort, the Wilderness Society's membership increased more than tenfold from the war's end to the conclusion of the campaign, totaling almost seventeen thousand in December 1960.[12] Unlike the other organizations, the society had, since its inception in 1935, advocated for wilderness on ecological grounds as well as for recreational, therapeutic, and aesthetic purposes. Its founding platform recognized the value of wilderness for recreation, as a "mental resource," and as a living museum of "primeval" natural processes. "It is manifestly the duty of this generation to preserve under scientific care," it stated, "as many, as large, and as varied examples of the remaining primitive as possible."[13] Although anthropocentric arguments would dominate the Wilderness Society's advocacy, ecological reasons for preserving wilderness were actually more important to the leaders who spearheaded the Arctic campaign.

Wilderness and the Emerging Environmental Perspective

By the beginning of the Arctic campaign, postwar advances in the natural sciences converged with concerns about the changing landscape to bring about the emergence of an ecologically based "environmental" perspective. Whereas the dominant utilitarian conservation-of-resources paradigm was commodity-oriented and focused on the efficient use and continued production of resources, this antecedent to today's environmentalism emphasized the ecological system, or as some would phrase it, the community of life of which humans are members. Underpinning this perspective was the notion that our species, like all others, must live within ecological constraints.

The concept of ecology, it should be noted, was not new, at least to biologists. The word was coined in 1866 by the German Ernst Haeckel, who defined it as

> the investigation of the total relations of the animal both to its inorganic and to its organic environment...in a word, ecology is the study of all those complex interrelations referred to by Darwin as the conditions of the struggle for existence.[14]

During the postwar boom "ecology" became more broadly known to the public. Most of those who were attentive to the concept conceived of it less as a field of scientific investigation following disciplined methods of study than as a new means of arguing for protecting nature from the adverse effects of industrialization. While they found appealing the principle of the interrelatedness of all life, including humans, many overlooked the evolutionary implications of ecology.

Thus, popular ecological thinking during the campaign years can be summarized as a generally scientifically informed point of view of nature's function and a concern for how modern developments were adversely affecting that function. Throughout the period, the language of ecology would be employed to counter threats, such as pollution, which directly affected the quality of human life, and to oppose actions such as predator control more related to the welfare of other species.

More holistic than conservation, the emerging environmental perspective recognized a wider range of values that landscapes could hold, both tangible and intangible. It was quickly incorporated into the evolving wilderness idea, and its associated concept, "ecological integrity," served as both a scientific and a philosophical precept of the Arctic campaign.

While the now ecologically informed wilderness concept was "new thinking," its grounding in century-old American romantic and transcendental philosophies continued. The writings of Thoreau, Muir, and others in these traditions underpinned the wilderness movement and were formative influences for many of the new paradigm's vanguards. The ideas and statements of the early nature philosophers would often appear in the writings and testimony of the Arctic proposal's supporters.

Romanticism, a nineteenth-century European import, was both a product of the scientific rationalism of the Enlightenment and a reaction against the mechanistic materialism that characterized much of its scientific approach.

The movement extolled the aesthetic and psychological value of unaltered nature and, particularly, of that found in places with characteristics exemplified by the Arctic proposal: great height or depth, and vast scale. Monumental features and expansive vistas were characterized as sublime; approached with receptivity, they were said to evoke awe and wonder, instill humility, provide therapeutic benefits, and inspire spiritual experience.

Transcendentalism (1830s to 1860s) further expanded, popularized, and Americanized romantic notions of wildlands. Particularly relevant to the Arctic campaign was the fact that, preceding the coinage of the word *ecology* by decades, transcendentalism offered a profoundly ecological interpretation of the human-nature relationship. Its most influential spokesman, Henry David Thoreau, wrote of nature as an interrelated system, with humans being dependent and obligate members of the larger community of life. Wilderness, Thoreau taught, provided a physical and psychological distance from society's norms and pressures for conformity that yielded fresh perspectives, including the humbling yet ennobling recognition of human relatedness to the natural world. In describing untrammeled nature as a setting conducive to reflection upon one's role in the larger scheme of things, transcendentalism established wilderness as a cathartic, spiritually inspiring setting for the overcivilized.

But romanticism and transcendentalism were more than fonts of alternative ideas; they were reactionary movements. Much of their content was antimodernist, arising from misgivings about the social, psychological, and environmental effects of the Industrial Revolution. Similarly, the Arctic campaign was a reaction to changes wrought by the postwar order. It, too, was led by those who questioned whether the material gains of modernity were worth the cost of a degraded environment and alienation from the natural world.

Representative of these concerns is one of Wilderness Society president Olaus Murie's justifications for wilderness preservation. Expressing a notion that would recur throughout the campaign, he wrote that wilderness "is important for our happiness, our spiritual welfare, for our success in dealing with the confusions of a materialistic and sophisticated civilization." The psychological and spiritual benefits that wilderness offers the modern world, he believed, were "not to be lightly discarded in the modern reach for ease and gadgets."[15] Similarly, Murie's associate, the pioneer ecologist and wilderness philosopher Aldo Leopold, characterized the wilderness movement as "a disclaimer of the biotic arrogance of *Homo americanus*. It is one of the focal points of a new attitude—an intelligent humility towards man's place in nature."[16]

FIGURE 3. Aldo Leopold (left) and Olaus Murie at a Wilderness Society governing council
meeting in 1946. Leopold's *A Sand County Almanac* and other writings significantly
influenced the philosophical and ecological orientation of the Arctic campaign.
Photo by Charles G. Woodbury; courtesy of the Murie Center.

The book that would become the standard text of the emerging environmental movement was published in 1949, on the eve of the arctic campaign.
Leopold's *A Sand County Almanac* brought contemporary relevance and
scientific legitimacy to the underlying transcendental and romantic notions
of wilderness. Arctic proponents' recognition of the interrelated ecological, evolutionary, experiential, aesthetic, and ethical aspects of wilderness
clearly reflects the influence of Leopold's synthesis of scientific thinking
and preservationist values. Though it would not become popular until the
late 1960s, many proponents cited the now-classic book, and one Alaskan,
Virginia Wood, kept it on her bed stand for reference throughout much of
the campaign.[17]

The Arctic campaign reflects the emerging importance of the environmental
perspective in postwar American conservation and the expanding boundaries
of the wilderness concept. While retaining its roots in romantic naturalism and
transcendentalism, the wilderness idea was meeting new needs and embracing
a far wider range of values by the 1950s. Wilderness was supporting a greater
variety of recreational activities, and providing more diverse experiential benefits. Increasingly, it was being seen as a cathartic resource, a place of escape

and where one might find respite from the stress of modern living. As concern about pollution mounted, wilderness was becoming valued as a source of clean air and water. The scientifically oriented were coming to recognize it as a repository of ecological and evolutionary process. For the growing minority of those concerned about the environmental effects of the postwar order, the wilderness concept was coming to symbolize the need to measure the human, wildlife, and environmental costs of industrial and technological progress.[18] Their concern was well summarized by Virginia Wood:

> [L]ogged-over land, dust bowls, polluted streams, smog-ridden cities— all connected by billboard-bedecked, litter-strewn super highways. This is the price we have paid for our high standard of living and unparalleled industrial leadership, all achieved in the name of progress.[19]

To a large degree, the effort to embody the expanding wilderness construct in the northeast corner of Alaska was a product of the emerging environmental movement. But so, too, in focusing public attention on the concerns and values the movement represented, the Arctic campaign played a role in its advance. In fact, probably more than any other event, the Arctic campaign introduced the emerging environmental perspective to Alaska. This controversy first introduced many residents to the ecological arguments and vocabulary of wilderness debate that would reverberate through the acrimonious Alaska National Interest Lands Conservation Act of 1980, and continue in the equally contentious conflict over the question of whether the Arctic Refuge's coastal plain should be drilled for oil or protected as wilderness.

Bob Marshall and the Precampaign Years, 1936–1950

Bob Marshall never came within the boundary of what became the Arctic Range, and he died a dozen years before the campaign began. Nevertheless, his influence on the outcome was great, and his life illustrates the philosophical and psychological developments that were central to the effort.[20] By profession, Marshall was a forester with a Ph.D. in plant physiology. But his specialty in the Forest Service was outdoor recreation and, by inclination, he was what might be termed a wilderness psychologist. Understanding the resonance between wild nature and human nature was a compulsion. His scientific justification for first going to the Central Brooks Range in 1929—to research the northern limits of tree growth—was, he later admitted, secondary to his urge to experience "the joy of exploration in untrammeled lands ... the joy of exploration into mental continents."[21]

FIGURE 4. Bob Marshall in Wiseman, 1930s. *Courtesy of Jonathan Marshall.*

Marshall's influential writings extolled adventurous and character-enhancing experiences that would repeatedly be referenced during the Arctic campaign, particularly the psychic benefits of challenge, exploration, and natural beauty. They also resonate with references to the cultural heritage value of wilderness as a place where "the feeling of the pioneer finds full expression." Echoing historian Frederick Jackson Turner, Marshall called for preservation of "that wilderness which has exerted such a fundamental influence in molding American character."[22] Marshall's ideology would become a seminal influence in the emerging national wilderness movement. His early call for preservation of the Brooks Range would become a standard reference for the Arctic campaign and subsequent wilderness designation efforts there.

The recreational, aesthetic, and cultural heritage values Marshall found in wilderness served what he described as fundamental human needs that modern society left unsatisfied. His most original and significant contributions to the wilderness movement grew out of his pioneering use of the emerging science of psychology to understand and promote the restorative and self-enhancing benefits of nature celebrated by the early romantics and transcendentalists.

When Marshall returned to the Brooks Range settlement of Wiseman in 1930 for a fourteen-month study of its wilderness-dwelling inhabitants, he brought psychology textbooks. His popular book about the experience, *Arctic Village*, lauded their life "200 miles beyond the edge of the 20th century." It analyzed the community's preindustrial environmental conditions and social patterns, which contributed to, as the book concluded, "a life filled with an amount of freedom, tolerance, beauty, and contentment such as few human beings are ever fortunate enough to achieve." [23]

Arctic Village was appealing to a nation in the midst of depression, questioning, like Marshall, what had been lost to industrial civilization. It became a Literary Guild selection and minor bestseller. Characteristic of the era's anthropological studies of primitive cultures, the book revealed the shortcomings of the modern order. In doing so, it drew upon Sigmund Freud's ideas about the harmful effects of suppressing primal urges. The freedom and happiness Marshall found among his Wiseman subjects supported his Freudian notion that the pressure to conform to the norms and roles imposed by modern society suppressed some formative and fundamental aspects of one's humanity.

Marshall advocated preserving areas that might provide the opportunity to "return to the life which the human race had known for countless centuries before." This was a reactionary position, an antimodernist response to "the strangling clutch of a mechanistic civilization." [24] Wilderness provided an antidote. In satisfying "the craving for adventure," "the longing for physical exploration," and the "opportunity for complete self-sufficiency," he believed the wilderness adventurer might find "heartiness of character" and relief from the "neural tension of modern existence." [25] His descriptions of "breaking into unpenetrated ground, venturing beyond the boundary of normal aptitude, exerting oneself to the limit of capacity" began the association of Brooks Range travel with the mythical journey quest whereby one's outward adventures contribute to inner discovery and growth. [26]

Many of the psychological benefits Marshall espoused were dependent on the "virgin" character of the Arctic wilderness as well as its "ocular beauty," that is, its mere scenic appearance. Being free of the physical manifestations of modern civilization, virgin wilderness fostered an escape from its social conventions, allowing one to more fully experience the cathartic effects of nature. His writings suggest that just knowing nature is free from the control of society helps free the mind from its controlling influence. Thus the physical and psychological aspects of wilderness were inseparable in Marshall's thinking; wilderness benefits, he wrote, "depend not only on what one can see and hear, but also on what is in the back of one's mind."[27]

Bringing a new psychological rationale to an early transcendental idea, Marshall wrote that the many values of wilderness "are blended with the dominant value of being part of an immensity so great that the human being who looks upon it vanishes into utter insignificance."[28] Attaining a sense of proportion in the larger scheme of things, he believed, was the initial experience that opens one to the ultimate benefits of wilderness.

Marshall's accounts of his transformative Brooks Range experiences contributed ideological depth to the growing wilderness movement underpinning the Arctic campaign. And for many who would become involved in the conflict, Marshall's writings about the region provided their first impression of its value as wilderness. As well, his notion that wilderness preservation served to mitigate the effects of an increasingly mechanistic and materialistic age would resonate through the Arctic campaign.

George L. Collins's Vision

In 1936 the young National Park Service planner George L. Collins ran into Marshall on a hiking trail in northern Michigan. Thereafter, Marshall made it a point to visit Collins during his frequent visits to the agency's Washington, D.C., headquarters to lobby against the construction of roads and facilities in the wilder sections of parks. They became close friends, and Marshall's ideas would leave a lasting impression on Collins. So did his stories of adventuring in the Brooks Range. A decade after Marshall's premature death in 1939, Collins was in a position to initiate an effort to fulfill much of Marshall's early vision for a vast Arctic wilderness.

In 1949, the American Association for the Advancement of Science sponsored the first Alaska Science Conference. Scientists, government officials, and other participants recommended a territory-wide study of natural areas worthy of some form of federal or territorial protective status. The National Park Service took the lead role in what became the Alaska Recreation Survey. The agency's director selected George Collins, who now held the position of senior project leader for studies of new park areas, to oversee the initiative.[29]

From 1951 through 1953, Collins's survey team examined a wide spectrum of areas throughout Alaska with special potential for recreational use, historic preservation, or scientific research. Collins personally visited 147 of them and oversaw completion of the comprehensive 1955 report, *A Recreation Program for Alaska*.[30] But for Collins, the northeast corner of Alaska held special promise. He believed it had the greatest potential to fulfill what became his career-culminating ambition: "to locate the one preeminent region that was most representative of park values."[31]

To understand the "park values" that Collins sought, and the perceptual lens through which he saw northeast Alaska, it is worthwhile to consider why he came to be aptly described as "one of a small band of Park Service 'dreamers of the biggest dreams.'"[32] Collins's Park Service career extended from 1927 to 1960, ending a few weeks after the establishment of the Arctic Range. Having worked his way up as a ranger and park superintendent, he was thoroughly grounded in his agency's tradition and culture. But Collins was not content with the rather limited focus on scenic, recreational, and heritage values of the National Park Service. An explorer of the human nature–wild nature relationship, he sought to understand the fuller range of wildland values through transcendental and romantic concepts and new perspectives,

FIGURE 5. George L. Collins looking over potential parklands from a PBY aircraft during the Alaska Recreation Survey, June 1951. *Photo by Lowell Sumner; courtesy of the National Park Service.*

FIGURE 6. George L. Collins in Southeast Alaska during the first year of the Alaska Recreation Survey, May 1950. *Photo by A. Kuehl; courtesy of the National Park Service.*

particularly those of his friends Marshall, Leopold, and Murie. The opportunities he saw in northeast Alaska reflect their influence.

Collins's son, ecologist Joshua Collins, believes the ultimate park values his father sought in northeast Alaska were best expressed in a treatise his father wrote describing "our heritage from our earliest ancestry":

> We go to the wildlands to experience the power and beauty of elemental scenes and forces that bring us physical pleasure and spiritual stimulation. It is as simple as that—a reawakening, a revelation, an inspiration.[33]

This statement reflects Collins's belief that an evolutionary heritage underlies the spiritual and inspirational benefits that wildlands can provide. It reveals his transcendental notion that wild nature had the capacity to reawaken one's sense of being part of a larger, more encompassing reality. The belief that monumental features or vast vistas might inspire such spiritual insights was not uncommon in the agency. But Collins went beyond conventional Park Service philosophy in his belief that the source of this stimulation was deeper than scenery. Transcending the visual qualities of the surface, he believed, was the effect of knowing that ecological and evolutionary processes—those "elemental scenes and forces"—continue. Collins brought to northeast Alaska the belief that the highest experiential values of wild areas derived from understanding that natural processes "are ongoing, they are evolving, they are beyond good or bad. They are 'right' because they are right unto themselves and can evolve naturally without the medium of man."[34]

Collins also brought to the Alaska Recreation Survey a sense of urgency grounded in the fear that the nation's postwar rush for development was resulting in an irretrievable loss of some of the finest remaining repositories of such qualities. It was not just the environmental degradation that concerned him; it was also the attitude toward nature that it represented. Reflective of his thinking is a post-establishment article about the Arctic Refuge in which, using language reminiscent of Marshall's reactionary pronouncements, Collins decried "man's enormous technological capacity to conquer, and his willingness to go it blind, if necessary, in converting natural resources into material values."[35] And, reflective of Leopold's melding of ecological, aesthetic, and ethical values into a land ethic, Collins concluded that

> we are searching for a state of ecological adequacy in the Arctic, an ... area of reference, scientifically and aesthetically.... Ecological well-being—a state in which man will not over-program, subjugate and sabotage his surroundings—is the ideal. It can be realized again and again and strengthened to the everlasting benefit and enjoyment of man in the goal of an Arctic International Wildlife Range as one of the world's truly great examples of its kind.[36]

Before the Alaska Recreation Survey's fieldwork began in 1951, Collins knew the embodiment of the ideal he sought would be found in the Brooks Range. He remembered Marshall's descriptions of the Central Brooks Range, most of which is now within the Gates of the Arctic National Park. He had studied *Arctic Village* and Marshall's many articles extolling the experiential and heritage values of the region.

Prior to extending the Survey's work to northern Alaska, Collins met with officials of the U.S. Geological Survey in Washington, D.C. The agency's arctic expert, John Reed, advised him to focus on the eastern sections of the Brooks Range. In an extensive series of oral history interviews published as *George Collins: The Art and Politics of Park Planning and Preservation*, Collins described how Reed had told him this region was unlikely to have petroleum reserves, as did areas to the west:

> [T]hat's where the finest relief, the highest mountains in the Alaskan Arctic, and the greatest relief are, because it escaped most of the last ice age. So *evolution* has been continuous over a long period of time.

"He opened my mind to a vision that was way beyond anything I'd had before," Collins said, adding, "he gave me ideas about possibilities there that made me tremendously happy."[37] This remote corner of Alaska, Collins believed, held the possibility of a reserve large enough and intact enough to enable its life forms and the large-scale processes in which they were embedded to remain as they were or become what they would. If free of the human intention to alter, manipulate, or control, this place could thus epitomize the root concept of wilderness. Such is the reasoning behind the statement that perhaps best encapsulates Collins's intent here. This area, he said, "ought to be preserved as it was. For no other reason but for there it was, as it had always been."[38]

Lowell Sumner, Maverick Biologist

Another pioneer of the emerging environmental paradigm, a biologist who would integrate early notions of the psychological/spiritual benefits of connecting to the natural world with postwar ecological science, was Collins's close friend and partner in the Survey, biologist Lowell (Doc) Sumner.

Sumner joined the National Park Service in 1935 after completing his graduate work under University of California professor Joseph Grinnell, the first proponent of ecologically based management of national parks. He soon became outspoken within a minority faction of biologists that challenged the agency's interpretation of its Organic Act's statement of national park purposes. The 1916 act directed the agency to conserve scenery, natural and historical objects, and wildlife in such a manner "as will leave them unimpaired for the enjoyment of future generations."[39]

Since the act's passage and through the Arctic campaign years, the Park Service had interpreted "unimpaired" largely within the context of public use. In managing for desired appearances and experiences, the agency interrupted natural processes by stocking naturally fishless lakes, placing salt blocks to lure elk within view of tourists, and spraying DDT to kill insects that annoyed visitors and altered scenic tree stands. Sometimes service personnel killed predators to enhance populations of sport fish and viewable ungulates such as elk, moose, and deer. Sumner was among those who resisted what Park Service

FIGURE 7. Lowell Sumner, left, with National Park Service director George Hartzog. The year before he retired, in 1967, Sumner was recognized for his exceptional contributions with the Interior Department's Meritorious Service Award. *Courtesy of the National Park Service.*

historian Richard Sellars has described as the era's "façade" management of parks: "protecting and enhancing the scenic façade of nature for the public's enjoyment, but with scant scientific knowledge and little concern for biological consequences."[40]

In contrast, Sumner took "unimpaired" to mean that primacy should be given to maintaining ecological integrity and evolutionary processes. At a Park Service conference in 1950, he admonished his agency to focus on "watching natural processes unfold" and "letting nature alone."[41] While Sumner's position was regional biologist, he came to function more as an ecologist. His perspective that nature was neither static nor in balance, but dynamic and ever-changing—going somewhere—suggested that he is better described as an evolutionary ecologist. Sumner's approach to natural landscapes can be characterized by his phrase "zoom lens ecology," that is, "being able to zoom in and zoom out of scale in time and space; seeing relationships in different scales of time and space." His prescient (1948) warnings about the potential effects of the agency's use of DDT reflect his capacity to "see what it might be like a hundred or a thousand years from now."[42] This is probably why, according to Collins, Aldo Leopold considered Sumner "one of the greatest field biologists he ever knew."[43] Nevertheless, the tolerated maverick biologist was among those whose contributions, as he wrote, were limited by the agency's leaders, who believed that "biologists were impractical, were unaware that 'parks are for people,' and were a hindrance to large scale plans for park development."[44]

As with Collins, the wilderness concept provided much of the framework for Sumner's park philosophy. But while Collins, much like Marshall, felt the central value of wilderness preservation was its beneficial effect on individuals and society, Sumner, more the ecocentrist, brought "a stricter sense of ecological right and wrong." For Sumner, "the value of land did not need to be translated into human terms."[45]

Even more so than Collins, Sumner's perspective on wilderness cannot be correctly understood with reference to the anthropocentric versus biocentric dichotomy used to categorize wilderness management approaches. *Wilderness Management*, the standard textbook of the field, characterizes this misleading distinction as "wilderness for people's sake" as opposed to "wilderness for wilderness's sake."[46] Sumner's approach was biocentric in that he believed that wilderness had intrinsic value and within it, human uses should be subordinate to maintaining natural conditions and processes. In fact, he was probably the first to propose specific limitations on the types and levels of recreational use in wilderness. Yet Sumner's perspective was also anthropocentric in that he believed that a higher level of human benefit accrued when, going beyond the enjoyment of scenery, one perceived the landscape through his friend Aldo Leopold's land aesthetic: Beauty is found in knowing the land is free from human interference and that the natural processes of its genesis continue.[47] To Sumner, the wilderness perspective provided a sense of scale that instilled humility and led to more respectful treatment of the natural world.

When Sumner retired as the Park Service's chief research biologist, he reflected on his distinguished career and declared that his role in the Arctic campaign "was the crowning achievement of my professional life."[48] Looking back, he recalled his hope that in this northeast corner of Alaska, "the majestic story of evolution" would continue. This could be a place "where we can learn to appreciate and respect the intricate and inscrutable unfolding of the Earth's destiny." Inclined to express evolutionary insights with an eloquence uncharacteristic of biologists, Sumner expressed the hope that this place might always have the

> freedom to continue, unhindered and forever if we are willing, the particular story of Planet Earth unfolding here ... where its native creatures can still have freedom to pursue their future, so distant, mysterious.[49]

2

To Northeast Alaska

The experience gratifies in us some fundamental longing for
spiritual refreshment and for intellectual composure.

—Lowell Sumner and George L. Collins[1]

1951: The Embodiment of an Ideal

owell Sumner's perspective on wilderness was at odds with that of the agency with responsibility for managing wildlife in the region. This was made clear to him in April 1951. The U.S. Fish and Wildlife Service's Alaska regional director and pilot Clarence Rhode had invited Sumner to participate in the agency's aerial survey of "game conditions" in Arctic Alaska. The singular focus of the survey component of the program was hunted species, primarily caribou. The secondary purpose was to kill wolves. While on the survey, Sumner witnessed Fish and Wildlife Service personnel shoot a wolf and drop poison bait among wolf packs. One day he saw five dead wolves

◀ FIGURE 8. Peters and Schrader lakes. *Photo by Averill Thayer.*

being brought into base camp. The treeless Arctic and its wild inhabitants were highly vulnerable to the agency's airborne predator killers.

Sumner wrote a brief report on the survey in which he broached his and Collins's idea of "setting aside, as an inviolate wildlife sanctuary for all species, a sizeable chunk of the Arctic slope and Brooks Range." He described boundaries roughly approximating the region that would become the Arctic Range.

Afterward, Sumner wrote to their friend, Wilderness Society director Olaus Murie, with whom they had previously discussed the area's potential. He told Murie how he and Collins were "deeply impressed with the wilderness qualities of the area" and that they "feel strongly that its highest destiny would be permanent preservation as one of the most spacious and beautiful wilderness areas in North America."[2]

Sumner's rhetoric in these first known written references to establishing some form of reserve is worth noting here. "Wilderness," "preservation," "highest destiny," "inviolate," and "sanctuary for all species" were his emphases. Noticeably absent was the more popular utilitarian focus on "conservation of resources" for hunting, recreation, and tourism that had been prominent in the establishment of other conservation units in Alaska, such as Mount McKinley National Park and the Kenai National Moose Range.

Sumner emphasized a sanctuary for all species—as opposed to one that placed priority on species favored for hunting or viewing. This emphasis was a response to the predator control activities he had witnessed and the attitude toward natural processes such activities represented.

Indeed, Sumner's focus on all species needs to be understood in the context of the widespread predator control programs conducted by the Fish and Wildlife Service, both in Alaska and in the western states.[3] These programs were the antithesis of Sumner and Collins's perspective that in wilderness, all life forms had intrinsic worth, independent of any utility or benefit to humans. This idea would be most pronounced in the early years of the Arctic campaign, before political realities required a shift in orientation from a park-type wilderness to a wildlife refuge. But the volatile issue of whether predators—especially wolves—should be treated as villainous competitors or venerated symbols would recur throughout the effort.

Profoundly unecological, Clarence Rhode's predator control program was popular with hunters, the agency's primary constituency in the territory. As Sumner cynically noted in his 20 April 1951 journal entry, "wolf control is a major FWS activity in large part because it pleases Alaska residents."[4] Collins was also troubled by the program. In his journal, he noted that "Rhode says he would not mind seeing all wolves exterminated." He later wrote, "My impression is that F & W's policies are those of game farming of all wildlife. It seems to me that at the hands of our Government the Arctic is a very perishable place." Expressing dismay that ecological considerations were so insignificant in the agency's program, he later wrote that the Fish and Wildlife Service's "game management and predator control activities seem not to be based upon scientific work as much as on claims of spectacular success in killing things."[5]

The Fish and Wildlife Service's Alaska predator control program *was* highly successful at killing wolves—and, incidental to that, many nontarget animals. That year, 1951, the Service reported having recovered 287 predators it had killed, 18 of which were wolves from the north slope operation Sumner had observed. Many more, the agency claimed, were killed but not recovered. These were mostly victims of its poisoning effort—strychnine-laced baits dropped from planes in winter and baited cyanide explosive charges placed in the spring. The numbers of foxes, bears, and other animals that found the baits and fell victim were largely unknown and not mentioned in the agency's reports.[6] Richard Carroll, a Native trapper, chief of the Fort Yukon Village Council, and local magistrate at the time, recalls his opposition to what he considered the agency's

FIGURE 9. Early in the Arctic campaign, the wolf came to symbolize the area's wilderness and the need to protect it from the attitude toward nature represented by government predator control programs. An Olaus Murie drawing from *Two in the Far North.*

indiscriminate use of strychnine. He had generally supported wolf control and confesses to having used poison baits at selected locations, but "throwing them out of airplanes kills the mice, martens that eat them, and everything else in the country. We knew that, so why was Fish and Wildlife doing it?"[7]

Extended to Alaska in 1948, the federal wolf control program had been initiated in response to a decline in caribou and other game animals. Its popularity in the last frontier was rooted in a deep enmity for the species that some believed reached back to prehistory. Illustrative is a feature article printed in *Alaska Sportsman* magazine shortly after Sumner's experience. After lauding Fish and Wildlife's campaign against the "vicious" wolves howling "a chorus of evil and death," author Larry Meyers explained that

> [d]estructive as they are of valuable wildlife, the wolf is universally hated
> in Alaska. It is hated with an intensity which seems to be handed down
> from our primordial ancestors—an instinctive hatred tinged with fear.[8]

Also popular in the territory was the bounty system. Begun in 1917, by 1951 it offered fifty dollars for each wolf and fifteen dollars for each wolverine killed. Although appropriation requests cited economic benefits to rural Natives, Rhode acknowledged that the majority of payments went to bounty hunters in private planes. They were particularly effective north of the Brooks Range, where Rhode estimated they killed at least 1,500 wolves during the early and mid-1950s.[9]

Rhode knew the decline in caribou and some other game populations was due in part to natural fluctuations and increased hunting pressure, including that brought by the increasing use of planes for hunting. But he had to work within the Alaska political scene. Shortly before initiating the 1951 program, Rhode received a letter from Territorial Governor Ernest Gruening calling for more control. "[T]he wolf works 365 days in the year," Gruening complained, "the matter of predation is so serious that no aspect of it should be left without action."[10] Attributing declines to hunters and restricting their take was not a popular response; blaming and killing wolves was. The attitudes underlying the agency's action led Collins to muse upon the underlying symbolic importance that preserving the area's wildness would have:

> Its intrinsic value alone, without any development at all, will be so great
> in time that it will become the physical heart of principles and standards
> of culture and beauty in far greater measure than ever before.[11]

Collins and Sumner believed that, more than a repository of natural conditions and processes, this area could serve as the embodiment of emerging environmental ideals. By this time, American history, culture, and scenic beauty were well integrated into their agency's heritage-keeping function. National parks had long served to create and support a distinctive national identity; they were promoted as repositories of the conditions that formed and shaped us as a nation.

But for Collins, the times called for a place that might also serve as an antidote to the attitude of conquest, control, and domination of nature that characterized this pioneering heritage. What he envisioned here was a place set apart from the utilitarian and commodity orientation that dominated the major part of America's relationship with nature. As such, some form of wilderness preserve here might expand Americans' thinking about their relationship to the natural world. This place, he hoped, might serve as a point of reference for establishing a legacy of restraint, a prerequisite for attaining a sustainable relationship with the natural world that formed and shaped us as a species.

It is fortunate that Collins kept a journal during the course of his fieldwork and travels and required those he supervised to do so as well. These records reveal an idealism and an enmity toward the Fish and Wildlife Service that they dared not place in their official correspondence or later magazine articles. Collins and Sumner's entries, corroborated by correspondence and personal interviews, show that by mid-1951 the Arctic project had become a personal mission for them that far exceeded the scope of the Recreation Survey. Its purpose, Collins wrote, is "worth every success, every effort, all our faith."[12]

Collins and Sumner's integration of scientific concepts and preservationist values appealed to a small but growing number of conservationists. But outside a small cadre of biologists, few people within the Park Service were willing to advocate for applying the emerging ecology-based environmental perspective to park management. The recent appointment of director Conrad Wirth, who emphasized park development, de-emphasized science, and would come to oppose designating wilderness in parks, had a dampening effect on those who supported the pair's vision for the area. As Collins kindly said of the slowness of his agency's leaders to adopt more holistic thinking, "Nobody had the time to concentrate on what Doc [Sumner] and I had evolved in our thinking."[13] Sumner stated and restated in his correspondence to Murie that the idea of an inviolate sanctuary was "strictly unofficial" because the Park Service was "not in a position to advocate or initiate any proposal along these lines."

"Such a proposal would have to come from the people themselves," Sumner told Murie, "that is to say the conservationists and lovers of wilderness throughout the country."[14] Popular support would ultimately lead to the area's establishment. But it was the vision, commitment, and eloquent articulations of Collins and Sumner that attracted the conservation leaders who would enlarge the campaign's base of support.

At its annual meeting in October 1951, the Wilderness Society passed a resolution supporting Collins and Sumner's idea for northeast Alaska. In a letter to Interior Secretary Oscar Chapman, the society called for protection of the region as "a wilderness area free from exploitation that would disturb its primeval character." Their letter made clear that the organization was familiar with the wilderness values described in the Recreation Survey's report. It cited their principal founder Bob Marshall's writings about the Central Brooks Range to the west of the proposal. It also mentioned the biological expeditions of Olaus and his brother Adolph Murie there in 1922–1923, and that of Olaus and his wife Margaret in 1924. Their letter went on to "urge that your appropriate agencies carefully study the reports of the Alaska Recreation Survey and take all necessary steps to insure the preservation of such an area in northern Alaska."[15] In this first known statement of organizational support, the Wilderness Society did not recommend the Park Service as the appropriate steward for the area. Nor did it suggest director Murie's former employer, the Fish and Wildlife Service, which he had left in 1945, in part because of his disgust with its policy on predator control.

1952: A Primeval Wilderness

In July 1952, Collins and Sumner began a ground survey of the region. They received logistical assistance from the Office of Naval Research's Arctic Research Laboratory in Barrow and were able to work out of its base camp at the mountainous junction of Peters and Schrader lakes.

Their surroundings were "enthralling" and "beyond description." But their interest in the region went beyond the scenic sections more associated with national park purposes and the focus of the Recreation Survey. A reserve here, they decided, should take in the "tundra plains" and then "go out to the sea, take in the habitat of the beluga whales and the migrating creatures that live by land and sea both."[16]

Their desire to incorporate the flat coastal plain contrasts with Bob Marshall's earlier, almost singular focus on the mountainous areas of the Brooks Range. From mountaintops, Marshall had seen the "arctic prairie." But he hadn't been inclined to venture into it. Nor did he describe it with his usual wilderness effusiveness. In large part, Collins and Sumner's broader landscape interests reflect the expansion of the wilderness concept that occurred during the decade following Marshall's death in 1939. His focus on the inspirational effects of monumental features and rugged topography corresponded to what

FIGURE 10. A Norseman supply plane overflies the camp at Peters–Schrader Lakes shared by the Office of Naval Research, National Park Service, and Conservation Foundation researchers, July 1952. *Photo by George L. Collins; courtesy of the National Park Service.*

FIGURE 11. George L. Collins at Peters–Schrader Lakes camp, July 1952. *Photo by Lowell Sumner; courtesy of the National Park Service.*

Aldo Leopold, with the benefit of greater ecological insight, later described as "that under-aged brand of esthetics which limits the definition of 'scenery' to lakes and pine trees."[17] Leopold's "land aesthetic" was premised on the notion that "[e]cological science has wrought a change in the mental eye."[18] Beauty, he had written in *A Sand County Almanac*, derives from what is both seen and unseen: Just knowing that an area's timeless evolutionary and ecological functions continue can be a source of aesthetic inspiration.

While the experiential, scenic, and cultural values Marshall espoused had, to a large degree, shaped Collins's early conceptualization of wilderness, Leopold's thinking about the role of natural processes and ecological wholeness was now the greater influence. In 1999 Collins looked back on Leopold's influence and declared, "It was his ideas we brought to Alaska.... If he hadn't lived, I don't think the Arctic Refuge would be what it is today."[19]

Heightening the pair's conviction that the area needed protection was the large-scale predator control project the Fish and Wildlife Service had concluded just two months earlier. Manifestly incongruent with Leopold's pleas for the government to accept ecological and intrinsic values of wolves, "Operation Umiat" involved three teams of skilled pilots and gunners hunting across the northern plains of the Brooks Range. In his report on the operation, Rhode lauded the effectiveness of "modern control methods"—strychnine, cyanide, and the use of the high-performance Super Cub aircraft with gunners firing specially loaded twelve-gauge magnum buckshot shotgun shells. Their known tally: 223 wolves shot, 36 poisoned, and 74 unborn pups destroyed. Not mentioned were the other wolves and other species that were sickened or killed by their poison baits, and the chemicals' potentially lingering ecological effects.[20]

Sumner was also involved in the politically volatile wolf control issue in McKinley National Park that summer, a controversy that would soon contribute to many Alaskans' opposition to any type of Park Service–associated reserve in the Arctic. Since the mid-1930s the small contingent of ecologically oriented agency biologists with which Sumner was aligned had been making progress in moving park management toward a position described as "preserving all forms of wildlife in their natural relationships." While the Fish and Wildlife Service's limited attention to ecological research was focused on applying scientific findings to its game propagation programs, the Park Service was bringing ecological principles to the task of maintaining or restoring the appearance and "balance" of nature as they were thought to have existed prior to European settlement.

Drawing upon studies conducted by Olaus Murie's brother Adolph on the ecology of wolves in McKinley, Sumner and his associates sought to terminate the park's limited predator control program. Sportsmen's groups and territorial politicians, whose notion of conservation was largely limited to the protection and propagation of game animals, were outraged at the prospect. They blamed wolves for a decline in the park's Dall sheep. Worse, they alleged, the park served as a breeding ground from which sanctuary wolves raided other game populations. Apparently the Fish and Wildlife Service agreed, as their planes dropped poison baits outside the park boundary. While many proponents of predator control sought to reduce the number of wolves in McKinley, others, including Governor Gruening, called for their extermination.[21]

In 1949 Sumner had used the inflammatory S-word in calling for McKinley Park to become "a sanctuary for wolves just as the other parks are now sanctuaries for buffalo, bighorn, grizzlies, wolverines, and trumpeter swans in the States."[22] In the summer of 1952 he conducted a sheep survey in the park, and while there made a recommendation that the park's wolf control program be temporarily suspended. Stimulating his recommendation was a proposal by filmmakers Herb and Lois Crisler to film a wolf family at a den site in the park.

The Crislers had been commissioned by Walt Disney to film northern and Arctic animals for the popular True-Life Adventure documentary series. The couple were strong wilderness supporters and Sumner knew they planned to portray wolves sympathetically. Since park policy at the time required rangers to shoot wolves they saw—though some disregarded the order—biologists would not be able to identify a suitable den for them without a suspension of the wolf-killing policy. Fearing "another public relations problem," McKinley superintendent Grant Pearson refused to act on Sumner's recommendation. But someone elevated the issue to the new Park Service director, Conrad Wirth, who overruled Pearson. The temporary suspension of wolf control continued until 1954, when Wirth made it permanent.[23] Angered by the termination, Fairbanks sportsmen charged that park management was contrary to proper wildlife (i.e., game) conservation. Their arguments and rhetoric against maintaining a balance of nature would soon figure prominently in opposition to the Arctic proposal.

While at Schrader Lake, Collins and Sumner were joined by two of the most noted pioneers of the emerging environmental perspective. One was Aldo Leopold's son, A. Starker Leopold. Following in his father's footsteps, Starker was a professor of biology, an authority on wildlife management, and an advocate of maintaining ecosystem process. The other was the eminent Scottish ecologist Sir Frank Fraser Darling, an early proponent of studying wildlife and human–environment interactions from an ecological perspective. Sierra Club director David Brower considered him "the Einstein of ecology."[24] Both men, and their sponsoring organizations, the New York Zoological

Society and its adjunct, the Conservation Foundation, soon became active and influential advocates in the Arctic campaign. Their book, *Wildlife in Alaska: An Ecological Reconnaissance*, was published the following year. It endorsed establishment of an "Arctic Wilderness Area ... to protect an adequate reserve in that wonderful primitive region for posterity." The authors described the wildlife values associated with recreation, tourism, aesthetics, and subsistence. But, like Collins and Sumner, they also noted an intrinsic value of the area's wildlife: "[T]he animals exist, also, in their own right and we should acknowledge this as part of the national responsibility."[25]

Certain that the region should be preserved, Collins, Sumner, Leopold, and Darling contemplated the advantages and disadvantages of alternative forms of "protective custody" for it.[26] Which agency, they wondered, should be the area's steward, and what designation would be most appropriate?

Because Collins and Sumner worked for the National Park Service, and because Collins frequently referenced "park values," most of those becoming interested in the area assumed they had been initially intent on establishing a national park. But that wasn't necessarily the case. Although Collins later reported that "it was a park to us, always was, and still is," he acknowledged using the word *park* generically, as an adjective describing wilderness

FIGURE 12. Scottish ecologist Frank Fraser Darling and biologist A. Starker Leopold at Peters–Schrader Lakes, July 1952. *Photo by Lowell Sumner; courtesy of the National Park Service.*

conditions.[27] While the Park Service had the lead role in the Recreation Survey, it was actually a broader Interior Department initiative. Collins's thinking transcended agency jurisdictions and he was well connected at the department level. "So I looked at this whole thing from a departmental standpoint," he said, "[from] the Secretary's office, not from the National Park Service."

In fact, early on, according to Collins, "We didn't think that the National Park Service was the best agency of the federal government to administer whatever might be identified and set forth as a piece of country that ought to be preserved for itself."[28] Collins initially felt his agency's emphasis on recreation and tourism would not be compatible with such a nonutilitarian purpose. But by the time he and Sumner left Schrader Lake, he had reconsidered. In a letter dated 15 September to another future proponent, the noted Arctic archaeologist Louis Giddings, Collins wrote:

> While we were out in camp with Leopold and Darling we had many discussions about this park idea. Every one of us came to the same conclusion—that a national or international park is the only solution. No other form of land use is a sufficient guarantee of security, in our opinion.

In spite of his frustrations with the agency culture he sought to enlighten, Collins became convinced that park status was the most protective classification available. Collins also knew a park proposal would be controversial and that advocacy would be personally demanding. His letter to Giddings continued:

> At first, a year or so ago when I first got into this matter, I didn't want to get involved in another park campaign. I've been through several of them. But now I don't care. This job needs to be done.[29]

In August Collins and Sumner were flown across the Brooks Range divide to explore the mountains and foothills of the south side. They set up a base camp on the upper reaches of the Sheenjek River within its sparkling "Valley of Lakes." Camp was located on the drainage's most northerly lake accessible by floatplane, later appropriately named Last Lake. Here the pair began mapping preliminary boundaries for some form of park. Delineating a western border was most troubling. The central section of Alaska's Arctic coastal plain was considered a likely prospect for oil development. So they reluctantly chose the Canning River. U.S. Geological Survey geologist John Reed had told the pair that if they stayed east of Naval Petroleum Reserve Number Four, south of Barrow, and east of the Canning, "we'd be out of the oil people's hair, because there isn't anything there that they want."

FIGURE 13. Gyrfalcon over Sheenjek River "Valley of Lakes" was among the many drawings by George Collins that accompanied his and Sumner's articles about the Arctic proposal. This is from "Arctic Wilderness," 1953. *Courtesy of the Collins family.*

Collins later regretted not including the Canning River's entire watershed, but "not wishing to make our relations with industry and the Geological Survey more sensitive," he decided not to include the river's western ridgeline. Mindful of the industry opposition their proposal would surely generate once a public campaign for preservation was launched, he said, "We can't justify any more than we're taking in, which is already about ten million acres."[30]

That was more than four times the acreage of Yellowstone Park, which would become the often repeated standard of comparison for the Arctic proposal, in terms of purpose as well as size. While ten million acres seemed the far limit of what might be designated for preservation in Alaska, Collins and Sumner's vision did not stop at the international border. Their aerial surveys had included unauthorized excursions into Canada's northern Yukon Territory. Seeing the region as a vast unbroken ecosystem, Collins reported that "[w]e started thinking of it not only in terms of a national park, but...as a great international park, the first one, really, of any consequence on any U.S. border."[31]

In the fall of 1952, Collins and Sumner issued a "Progress Report" based on their fieldwork. Supposedly a report of findings, it was more a piece of advocacy. "The study area," they concluded, "includes probably the most completely undisturbed large wilderness remaining in North America together with some of the most unusual and inspiring Arctic scenery." The authors were not reluctant to point out that the landscape and wildlife were vulnerable to inappropriate uses. One of their conclusions offered the first formal statement of the "scientific value" argument for preserving the area. After describing how the area's animals "maintain their primeval numbers," it went on to state that the region

> if it can be kept free of artificial disturbance, will continue indefinitely to offer outstanding research possibilities in many branches of ecology and natural history, including studies of cyclic population fluctuations. It can also be used as a "control" area for comparison with other areas devoted to game, fur and fish management.[32]

This "control" function, the notion that the area would serve important scientific purposes beyond its boundaries, would figure prominently in the campaign. In *A Sand County Almanac* and other writings, Aldo Leopold had popularized the idea of protecting some areas to serve as a "baseline of normality for healthy ecosystems." Wilderness, he had declared, was the "most perfect norm."[33] This ecological value was becoming an increasingly prominent justification for wilderness preservation during the postwar years. In 1950,

Wilderness Society president Benton MacKaye had advanced Leopold's ideas in *Scientific Monthly* magazine. His point was that the "primeval organic land, the aboriginal food chain" is characterized by perpetual self-renewal, and that knowing how such natural processes operate can aid in maintaining sustainable land-use practices. Stating the scientific principle in terms reminiscent of John Muir, MacKaye concluded that "wilderness is a reservoir of stored experience in the ways of life before man."[34]

The idea of establishing large reserves for the purpose of ecological research was not entirely a postwar development, however, nor was its application most advanced in America. In 1917 the newly formed Ecological Society of America had begun to identify and seek preservation for areas retaining their original flora and fauna for scientific purposes. At the same time, under Lenin, the Soviet Union began a system of "natural laboratories" called *zapovedniki*. By the late 1930s some of them were strictly administered so that large-scale and long-term natural processes could be studied without interference. Recreation was not allowed, and for the most part, commercial activity and consumptive use were banned. The Arctic proposal's scientist-advocates were, to varying degrees, aware of these *zapovedniki*, and at least one, University of Alaska biologist William Pruitt, considered them something of a precedent that helped shape his thinking about potential research uses of an Arctic reserve. But no campaign writings would reference the *zapovedniki*. As Pruitt recalls, because descriptions of *zapovedniki* were unavailable in English, they were unknown in the United States outside the small ecological research community. Perhaps more significant, he said, was the fact that these areas were established by the communist regime and resulted from the taking of individuals' rights. During this cold-war era, that would have elicited extremely unfavorable comparisons.

The conclusion of Collins and Sumner's report reveals that beyond any form of use, including scientific, their primary concern was the maintenance of natural conditions and processes. Providing recreational opportunities, while given greater emphasis in subsequent documents, was here described more as a means of gaining public understanding and support for protecting what they considered the area's higher purpose:

> The permanent preservation of this wilderness in a primeval condition.... Recreation use, sufficiently provided with safeguards and restrictions to avoid disturbing the natural features and ecological balance of the area ... should increase public appreciation of the special scientific and inspirational values of the area and thereby assure the permanency of its primeval status.[35]

The repeated use of the word *primeval* by Collins and Sumner, and soon by other proponents, illuminates their conception of the area and the experiential and symbolic functions they believed it would serve. This evocative label would continue to be effectively employed to evoke images and trigger associations that helped attract public support for preserving the area.

The primeval construct linked northeast Alaska to the romantic ideas of the early wilderness literary tradition. In 1932, Bob Marshall had combined the old image of wilderness as untouched virginity with the emerging interest in ecological and evolutionary processes to author a U.S. Forest Service definition of "Primeval Areas." These were "tracts of virgin timber in which human activities have never upset the normal process of nature."[36] Three years later, the Wilderness Society expanded upon Marshall's definition, describing *primeval* in terms of "the culmination of an unbroken series of natural events, stretching infinitely into the past...not only of surpassing value from the standpoint of scenery, but of great scientific interest."[37] These definitions reflect a departure from the notion that nature undisturbed by man is unchanging. The concept of "primeval" began to convey the emerging understanding that it was dynamic evolutionary and ecological processes, more than landscape features, that were timeless.

In the decades immediately preceding the Arctic campaign, the National Parks Association revived the term to distinguish the large, wild, and monumental parks from those that were less inspiring. Primeval landscapes were now being described both as surviving relics of a disappearing natural world and as touchstones to man's distant past. In contrast to the cultural heritage connotations of the word *primitive*, with its implications for re-enacting the experience of the first Euro-Americans, *primeval* related more to humankind's evolutionary heritage. It echoed the human species' origin as creatures of the wild and conveyed the notion that in untouched landscapes, one might experience and respond to the natural world much as one's more distant ancestors had. For visitors prepared for the experience by the wilderness literature, such associations enhanced the capacity of a landscape to inspire. They contributed a spiritual dimension to the wilderness experience by connecting visitors to processes and time scales far beyond their life and lifetime. Appealing to non-visitors as well was a moral value that attaches to the protection or destruction of objects of antiquity. Thus, association with the primeval concept contributed a more widely appreciated ethical dimension to the preservation effort.

The primeval construct played a significant role in the successful 1949–1956 campaign to prevent construction of a dam within Dinosaur National Monument in Utah.[38] Concurrent with the first half of the Arctic campaign, this pivotal conflict involved many of the same proponents and organizations, whose similar rhetorical associations and political strategies were used to gain support for the Arctic proposal.

A copy of Collins and Sumner's "Progress Report" that Margaret Murie provided to the Fish and Wildlife Service following the death of her husband, Olaus, in 1963 includes the parenthetic notation, "reproduced and distributed by the Sierra Club." Collins and Sumner had wasted no time in providing—or leaking—the in-house document to supporters. In a letter to Interior Secretary Chapman only a few weeks later, Collins's close friend, Sierra Club secretary Richard Leonard, announced the club's endorsement of the report's recommendations. Highlighting ecological values and the importance of all species, Leonard said the area would "bring the highest returns to the nation if kept free from artificial disturbance or management."[39] At the time the Sierra Club's interest in natural areas was still largely focused on their recreational potential, yet recreation was not even mentioned as a basis of their recommendation.

Considering the author of the letter, the ecological focus of the club's endorsement is not surprising. Richard Leonard was an attorney who had served on the club's board since 1938 and would soon become its president. Also on the Wilderness Society's governing council, Leonard was considered a wilderness purist in the tradition of John Muir. Along with his friend Lowell Sumner, he was one of the Club's leading advocates of ecocentrism. For the next eight years, Leonard would direct the Sierra Club's influential involvement in the Arctic campaign.

In 1953, the Izaak Walton League, an early sportsmen's organization with which Olaus Murie also had a leadership role, endorsed the idea of an "Arctic Wilderness." Later, Dr. Edgar Wayburn, president of the Federation of Western Outdoor Clubs, announced his organization's resolution to support the creation of an "Arctic wilderness preserve" to perpetuate its "primeval values."[40]

In November 1952, Collins and Sumner completed the first formal proposal to establish a reserve in northeast Alaska. The twenty-three-page, photo-illustrated document was titled *A Proposed Arctic Wilderness International Park: A Preliminary Report Concerning Its Values.* The in-house report effusively described the scenic, recreational, historic, wildlife, ecological, and scientific values of the region. It made what would become an often-repeated comparison of the region's caribou herd to the vanquished buffalo herds of the last century. It included a warning that would recur through the upcoming campaign: "Unless an adequate portion of it can be preserved, in its primitive state, the Arctic wilderness will soon disappear." Suggesting the primacy of ecological values, they recommended that this superb area should be preserved "as a scientific field laboratory and also for the education, enjoyment, and inspiration of all outdoor-minded people."[41]

This first official proposal recommended incorporation of a large portion of Canada's Yukon Territory into the wilderness area. Though not successful, the international aspect of the proposal became central to Collins's advocacy throughout the first half of the campaign. Following the area's establishment in 1960, and Collins's retirement soon after, expansion of the range into Canada became a central focus of Conservation Associates, the nonprofit organization he and Richard Leonard's wife, Dorothy, and Dorothy Varian formed. Looking back, Collins explained:

> We saw the fallacy of having a park, or whatever you want to call the area, divided by an international boundary when you had so many migratory species, both marine and terrestrial, that used both sides of the line. It was one habitat.[42]

The report included little information specific to Canada because no formal discussions had yet been held, but it stated, "[I]t definitely is intended herein to stimulate the widest interest and discussion of a complete, self-sustaining area which by reason of geography naturally falls across portions of both countries."

The report's concluding statement indicates that by late 1952 Collins and Sumner were fully supportive of park status. "Only one type of land classification appears to assure these essential land-use objectives—that of 'Arctic Wilderness International Park.'"[43]

A Last Great Wilderness

The authors emphasize that the northeast Arctic wilderness

offers an ideal chance to preserve an undisturbed natural

area large enough to be biologically self-sufficient.

—Lowell Sumner and George L. Collins[1]

1953: Problems with a Park

In the summer of 1953, George Collins wrote a letter to Olaus Murie describing plans to help prepare Murie and Starker Leopold to take over the Arctic campaign. Revising his previous position, Collins stated, "I do not advocate any description incorporating the word 'park.'" Instead, he suggested the title "The Arctic International Wilderness." The objective, Collins said, was "to save some wilderness through the best organization available for that purpose." The Park Service, he added, was "not necessarily well enough qualified at present."[2]

◄ FIGURE 14. Quiet moment amid limestone columns, East Sadlerochit Mountains, 1998. *Photo by Roy Corral.*

Why? Collins was concerned that the Park Service's increasing emphasis on promoting recreation, developing visitor facilities, and perhaps even accommodating auto tourism might be extended to northeast Alaska. This concern developed in the context of the tourism explosion that began in the early 1950s. Being in the inner circle of national park system planning, Collins was well aware of pressures leading to "Mission 66," the agency's billion-dollar, ten-year initiative to expand park infrastructure to accommodate increasing tourism. The initiative was planned to extend from 1956 to 1966, the golden anniversary of the 1916 National Parks Act.

Mission 66 would expand the national park road system, develop more campgrounds and picnic areas, and construct administrative and visitor facilities, including amphitheaters, visitor centers, and roadside exhibits. The initiative also promoted concessionaire services, resulting in more stores, lodges, and other corporate developments.[3] Distrustful of science, Park Service director Conrad Wirth allocated minimal funding for study of the ecological effects of the program. As Olaus Murie stated in a letter to Lowell Sumner, the development initiative was politically expedient, but a setback for those working to elevate the role of biology in park management decisions.

Since the mid-1930s a small contingent of Park Service biologists and Murie's Wilderness Society had been criticizing the agency's accommodation of auto-based and convenience-oriented tourism. Now the controversy extended to Alaska, increasing concern that, if designated as a park, the ecological condition and wilderness character of northeast Alaska would be jeopardized by developments.

Shortly before Collins's change in strategy, his boss, Director Wirth, received a letter from territorial Governor Gruening, who wanted assurance that the Park Service would accommodate the "tremendous influx of automobile bearing tourists" he eagerly hoped would drive the new Denali highway to McKinley Park. Although later, as a senator, Gruening would become one of the Arctic proposal's most formidable opponents, he had been an influential supporter of Collins's Alaska Recreation Survey because of its potential for expanding Alaska's fledgling tourism industry. Gruening wanted the agency to seek $150,000 for road and bridge construction in McKinley. Hotel and lodge construction was also on his agenda. Wirth, who lacked the preservationist sentiment of his predecessor Newton Drury, agreed with Gruening and sought funding for tourist accommodations inside the park.

The most outspoken critic of development within McKinley was Olaus Murie's brother Adolph, a Park Service biologist who conducted research on predator–prey relationships in McKinley and Yellowstone Park. He opposed the expansion of tourism developments in Yellowstone and, as many Arctic proponents would, used Yellowstone management practices as examples of what to avoid in Alaska wilderness areas. He argued that the agency should both preserve the park's ecological integrity and avoid "intruding and injuring the spirit of wilderness."[4]

In a 1953 report on his fieldwork, Adolph described an aspect of this spirit, little recognized by the Park Service, that his brother Olaus and others would seek to preserve in the Arctic proposal. Adolph objected to the installation of interpretive signs within the park, and referring to their labeling of features, he told his agency that

> [t]here is the stark label—one might think he were looking at a museum showcase. The opportunity to discover the trails for oneself, to wonder about them—what animal made them and why and where he was going—had been taken away.[5]

Extolled by Bob Marshall, the feeling of mystery and unknown, the sense of exploration and discovery, were among the intangible attributes of the

FIGURE 15. Three wilderness movement leaders: Olaus Murie, Howard Zahniser, and Adolph Murie in McKinley Park, 1961. Predator control and recreational developments in McKinley and Yellowstone parks provided them with examples of the type of administration that must be avoided in the proposed Arctic wilderness.
Courtesy of the National Park Service.

wilderness experience many felt were at risk in Park Service administration of the Arctic proposal. Celia Hunter and Virginia Wood were among those whose McKinley experiences convinced them that their friend Adolph was right. The Park Service's reluctance to manage for the adventurous, self-reliant experiences they valued was a primary reason they would later hesitantly favor wildlife range rather than park status for the area.

George L. Collins, it should be noted, generally supported Wirth's goal of accommodating increasing numbers of vacationers in national parks. In fact, the year before, in 1952, he had even approved plans for developing a number of visitor conveniences in Alaska's Katmai National Monument, including a road to the Valley of Ten Thousand Smokes. But Collins did not believe that altering the landscape to accommodate visitors was appropriate in all parks or park-type reserves. Collins thought of conservation units broadly; each park, monument, refuge, or forest was part of a national system providing a wide range of conditions and recreational experiences. Northeast Alaska, he believed, should represent the far end of the paved to pristine spectrum.

With a national park here, Collins feared, "[Y]ou would have to endorse the idea of all kinds of people going up there. And I didn't want that." Concerned with the increasing commercialization of national parks, and the growing influence of concessionaires, he added, "What Doc Sumner and I were after wasn't going to make any money for anybody." In sharp contrast to his agency's dominant parks-are-for-people orientation, this area, Collins said, "would be established for the purpose of simply protecting it, and letting it alone, as it was."[6]

A second reason Collins was reluctant to propose park designation was his concern for the rights of Native peoples, a concern not yet widely held within the agency:

> We had indigenous people in the area.... I wanted those native people to be there and to continue to have their subsistence economy out on the land. ... We would have to allow them hunting and trapping privileges, such as they'd always had.[7]

The Arctic wilderness Marshall had envisioned would have done so. Earlier, Collins had believed that, given the uniqueness of northeast Alaska, the Park Service would have the flexibility to accommodate the traditional activities of the region's Gwich'in Indians and Inupiaq Eskimos. But there was no such precedent in the national park system. He came to accept that the agency was not yet ready to break tradition and accept any form of hunting or trapping within national parks. (Fishing was an accepted public use in parks; there would be no mention of it as a concern during the campaign.)

Finally, as a matter of strategy, Collins realized the very word "park" would heighten opposition in Alaska. The Arctic campaign occurred in the context of widespread resentment of federal control of territorial resources and the drive for statehood, a dominating issue in Alaska during the 1950s.[8] Federal conservation policies and land withdrawals, where lands were removed from the public domain for conservation or military purposes, were chief concerns of statehood proponents, who resented what was often referred to as "colonial treatment" by distant Washington bureaucrats.

The Drive for Statehood

Many Alaskans decried the Interior Department's cautious approach to resource development, claiming it prevented the territory's full benefit from the postwar economic boom. In Interior Alaska, the Park Service's resistance to local demands for wolf control in McKinley Park represented perceived governmental deference to balance-of-nature-oriented conservation interests located outside the territory. During a statehood hearing, the territory's attorney general and future congressman (and range opponent) Ralph Rivers included management of McKinley Park in his litany of complaints against the federal government. If Alaska had been a state, he claimed, the park would not have become the "breeding ground for hundreds of wolves" that his constituents so resented.[9]

In fact, arguments against the Arctic proposal echoed many of those for statehood. On the national level Ernest Gruening was the leading proponent of the statehood movement. He soon became one of the most formidable opponents of the Arctic proposal. Gruening had been appointed territorial governor by President Franklin Roosevelt in 1939, and Alaskans elected him to be one of the state's first two U.S. Senators in November 1958. A Harvard graduate and former newspaper editor, Gruening was an energetic and liberal crusader who soon became known throughout the territory. A staunch civil rights advocate, he had lobbied the territorial legislature to win passage of the controversial Alaska equal rights bill, which outlawed discrimination against Alaska Natives. Gruening was also, in his words, "a fervent conservationist." One of his first actions as governor was to initiate a controversial but successful effort to repeal legislation authorizing the bounty-killing of bald eagles, which were widely believed to be detrimental to salmon populations.[10] By the early 1950s Gruening's efforts were focused on promoting economic development, which, he believed, was critical to attaining statehood.

FIGURE 16. U.S. Senator for Alaska Ernest Gruening. *Courtesy of the Archives, Alaska and Polar Regions Department, University of Alaska Fairbanks, acc. no. 87-065-08.*

Gruening spoke for many when he described Alaska as "still a frontier." He compared the Alaska experience to "the westward trek of peoples in search of greater freedom and greater economic opportunity."[11] The barrier to this frontier freedom was "federal obstructionism." While the most onerous federal policies were those allowing powerful outside fishing and mining interests to exploit Alaska's resources without contributing to the territory's meager economy, Alaskans also resented federal conservation withdrawals and wildlife regulations. In 1955, Gruening delivered his passionate "Let Us End American Colonialism" speech before the constitutional convention, convened in Fairbanks to draft a constitution for the future state. His ideas found expression in Article 8, which declared that Alaska would "encourage the settlement of its land and the development of its resources by making them available for maximum use consistent with the public interest."[12] To territorial leaders and most of their constituents, this public interest was sorely at variance with the national interest in Alaska. Article 8 became the formal basis of Alaska's natural resource policy. Range opponents seized upon this fact and their references to it would echo through subsequent preservation efforts.

Not all residents favored statehood, however. One opponent was future governor Jay Hammond, a Fish and Wildlife agent from 1949 to 1956 and later hunting guide and commercial fisherman. "Environmental degradation" in the lower states was one of the reasons he came to Alaska after the war. Looking back, Hammond saw statehood proponents as the "advocates of aggressive, no holds barred growth." He found their perspective "at odds with what I thought was the best destiny for Alaska."[13]

But Hammond's was a minority viewpoint and Collins was painfully aware of the popularity of the dominant frontier land ethic. He also knew how threatening the park concept was to those who held it. His journal at the time contains numerous references to the incompatibility of "Alaskans' philosophy of independence and freedom of action" with the restraint and humility required for wilderness preservation. The opposition would be formidable. There were many residents like his friend University of Alaska professor Ivar Skarland, who, Collins wrote, stood "ready to tear the Govt. apart because of large land withdrawals."[14] A park withdrawal would preclude not only settlement and mining, but Alaska's revered hunting and trapping traditions as well. It was becoming apparent that, politically, a park withdrawal was the least likely (though not impossible) means of preserving the area.

In early June 1953, part of Collins's survey team returned for a summer of field investigation. Sumner was the leader, bringing with him landscape architect William Carnes, archeologist Alex Ricciardelli, and U.S. Geological Survey geologist Marvin Mangus. The group established a base camp at Joe Creek, a tributary of the Firth River which crossed the Canadian border. Collins, who was also supervising other Alaska projects, could only stay two weeks. But his days in this most remote section of the proposal were among the most memorable of his career. Shortly before his death, the ninety-three-year-old Collins told a *Smithsonian* writer, "I think about Joe Creek every day of my life."[15] Having obtained a Scientists and Explorers License from the Yukon Territory Commissioner, the group was able to extend its ground reconnaissance into Canada. On July 16, they broke camp and began a five-week float-based examination of the Kongakut River valley.

A lengthy report incorporated the season's findings with those of their previous reports and information from other agencies. *A Preliminary Geographical Survey of the Kongakut–Firth River Area, Alaska–Canada* detailed the archeological and historic significance of the area as well as the previously described ecological and recreational values. In contrast with previous statements, a geology section included the single, unreferenced speculation that "it is very

FIGURE 17. National Park Service survey team archaeologist Alex Ricciardelli searching
for evidence of the early human migration from Asia to the New World in a cave near Joe
Creek, June 1953. *Photo by Lowell Sumner; courtesy of the National Park Service.*

possible that good...petroleum traps may be present...in the coastal plane [*sic*] between the Aichillik and Canning Rivers."[16] A few opponents would later mention that possibility, but it would not become a significant issue until the 1970s.

The report predicted an increase in use of the area by both scientists and vacationers and openly acknowledged that restrictive provisions (sure to be unpopular with many Alaskans) would be necessary to protect wildlife and wilderness conditions. To discourage consideration of the type of recreational infrastructure associated with parks, the report suggested that permanent developments were not appropriate here.[17] Like many aspects of the Arctic proposal, including its sheer scale, the idea of a vast park-type unit without any roads or facilities was essentially without precedent.[18]

The report's strongest recommendation concerned the function Collins and Sumner most hoped the area would serve—as a repository of ecological and evolutionary process where "every species would be left to carry on its struggle for existence unaided." The report left no doubt as to the incompatibility of the Fish and Wildlife Service's predator control with this vision. "No native species," it stated, "would be destroyed on account of its normal utilization of any other native animal unless the latter were in immediate danger of extermination."[19] In late August, Sumner joined Collins at their San Francisco office, where the two quickly incorporated information from this and previous reports into a high-profile magazine article intended to launch a public campaign to preserve the area.

"Northeast Arctic: The Last Great Wilderness" was published in the October issue of the *Sierra Club Bulletin*.[20] The twenty-four-page feature and addendum included photos by Sumner and drawings by Collins, a talented artist. The origin of that evocative—and enduring—characterization of the area as the "last great wilderness" is uncertain. In 1992, reflecting back forty years, Collins said he believed he and Sumner came up with it together, perhaps around a campfire at Joe Creek.[21] Perhaps they borrowed it from Frank Dufresne's 1946 book, *Alaska's Animals and Fishes*. A former Bureau of Biological Survey agent and Alaska Game Commission chief, Dufresne had warned that if Alaska were tamed, "we shall have destroyed our last great wilderness."[22]

The article began with a full-page tribute to Robert Marshall, who, it was noted, scarcely anyone agreed with when he was alive and "pioneering Alaska conservation ideas." But in reference to the nascent environmental perspective, Collins and Sumner wrote that "with our new natural resources consciousness," almost everyone should be able to appreciate Marshall's foresight. Citing Marshall's belief that "northern Alaska belonged to all the

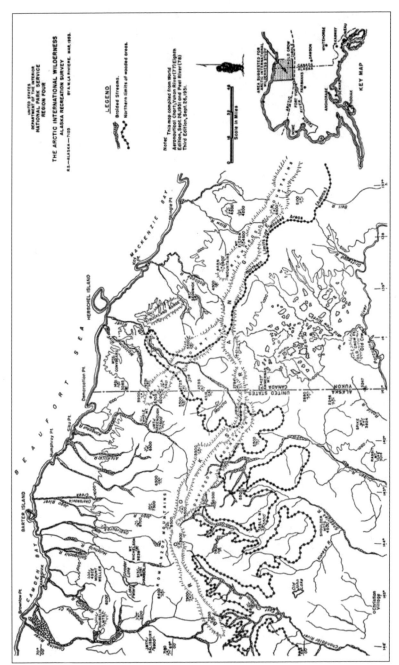

FIGURE 18. Accompanying the "Last Great Wilderness" article, this 1953 map shows the large section of Canada that George L. Collins originally hoped would be incorporated into an "Arctic International Wilderness." *Courtesy of the National Park Service.*

people of the nation as a frontier," the authors began explicating the area's values with "the cultural values of this land itself." It concluded on a similar note, stating, "[T]his area offers what is virtually America's last chance to preserve an adequate sample of the pioneer frontier, the stateside counterpart of which has vanished."[23]

An Arctic Frontier

The emphasis of Collins and Sumner on the preservation of frontier values in this first widely read description of the area is significant because frontier imagery became prominent in future articles, the testimony of supporters, and government press releases. But opponents, following Gruening's lead, also deployed frontier metaphors, analogies, and rhetoric to bolster their arguments against withdrawing the area. Indeed, the question of what kind of frontier Alaska was, or should remain, underpinned much of the disagreement between partisans.

Advocates of the Arctic proposal repeatedly referred to the wilderness frontier as something of a living museum of the qualities that forged the nation. Olaus Murie wrote that it represented some of "the original conditions that our pioneers found on this continent." One motive of the wilderness movement, he said, was a belief that "we are losing the last vestiges of that precious frontier atmosphere which helps to build a strong civilization."[24]

The notion that wilderness had been a "transforming influence" upon American character had been popularized by historian Frederick Jackson Turner's canonical 1893 essay, "The Significance of the Frontier in American History."[25] In the 1920s, Aldo Leopold drew upon Turner's ideas to argue that protecting some areas as wilderness served to perpetuate opportunities for the type of rugged, adventurous experiences that were believed to have shaped the nation. Although discounted by many historians today, the frontier thesis provided a popular means of interpreting the country's heritage. It was readily incorporated into the wilderness movement and used as an argument for preservation efforts. But proponents did not need to experience the frontier to benefit from its preservation. Like a national monument or historic artifact they might never see, they believed a cultural value was served in just knowing it was there, as a vicarious touchstone to America's past. Preservation of this area would help ensure perpetuation of that sense of a Great Beyond which, since colonial times, had been part of the American psyche.

Alice Stuart was a Fairbanks proponent and close friend of the late Bob Marshall who would reference Theodore Roosevelt and the frontier poetry of Robert Service and Rudyard Kipling to support her argument that "the

American wilderness, to a great extent, made Americans what they are." The
Arctic proposal, she believed, would "[l]et us Alaskans also pass on this secret
of our Americanism to future generations by preserving in the northeast corner
this Wilderness area."[26]

Concern for the potential loss of this heritage was accentuated by a
recently published report by the House Subcommittee on Territories and
Insular Possessions, which had responsibility for Alaska. The Hackett
Report, *Alaska's Vanishing Frontier: A Progress Report* lauded proposals
for new mines and industrial developments. It concluded, approvingly, that
"whatever frontier there is remaining in Alaska appears to be rapidly vanishing under the impact of progress."[27] Proponents used this conclusion to
bolster their case for preserving northeast Alaska as a remnant of a vanishing
cultural heritage.

Opponents of conservation withdrawals used the term "frontier" more
in its original context, as an area open for pioneering, where freedom of
action and economic opportunity prevailed. Their icons were the settlers and
miners who subdued and tamed the wilderness. Transforming an environment from a wasteland to one that served human progress was supported
by religious sanctions as well as the territory's dominant economic and governmental institutions.

Fabian Carey was a trapper, part-time construction worker, and amateur
historian whose childhood hunting and trapping adventures and formative
woodcraft and mountain-man readings had sparked an interest in Alaska. His
wish to prolong the frontier freedoms he had enjoyed since his 1937 arrival
would stimulate vocal opposition throughout the campaign.

A conservationist, Carey was not one to embrace development schemes proposed for the territory, and although a skilled bush pilot, the idea of shooting
wolves from the air didn't appeal to him. But as an outdoorsman seeped in
old-time woods lore, he found the type of restrictions imposed by McKinley
Park, just north of his trapping area, even less appealing. The park's prohibition of hunting, trapping, and prospecting led Carey to refer to the agency's
policy of nature preservation as "entombment," and another federal reserve,
he feared, was another step in the demise of a lifestyle he felt should remain
a living heritage.

Another opponent from Fairbanks, electrician Wenzel Raith, based his
adamant opposition to a "9-million acre sandbox" upon veneration for
"the trail blazers, men like Daniel Boone, James Bowie, Kit Carson, Davey
Crockett, and Jim Bridger." Alaska should be a refuge "for people with
guts and courage … like the old frontiersmen." To Raith, the "ridiculous
restrictions" and "paternal bureaucracy" that would accompany a wilderness

withdrawal would erode opportunities for the "rugged individualism" and "self-reliance" that made America and Alaska what they are. "By curtailing the opportunity for individual initiative," he wrote, "we dry up our vitality at its wellsprings."[28]

While the era of westward expansion was the stage of history opponents sought to prolong, "The Last Great Wilderness" article pointed out that this vision of the frontier was particularly unsustainable in the Arctic. It warned that as "today's profound changes continue to accelerate … opportunities for preserving original conditions decline." It compared the recent occurrence of "air expeditions" into the Brooks Range with the first arrival of automobiles in Yellowstone Park, predicting a similar loss of wilderness character if public use was not adequately controlled. Remoteness, it was apparent, would not remain the area's protection. Even by the early 1950s, its sense of farness was eroding. "Already," the authors lamented, "aircraft being what they are, it is easier to get into the heart of the Arctic than it was to get into the heart of Yellowstone 40 years ago."

FIGURE 19. Trapper Fabian Carey with a marten fur, about 1970.
Photo by Jerome Lardy; courtesy of Michael Carey.

As in previous reports, the article enumerated the scientific, ecological, wildlife, recreational, and aesthetic values of the region. But its greater
emphasis on cultural heritage values is notable. Although of concern to both
authors, this emphasis was more the contribution of Collins, who was trained
as a landscape architect and was highly attuned to the fact that the national
park idea had evolved to fulfill cultural needs as much as environmental or
recreational purposes. He knew that the national identity function of dramatic landscapes continued to be a significant source of public support for
their preservation.[29]

A veteran of working with the public on many park establishment efforts
and planning processes, Collins also knew that few readers of a popular magazine would be strongly interested in ecological concepts, which were still rather
esoteric in the early 1950s. Although Sierra Club members were interested in
wilderness recreation, few would see a trip to this distant place as a possibility
for themselves. Collins, like Marshall, recognized that a wider segment of the
public would appreciate the area as a remnant of America's vanishing cultural
heritage and support the proposal as a legacy to future generations.

Appending "The Last Great Wilderness" was a letter by Sumner expressing
"one individual's personal feeling about the wild world from the Brooks Range
north." Written from the Kongakut River and addressed to Richard Leonard,
"A Letter from the Arctic" began with the statement: "This wilderness is big
and wild enough to make you feel like one of the old-time explorers." It reiter-
ated the theme that this was a place in which one could relive the adventurous
experiences of the nation's formative era.

Sumner's letter provided the first published account of the spectacle that,
throughout the campaign and later in the area's future conflicts, would serve
as the symbolic representation of the area's wildlife and wildness: "We came
upon whole valleys, hill slopes, ravines and tundra flats *crawling* with caribou.
They flowed up and down the slopes in all directions."

In response to the drama, Sumner wrote, "One feels one has lived, and
seen some of the world unspoiled, as it was intended people should see it." He
used the experience to develop an analogy that would recur throughout the
writings and testimony of the campaign's supporters:

> Now we knew what it must have been like to see the buffalo herds in
> the old days; we knew more vividly than ever what we have lost forever
> in the states. And are losing fast up here too.[30]

Postwar conservation writings regularly drew upon national guilt regarding
the wanton destruction of the buffalo. The evocative buffalo-caribou analogy,
with its strong historic and emotive associations, enhanced the ideological

FIGURE 20. "Caribou in the Kongakut Country." This drawing by George Collins accompanied his and Sumner's 1953 article. Emulating the Hudson River School of Art style, Collins's drawings gave visual expression to textual accounts of the area's iconic wildlife and dramatic features. *Courtesy of the Collins family.*

significance of the campaign. The specter of losing "forever" a spectacle "[l]ike the buffalo of 100 years ago" lent a sense of urgency. This "last" wilderness was an opportunity for the nation to avoid, and perhaps atone for, such mistakes from its past.

A few months later, Sumner and Collins furthered public awareness of the proposal by publishing a second feature article, this one in *Living Wilderness* magazine. Sumner was the lead author of "Arctic Wilderness," based on his summer experiences at Joe Creek. The article described the natural processes of "this primeval land," drawing upon the well-established association of wilderness with timelessness and antiquity. The authors compared the valley's cycles of life to human events, from the construction of the Egyptian pyramids to the first-known aircraft landing in the valley in 1947. Then "we reflected that against the background of Joe Creek's leisurely rhythm, all of recorded human history was but a recent incident."[31] In placing civilization within the vaster time frame of the valley, the authors conveyed the spiritual notion that here one might see one's life in proportion to processes and time scales far beyond one's lifetime.

"Who cares about an Arctic Wilderness?" they rhetorically asked. Those with ecological and scientific interests, and potential visitors with "some fundamental longing for spiritual refreshment" were mentioned. But recognizing the intrinsic, non-use values they believed inherent in the area, the authors also included "the animal inhabitants of Joe Creek and the surrounding Arctic wilderness," adding that "man has not been notably in the habit of considering their feelings." As to what designation and which agency would protect such opportunities and values, "we would not venture to say here."[32]

With no consistent title or designation associated with it, nor an agency affiliation, the Arctic proposal lacked the name recognition needed to attain widespread support. Unlike previous national park, forest, or refuge proposals, this obscure place had no constituency of visitors. In fact, it had no known history of recreational use. But with publication of these articles, it now had an identity. It was a Wilderness. Just as Yellowstone epitomized the national park idea, this Last Great Wilderness was portrayed as the embodiment of the concept that many of the leaders of the Arctic campaign concurrently sought to codify in legislation as the Wilderness Act.

In October 1953, Collins received an inquiry from the Alaska Development Board concerning what it heard was a proposal to create an "Arctic National Monument."[33] A second letter from the board, foreshadowing strident territorial opposition, requested that a survey of the area's resources be conducted, "before any consideration whatsoever should be given to the establishment of a park in the area."[34]

Collins immediately responded to what he surely knew was only the first official objection. He wrote the governor and, referencing the board's concerns, assured him that the Park Service was not planning either a monument or a park. "We think of the country by name as the Arctic International Wilderness," Collins wrote, again avoiding mention of any specific land status or administrating agency. He highlighted the need to protect the area from military activities associated with the cold-war buildup of defense facilities along the coast. These sites, and the all-terrain-vehicle "weasel" tracks scarring the tundra around them, were the most visible threat in the region. More important, because of unpopular military withdrawals and activities near Fairbanks, the potential military threat was the argument for a reserve that Alaskans were most likely to be receptive to. And in what must have been a painful statement for Collins to write, he told the governor that proponents were fully aware that in any plan to protect the area, prospecting and mining would have to be "freely permitted."[35]

By now, it was apparent that political reality would thwart his vision for an inviolate wilderness. To minimize the gathering opposition, Collins and sponsoring organizations decided not to oppose prospecting and mining. Their publicity, in some cases, even emphasized that the area would be open to mining. However, they believed this was a concession with few tangible consequences. The region was believed (correctly) to have little mineral potential. Its extreme distance from any markets would discourage development of any but the richest deposits. Further, they were confident that establishing legislation could be written that would limit mining rights to the subsurface estate, preventing the patent of what had in other areas become privately owned inholdings within conservation units.

In late fall, Collins and Sumner met with Olaus Murie, Howard Zahniser, Richard Leonard, Starker Leopold, and others to "discuss the political angles of setting up such a reserve."[36] They decided that Leopold would initiate formal correspondence with Canadian officials to discuss some form of international wilderness. While his letters to them were optimistic about the proposal, he acknowledged that the necessary support from American authorities was by no means assured. Because of Alaskans' attitude toward federal land withdrawals, he told one official, "we anticipate some rather severe opposition to the idea, both in Alaska and Washington." He went on to tell the Canadians that "it might be politically impossible to exclude mineral exploration and mining," adding that there seemed little likelihood of such activities.[37]

Although several Canadian officials expressed support for the idea of an international reserve, the adjacent Canadian areas were currently better protected than the Alaska lands encompassed by the proposal. Because there was no immediate need for more protection, the official Canadian response was, in the words of one official, "something less than enthusiastic."[38]

1954: Controversy Begins

The Arctic proposal became a polarized public issue in Alaska in January 1954, when the Fairbanks newspaper published an article summarizing Collins and Sumner's "The Last Great Wilderness" article. A flurry of letters to the editor immediately responded to "Would Set Aside Wilderness Area in Northeast Alaska."[39] They put forth the main arguments for and against establishment of a wilderness area, and set the tone that the local debate would take for the next six years.

First in opposition was the locally prominent hunting guide, pilot, and newspaper printer, Charles Gray. He warned Fairbanks residents about the Park Service's "propaganda campaign" which had "mustered plenty of support"—most of which, he pointed out, came from outside Alaska. While Gray complained the proposal would prevent oil and mineral prospecting, his main objection was that game management would be precluded. Gray led hunts for sheep, bear, moose, and caribou within the proposed wilderness, and polar bears just offshore of it. He was likely the individual most knowledgeable of the region and the hunting opportunities it afforded. He predicted that hunting pressure in the Arctic would increase to the point where predator control would be necessary to insure a sufficient number of game animals. Then, he argued, "this area would become a wolf haven."[40] Opposing the proposal wasn't Gray's only action to prevent that. A skilled aerial wolf hunter, he and a fellow pilot killed fifty-six wolves in the Brooks Range and north slope the following spring.

Gray, it should be noted, was a committed conservationist and a former territorial game warden. In the dominant tradition of maximum sustained yield of game animals, his actions contributed to what was widely considered—and endorsed by the Fish and Wildlife Service—as the wise and appropriate management of natural resources. Looking back in 2003, Gray recalled that his initial opposition was less a response to the wilderness proposal than its association with the Park Service, which he believed to be too much of "a protectionist type of operation—favoring the animals over people."[41]

Sven Gustav Norder wrote a letter to the editor urging that "all Alaskans and friends of Alaska should fight land withdrawals such as that outlined." A withdrawal for such "nebulous purposes," he said, "would only tie up important resources, restrain travel and free enterprise." Scientific research, he argued, did not justify foreclosing development of the many economic and strategic minerals he presumed the region held. He urged opposition to a withdrawal "at the whim or whimsy of every individual with a hobby to pursue or an axe to grind."[42]

Carl Wilson was likewise critical of the "scheme to grab up the best part of the Brooks Range." Correctly anticipating proponents' strategy, he predicted that "the adjective-happy Park Service will try to pacify the mining fraternity by allowing prospecting and possibly certain mining."[43] Repeating, as many would, arguments developed during the McKinley Park wolf controversy, he stated that because "the Park Service sticks so close to the balance of nature theory," it was doubtful that the withdrawal could benefit wildlife at all. Opponents' use of the term *wildlife*, it should be noted, usually referred only to hunted species.

In a supportive letter, James Couch said the scientific significance of a "vast natural laboratory...is important beyond words." Characteristic of the post-war optimism about science associated with the campaign, he said the preserve might provide "new knowledge leading to a better world tomorrow."[44]

FIGURE 21. Charley Gray with a Dall sheep trophy taken near the Middle Fork of the Chandalar River, circa 1959. *Courtesy of Charles Gray.*

William Pruitt, Local Scientist Advocate

University of Alaska biology professor William Pruitt's influential involvement
in the campaign began with a letter pointing out the "misunderstandings" of
the area's scientific values caused by the newspaper accounts. He explained to
readers the concept of a "control" area whereby the animal ecology of regions
"where man's activities have upset natural conditions" could be compared
to natural areas. Pruitt advocated preservation of the area's scientific value
by pointing out that the small animals—mice, shrews, even invertebrates—
were of no less value than the more spectacular "big game." He argued that
the scientific values of the proposed wilderness "are so great as to make its
achievement worthy of the support of all Alaskans."[45]

Looking back fifty years, Pruitt recalled he had insisted that the area not
be referred to as a game range because "game implied that certain species are
more important than others." This area, he believed, "had its own rationale
for being." It should be allowed "to be what nature intended." Maintenance
of the area's full complement of life forms and their encompassing ecological

FIGURE 22. Biologist William Pruitt. *Photo by Les Viereck; Dan O'Neill Collection, Box 36, Folder
19; courtesy of the Archives, Alaska and Polar Regions Department, University of Alaska Fairbanks.*

and evolutionary processes was his reason for "agitating for the formation and preservation" of the area.[46]

Like several scientist-leaders of the campaign, Pruitt's professional development had been greatly influenced by the children's books of naturalist Ernest Thompson Seton. His organization, the Woodcraft Indians (later absorbed by the Boy Scouts), and his *Woodcraft Manual for Boys* extolled the recreational and character-enhancing benefits of camping and the practice of traditional outdoor skills. Pruitt became absorbed in Seton's popular *Wild Animals I Have Known* and *Two Little Savages*. In the tradition of Muir, they instilled in young readers a sense of moral order in nature and ennobled wild animals, particularly predators. "I just ate that up," Pruitt recalls.[47] Seton also connected preservationist, heritage, and romantic values to the Arctic. His book *The Arctic Prairies* (1911) was perhaps the first popular writing to feature the caribou–buffalo analogy. The North offered a second chance, an opportunity to avoid "a repetition of the Buffalo slaughter that disgraced the plains in the U.S."[48]

Not long after the Arctic campaign's conclusion, Pruitt attained some renown for being fired for his courageous stand against the University of Alaska–endorsed plan to use nuclear devices to blast a harbor in northwest Alaska. He went on to become one of Canada's leading Arctic ecologists and, as an advisor to the Ernest Thompson Seton Institute, Pruitt continues to perpetuate the ideals Seton espoused.

In response to supporters' letters, Charles Gray wrote again, this time urging resistance to "a land grab without precedent in the long history of withdraws in Alaska." George L. Collins's proposal for a wilderness area, he warned readers, was too large and it might "be completely inviolate by man for any purpose what-so-ever." Emphasizing that prospecting, as well as hunting and predator control, would likely be precluded, Gray stated that "we couldn't allow a prospector to be trampling on a flower while some scientist is studying it!"[49]

Pruitt quickly responded. "That is meant to be sarcasm," his letter retorted, "but in truth, it is exactly what should be the rule." Long after the mine has been exhausted and the prospector's money spent, Pruitt continued,

> the knowledge furnished by that flower, or that mouse, or that wolf which fed and survived in the region, that knowledge will still be used and will have become a part of our understanding of the arctic and will help all people live here.

Of course, the idea that research in this unaltered wilderness would provide ecological understandings that might contribute to a more sustainable relationship with the environment had been suggested by the Arctic proposal's early proponents. But the feisty Pruitt, the first Alaskan to strongly articulate this potential, was less inclined than they to avoid offense. His concluding remark, that the desires of a "few prospectors, miners, sportsmen, and guides must be sublimated to the scientist and his search for knowledge" undoubtedly fueled the controversy.[50]

Virginia Wood, Pioneer Environmentalist

Virginia Wood, soon to become one of Alaska's leading environmentalists, began her long involvement in the campaign with a detailed letter to the editor. She pointed out the intangible and heritage values of wilderness and suggested that Alaskans should look ahead and learn from those who established Yellowstone.

Wood addressed two issues that were becoming central to the Alaskan opposition. First was the concern that whatever form it might take, the Arctic

FIGURE 23. Virginia Wood in McKinley Park, 1969. Many of Wood's ideas for what became the Arctic Refuge came from her experiences exploring and guiding tourists in McKinley Park. *Courtesy of Virginia Wood.*

proposal would constitute a federal withdrawal. She acknowledged that Alaskans were "understandably resentful" of the many military and other withdrawals in the territory and agreed that some should be returned to public use. But she argued that associating the word "withdrawal" with the proposal created a misunderstanding. A distinction needed to be made, Wood said, as to "whether the land in question is to be withdrawn from the people or preserved for the people." Considering the many public uses that would be allowed, she told readers, "The creation of an arctic wilderness preserve would be giving land to the people rather than taking it away." Notably, Wood also stressed preservation, as opposed to protection or conservation.

Second, she addressed the continuing issue of the involvement of non-Alaskans in Alaska issues. "Opponents of the proposal," she noted, "resent outside groups such as the Sierra Club taking an interest in land that is 'none of their business.'" Concern about outsiders already had a history in the territory. Mount McKinley National Park, Katmai National Monument, and Glacier Bay National Monument had been established as a result of the efforts of non-Alaskan interests. The prospect of yet another huge withdrawal initiated by conservationists outside the territory made the Arctic proposal vulnerable to the criticism of statehood proponents that Alaska was being treated like a dependent colony.

Wood made the argument that outsiders had a legitimate stake in the future of the area, and not just "the vacationist seeking virgin lands to explore." Seeking to express the vicarious values that were becoming an underlying motivation of resident and nonresident supporters alike, she acknowledged that what happens to wildlife in Africa, or what happens in parks in the lower forty-eight states, might also be considered none of her business. But just knowing they were there was important. She compared the nonresidents' concern to how she would feel if the last lion or elephant were shot or if a dam were built in the Grand Canyon. Alaska wilderness, she concluded, was "for each of us and our posterity to enjoy."[51]

Wood became one of the most effective Alaskan supporters of the campaign. Although twenty-two years later she would become a recreational guide in the Arctic Refuge, at the time she had no notion of personally visiting it. Concerned about the mounting effects of industrial and technological growth, she was compelled by a sense that there needed to be "some places that nobody has done anything to." She traces such leanings to childhood adventures in the woods and to the writings of Ernest Thompson Seton and Henry David Thoreau. She and her partner, Celia Hunter, also a staunch supporter, had flown war-surplus planes to Alaska in 1947. A few years later they started Alaska's first ecotourism venture, Camp Denali, at the western edge of Mount

McKinley National Park. Wood vividly recalls discovering Marshall's writings
her first year in Alaska. "That really sparked my interest in wild Alaska," she
recalled, "his zest for adventure and seeing what's over the hill."

Shortly before her involvement in the campaign, Wood found a copy of
Leopold's *A Sand County Almanac* in a Park Service cabin while her ranger-
husband Morton was on patrol. She read it "over and over." Leopold, she
said, brought her to ecological thinking.[52] His philosophical interpretation of
ecological principles was appealing to her, especially his notion of the earth
as a community in which humans were citizens. Wood was among the many
nonscientists who would stress the area's scientific value. She later drew on
Leopold to provide what was probably the most succinct summary of the ecological argument for preserving the area. Such a wilderness area, she stated,
could be

> of the highest importance to science as a standard of reference—a natu-
> ral laboratory where biologists of today and the future can study to
> find the answers to the recurring question: What was the natural order
> before man changed it?[53]

While the Arctic proposal was being debated in the Fairbanks paper,
Collins received two letters regarding the response of the organization that

FIGURE 24. Conservationists and pilots Celia Hunter and Virginia Wood, circa 1950.
While landing in the northern foothills of the Alaska Range, their propeller hit the
ground, shearing off both tips. It was their only flying accident. *Courtesy of Virginia Wood.*

would come to play a pivotal role in the conflict. University of Alaska biology professor John Buckley, a supporter, had attended a meeting of the Fairbanks-based Tanana Valley Sportsmens Association and found the organization "was immediately up in arms over the proposal." This hunting and fishing organization was particularly annoyed by the fact that "The Last Great Wilderness" had been published in a California magazine (the *Sierra Club Bulletin*), while no notice was provided in Alaska.[54]

Soon after, Collins heard from Pruitt, who told him that the Sportsmens Association did not object to the proposed withdrawal so much as to "the fact that the program was instigated by 'outsiders.'" He advised Collins that attaining the support of local sportsmen's groups and Alaskan members of national conservation groups would be more effective than "more communications and publications by 'outsiders.'"[55]

Alaskans who opposed the proposal were rightly concerned about the influence of outside supporters. Their numbers were growing, and not just among the mainline conservation organizations. Paul Shepard, representing the National Council of State Garden Clubs, wrote Starker Leopold about the proposal, stating that he was "eager and prepared to sic 300,000 ladies on such an objective." Shepard, who would become a noted pioneer in the fields of human ecology and ecopsychology, knew of Alaskans' frontier attitude toward wolves and he knew that being surrounded by wilderness, they were least likely to understand its potential for loss. He probably represented many national conservation leaders when he told Leopold that "it does make some difference what the Alaskans themselves want, although I am frightened at the notion."[56]

The substantial increase in public interest stimulated by "The Last Great Wilderness" article coincided with a shift in leadership of the Arctic campaign. Collins and Sumner had been planning for the change for some time. Since their first explorations of the area, they had been unofficially strategizing with their friend Olaus Murie of the Wilderness Society. They knew that, as agency employees, they could not be perceived as advocates once the proposal became public. "As representatives of the National Park Service," Collins had written in late 1953, "we have felt ourselves to be limited to a descriptive and fact finding role with respect to this Arctic area."[57] Similarly, Sumner wrote that "in reporting the facts [regarding the area] we have met our responsibilities and it would be inappropriate for us to pursue the matter further."[58]

These were enormous understatements of the pair's overt advocacy. Collins acknowledged as much in an interview forty years later: "I talked whenever I could get an audience with or among people who I thought would be induced to be appreciative."[59] In regard to the Arctic proposal, the Park Service had allowed Collins considerable latitude to "define his job to embody the values that were emerging." There was at least the tacit knowledge that he "bent protocol a lot."[60] The Park Service director, according to Collins, "knew pretty well what we were up to officially"—but not, he implied, unofficially. With the issue becoming controversial, "it didn't take very much to get your bosses concerned. I'd get called in and talked to."[61] In December 1953 one of his supervisors, western regional director Lawrence Merriam, had written a memo to director Conrad Wirth regarding the agency's involvement in the campaign. Noting that "the implications are that it will become an exceedingly significant enterprise all over America," Merriam told the director the agency should continue to fund some research, but the initiative should now be considered the responsibility of the Wilderness Society and other organizations.[62] Collins and Sumner needed to be reined in before their proposal became more controversial. Early in January 1954, Collins concluded a letter to Olaus Murie discussing campaign details by stating

> Lowell [Sumner] and I are in perfect accord in feeling that we want to help the Wilderness Society take over the Arctic International Wilderness project. More importantly, I am sure that is what the Service wants.[63]

Howard Zahniser, Wilderness Ideologist

As Collins and Sumner assumed less visible roles, leadership of the campaign transitioned to the Wilderness Society during 1954. Although their mentors, the organization's principal founders Robert Marshall and Aldo Leopold, were dead, two philosophical heirs now shared leadership of the organization.[64] One was Howard Zahniser, the society's Washington, D.C.–based executive secretary. A persuasive lobbyist and brilliant tactician, Zahniser was adept at forming alliances with other conservation organizations and interest groups. His supporting role in the campaign was less visible than that of many others as he cultivated Capitol Hill contacts, coordinated strategy, and gave testimony.

But the scholarly Zahniser, described by environmental historian Stephen Fox as "one of the sharpest, best-stocked minds in conservation," contributed to the campaign's underlying ideology.[65] He was, foremost, a great synthesizer. He combined the insights of Thoreau and Muir with those of contemporary wilderness thinkers, particularly those of his friends Aldo Leopold, Robert Marshall, and Olaus Murie.[66] In 1949, the year Collins began planning for the Alaska Recreation Survey, Zahniser revived Marshall's idea of a federal wilderness law at the Sierra Club's First Biennial Wilderness Conference. In 1951 he proposed a national wilderness preservation system; his proposed Wilderness

Act contained concepts that would surface repeatedly as important attributes of the proposed Arctic wilderness:

> A wilderness, in contrast with those areas where man and his works dominate the landscape, is hereby recognized as an area where the earth and its community of life are untrammeled by man.[67]

The concept of an area and its community of life untrammeled by man describes a landscape condition that Zahniser further clarified as "not being subjected to human controls and manipulations" that interfere with natural forces.[68] This was essentially what Collins and Sumner had described as the area's freedom of ecological and evolutionary processes. This wilderness condition provided an important contrast with areas that humans dominate. One benefit of this contrast, discussed earlier, was the Leopoldian idea that wildlands provided a "baseline of normality for healthy ecosystems."

But Zahniser was not a biologist by either training or inclination. He came from a family of ministers and his orientation toward wilderness was more

FIGURE 25. Howard Zahniser, 1960. *Courtesy of the Zahniser family.*

spiritual than scientific. More important than the use of wilderness as an ecological comparison was the value of wilderness experience as a comparison to life in modern industrial society. Wilderness, Zahniser believed, provided a baseline of normality for the *human condition*. As a place where people yield their actions and uses to nature's primacy, wilderness provided the physical and psychological distance from modern society necessary to understand its effects. Zahniser summarized this antimodernist function of wilderness in his canonical treatise, "The Need for Wilderness Areas":

> Without the gadgets, the inventions, the contrivances whereby men have seemed to establish among themselves an independence of nature, without these distractions, to know the wilderness is to know a profound humility, to recognize one's littleness, to sense dependence and interdependence, indebtedness and responsibility.[69]

Olaus Murie, Campaign Leader

Zahniser's statement characterizes the philosophy of the Wilderness Society's charismatic director and president, Olaus Murie, who would come to personify the campaign and lead it to victory. Described as Lincolnesque, Murie had an air of humility and quiet authority that commanded respect even among the proposal's most strident opponents. His personal demeanor and stature as an acclaimed field biologist made him uniquely qualified to convey the varied purposes of the proposal to a diverse group of people, organizations, and officials, and persuade them to support it.

An early interest in natural history had led Murie to the formative influence of Ernest Thompson Seton's books extolling life in the wilds and the noble character of wild animals.[70] Murie's interests also took a practical bent; to help support his widowed mother and siblings, he became a skilled hunter and trapper. Murie earned a biology degree in 1913 and did fieldwork in the Pacific Northwest and Canada. In 1920 he was hired by the U.S. Biological Survey, predecessor of the U.S. Fish and Wildlife Service, to conduct a major study of the life history of caribou in Alaska and Canada.[71] For nearly seven years Murie conducted caribou research in the Alaska wilds, traveling by dogsled, boat, and foot. He also led expeditions to the Yukon Delta and Canada's Old Crow River to study waterfowl and conducted biological surveys on the Alaska Peninsula and throughout the Aleutian Islands. These experiences established him as an authority on the territory's wildlife and a master outdoorsman, a reputation that would serve him well during the campaign thirty years later. Also to serve him well was his 1924 marriage to a woman from Fairbanks,

Margaret "Mardy" Thomas, who would become his partner on the trail and throughout many conservation battles.[72]

Probably more than any other factor, it was the issue of predator control that first brought Murie to the forefront as a spokesman for the emerging ecology-based environmental perspective. Controversy among scientists and wildlife agencies in the 1920s and 1930s regarding the role of predators stimulated ecological thinking and changed public attitudes toward wildlife.[73] By the early 1950s the notion of maintaining the natural ecological role of even species such as wolves in some areas was prominent enough to become a significant factor in public opinion regarding the Arctic proposal.

Murie had been involved in predator control, including poisoning, before and while working in Alaska. But his field observations led to a systemic understanding of predators—and away from agency orthodoxy. During his early caribou work he wrote to his supervisor expressing a contrary perspective: "I have a theory that a certain amount of preying on caribou by wolves is beneficial to the herd."[74]

FIGURE 26. Olaus and Margaret Murie at Last Lake, Sheenjek River, 1956. *Photo by George B. Schaller; courtesy of the Murie Center.*

By 1929 he was overtly critical of his agency's killing of predators "in the spirit of hatred."[75] The subsequent censorship of some of his findings was a factor in Murie's decision in 1945 to leave the Fish and Wildlife Service to become director of the Wilderness Society, which he had served as a governing council member since his recruitment by Marshall eight years earlier. But his departure did not end his efforts to reform the agency he later recommended as the custodian for the proposed Arctic wilderness. In a 1952 letter of criticism, reflecting his evolving thinking, Murie argued that it made aesthetic and ethical sense, as well as ecological sense, to maintain what is now known as "biodiversity."[76] In an expression of his developing perspective, he told the Fish and Wildlife Service director it needed the best scientists, but "not specialists who are oblivious to *ecology*. We must consider *all* wildlife and all human aspirations." He prescribed a major shift in agency culture. The Fish and Wildlife Service, he wrote, needed personnel that are "psychologically adaptable to the strivings toward ideals in wildlife matters."[77]

Murie's concern with human ideals and aspirations reflects the fact that by the time he assumed leadership of the campaign, he had, like his friend Aldo Leopold, integrated tangible ecological concerns and intangible human values into a coherent wilderness philosophy. Derived from his wide-ranging observations and readings, and driven to advocacy by a visceral concern about his species' treatment of the natural world, his approach emphasized the need for humility and restraint in environmental matters.

This became a theme of the most detailed encapsulation of Murie's vision for the area, his paper "Wilderness Philosophy, Science, and the Arctic National Wildlife Range." Significantly, the title of the writing that most thoroughly describes his motivation for preserving the area placed philosophy before science. The paper, delivered at a science conference, described the scientific value of this "little portion of our planet left alone," particularly its "help to us for understanding of the natural processes in the universe." As a wilderness, the area could help people "to understand the basic energies which through the ages have made this planet habitable." But Murie's greater emphasis was on "what I consider human ecology … the importance of nature by which we live—not only physically, but esthetically and spiritually as well."[78] Not religious, Murie came from the perspective of a secular spirituality. Grounded in early romantic/transcendental precepts and enlightened by recent ecological and evolutionary insights, his ideology came to assume an innate affinity with the natural system based upon "a realization of a kinship with all life on this planet."[79]

Thus, in his paper's opening discussion of the impulse to protect wilderness, he offered that "we came by this urge through evolution … this urge has come down to us from the earliest time, and we must not ignore it if we believe in progress of the human spirit."[80] To Murie, nearing the end of his life, implicit in the wilderness concept was a recognition of an ultimate value, a larger reality encompassing human life and contributing meaning to it. It is therefore not surprising to find that throughout his later wilderness writings, and particularly those focused on the Arctic proposal, Murie placed preservation efforts in the context of the "world," the "earth," the "globe," and as "the universe measures time." Emphasizing this distant perspective served his purpose: to expand thinking about our species' role in the larger scheme of things.

As it had for Thoreau and Muir, wilderness protection to Murie symbolized an alternative to "the materialism and greed that has settled over our land."[81] As "a place to contemplate and try to understand our place in the world," wilderness provided an antidote to "the confused state of mankind's mind in this atomic age."[82] The centrality of ideals and human aspirations to Murie's advocacy is evident in what would be his most formal statement on the Arctic proposal. In testimony submitted to a Senate subcommittee hearing on proposed legislation to establish the Arctic Range, he stated that we need to make a living

> but we long for something more, something that has a mental, a spiritual impact on us. This idealism, more than anything else, will set us apart as a nation striving for something worthwhile in the universe.... It is inevitable, if we are to progress as people in the highest sense, that we shall become ever more concerned with saving the intangible resources, as embodied in this move to establish the Arctic Wildlife Range.[83]

Strategy

During his and Mardy's 1926 expedition to the headwaters of the Old Crow River, Olaus Murie had gotten just a few miles north of what became the proposal's southeast boundary. He later saw much of the area from the air, but at the time he assumed leadership of the campaign, he had only minimal experience on the ground. In 1953, at Collins's suggestion, he made plans to visit the Park Service team at Joe Creek, but last-minute commitments intervened. His priority for 1954 was to lead a summer-long expedition into the heart of the proposal in order to gain an ecological understanding of the area, photographing and sketching it

> with a view to demonstrating on the basis of detailed facts the value to science of this segment of Alaska. And, of equal importance, to interpret as well as we can the esthetic content of this sample of the

Arctic. We believe that we should be able to present to the public in a convincing way the desirability of insuring the preservation of this far north bit of wilderness.[84]

Murie planned to publicize the area through the context of a trip. The publications, slide shows, and films he expected to result would serve the same function that similar products were serving at the time in the fight to prevent construction of a dam in Dinosaur National Monument on the Colorado-Utah border. Overshadowing the Arctic campaign, the Dinosaur conflict was the most pressing preservation issue in the mid-1950s. It was the first of many postwar clashes that pitted the national interest against states' interests, and preservation against business, setting a pattern that the Arctic conflict and later conservation efforts would follow. Olaus and Mardy were among the leading organizers of that successful campaign. Their visit and raft trips through the canyon by associates contributed to the prose and photographs that, in historian Mark Harvey's analysis, "proved critical to awakening the public to this vast and beautiful preserve." Narrative and visual images would transform the unknown area "into a symbol of the nation's wilderness."[85] It was the Dinosaur strategy that Murie planned to repeat in the Arctic, and a similar symbolic transformation he hoped for.

Since the time of Thoreau and Muir, wilderness advocates had effectively employed the archetypal wilderness journey to such ends. Wilderness travel narratives often combined physical and mental adventure: One's physical passage became analogous to an inward passage, and outward discoveries corresponded to inner discoveries. Portrayed through the context of an expedition, northeast Alaska would appeal to a readership whose national history was steeped in journeys of exploration and discovery.

Another successful tactic of the Dinosaur conflict that Murie brought to the Arctic campaign was that of forging partnerships with groups outside the mainline conservation community. Recognizing that the thin base of Alaskan support needed to be broadened, he planned to visit with a number of Alaskan groups before beginning the expedition in May. In a letter to an associate summarizing his plans, he specifically mentioned his intent to meet with the influential Tanana Valley Sportsmens Association "for strategic reasons which I will tell you about some time."[86] Murie's statement underscores the strategic nature of the expedition that would become the defining event of the campaign. His reluctance to identify the role he foresaw for the hunting and fishing group hints at the caution with which he would approach sportsmen, whose support would be critical to success.

Both Murie and Zahniser knew that before widespread public support could be gained, they needed to determine which federal agency would serve as custodian and what the area's title would be.

The main problem was that no federal agency was fully qualified to manage land for the full range of values they sought to protect. The U.S. Forest Service was the most experienced, having had administratively established wilderness and primitive areas as early as 1924. These areas had fewer protective provisions than Murie and Zahniser envisioned. Further, without legislative mandates, any wilderness management guidelines of an area administratively established could be altered or abolished at any time by the agency. The fact that some 95 percent of the area was unforested was another reason they did not consider the Forest Service as a potential custodian. Although some organizations thought the area could be administered as a wilderness by its current administrator, the Bureau of Land Management, Murie and Zahniser did not recommend the BLM because its director did not think the agency could manage a wilderness area.

Zahniser favored the National Park Service, but deferred to Murie's preference for the Fish and Wildlife Service. Although he supported the Park Service, Zahniser did not want the area to become a national park. Nor did Murie wish it to become one of the Fish and Wildlife Service's national wildlife refuges or ranges. Rather, they shared the hope of protecting northeast Alaska through legislation that would specifically recognize the primacy of its wilderness qualities. In Zahniser's words, establishing legislation would ensure that "the particular requirements in such an Arctic wilderness were met in a special way for just that area." The legislation they envisioned would be unique to this area—and without precedent.

In 1954, Zahniser was in the early stages of formulating what would become the Wilderness Act, so he had been giving a lot of thought to protecting wilderness qualities by statute. He knew the limitations of protecting an area through administrative provisions that an agency could change on a whim. But he also knew that the administering agency might not follow legislative intent. Thus Zahniser advised Murie to consider appropriate management "conditions and requirements" during the planned expedition so that they could be incorporated into the specific legislation they believed was forthcoming. As to what to call such a unique area with such unique purposes, Zahniser agreed with Murie's new suggested title, "Arctic Wilderness Research Reserve."[87]

Given Murie's disdain for the Fish and Wildlife Service's predator programs, why did he support it as the custodial agency? One factor was probably that the Fish and Wildlife Service could accommodate Native hunting and trapping practices, whereas the Park Service probably would not. More important, he believed that recreational development by the Park Service posed a greater threat to the area. Murie was among the strongest critics of the Park Service's Mission 66 program. But until the end of his life, Murie was concerned about his choice of the Fish and Wildlife Service. Shortly before he died in 1963, Murie wrote, "It was concluded that [the area] would have the least development if we put it in the Fish and Wildlife Service.... I hope we were right."[88]

Murie's support for the Fish and Wildlife Service as the administrating agency cannot be taken as a softening of his concern about its approach toward predators. In fact, only a few months later he published an article taking its Alaska regional director, Clarence Rhode, to task for his recently published book, *Alaska's Fish and Wildlife*. In "Ethics and Predators," Murie protested the book's use of "only derogatory terms to characterize the carnivores." He complained that Rhode ignored the "ecological background for each animal," and characterized the wolverine as "a gluttonous killer," the weasel as "bloodthirsty," and the wolf as "preying on valuable big game animals."[89]

The book's appearance during the campaign reflects an attitude toward nature that was prevalent in the Fish and Wildlife Service and the Alaskan public. Murie's response to it did not endear him to many in the agency. Nor did his article published in the *Journal of Wildlife Management* about the same time. "Ethics in Wildlife Management" offered a thinly veiled criticism of wildlife managers who were "pretty good technicians but philosophical illiterates." It proposed to the profession "a philosophy about our relation with Nature, which grants Nature a right to exist, and reveals generosity toward wildlife."[90] Like his friend Aldo Leopold, Murie advocated for a land ethic less focused on human uses and more accepting of the otherness of life. Indeed, his writings about the Arctic proposal suggest that this area might serve as the embodiment of such an ethic.

A request by Murie for help financing the 1954 expedition to Alaska brought the prestigious New York Zoological Society and its affiliate, the Conservation Foundation, into the campaign. They had financed Starker Leopold and Frank Frazer Darling's territory-wide study described in their book *Wildlife in Alaska: An Ecological Reconnaissance*. Now they jointly committed $7,290, Murie's estimate for the fieldwork, public promotion, and territorial government lobbying in Fairbanks, Anchorage, and Juneau.[91] On the national level, public and political support came with the involvement of these influential organizations. Their leader, Fairfield Osborn, became personally involved, adding to the list of pioneers of the new environmental paradigm that would support the campaign.

Osborn's bestselling book, *Our Plundered Planet* (1948), is credited with launching the debate about the potentially apocalyptic environmental effects of unrestrained growth and development. Osborn warned of the "present terrific attack upon the natural life-giving elements of the earth." "There is only one solution," he concluded. "Man must recognize the necessity of cooperating with nature."[92] Osborn's involvement raised awareness of the Arctic campaign in the East, and furthered its association with broader concerns about the sustainability of the postwar order.

In March 1954, Murie traveled to Cumberland, Maryland, to join Supreme Court Justice William O. Douglas in leading a 186-mile walkathon of conservationists opposed to a proposal to build a highway along the scenic and historic Chesapeake and Ohio (C&O) Canal. Organized and publicized by Howard Zahniser, the trek brought Murie into a close friendship with the controversial liberal and conservationist judge.

The two had much in common. For both, outdoor adventures had provided formative experiences. Like Murie, Douglas was a conservationist-turned-preservationist who cited Thoreau and Muir regularly. Three years earlier, a 250-mile hike through the Himalayas culminating in a stay at

FIGURE 27. Fairfield Osborn. *Courtesy of the Wildlife Conservation Society.*

a Buddhist monastery had led to Douglas's spiritual awakening. Nature came to hold intrinsic value for him, and was a means for helping man "survive the mad rush of the machine age."[93] These paired values were the basis for Douglas's controversial proposal for a "Wilderness Bill of Rights" intended

> to protect those whose spiritual values extend to the rivers and lakes, the valleys and ridges, and who find life in mechanized society worth living only because those splendid resources are not despoiled.[94]

Within their respective professions, Murie the field biologist and Douglas the jurist were among the most publicly recognized of those who would employ antimodernist rhetoric to defend intangible wilderness values. Thus, Murie and Douglas had a lot to talk about during their eight days hiking together. One subject was the possibility of Douglas participating in the planned Arctic expedition, and perhaps lending his name, political influence, and writing skills to the effort to preserve the area.

In April Olaus wasn't feeling well and Mardy got him to go in for a checkup. He was diagnosed with tuberculosis, later determined to be tuberculosis-meningitis, an often fatal disease. News of Murie's illness alarmed the conservation community. Collins spoke for many when he wrote that the "biggest conservation project of all is the full and complete recovery of Olaus Murie."[95]

Olaus was hospitalized for several months in Denver, where Mardy was given a job at the Izaak Walton League's western office. Initially it was hoped that the expedition would just be postponed for a year. "And such it will be, Olaus," Fairfield Osborn wrote, "if you are a 'real good boy' and do what the doctors tell you." But progress was slow and recovery uncertain. By year's end it was apparent that Olaus would not be ready by the summer of 1955, if ever. Osborn began compiling a list, including Collins, Sumner, Olaus's brother Adolph, and Frank Darling, of those who might replace Olaus in leading the expedition.[96]

1955: Preparing for Alaska

By early 1955 Olaus began to improve. Although he had to dictate to Mardy because arm and shoulder pain made writing difficult, he contacted Osborn, assuring him he would be able to undertake the expedition the following spring. Because of the two-year delay, Olaus knew that the political stage of the Arctic campaign would coincide with the climax of the statehood campaign. Animosity toward federal management of resources would be more acute than ever. Attaining a designation with the words *wilderness* or *park* in the title, he knew, would be more problematic. Broadening the base of Alaskan support became ever more important, and more challenging.

One of Olaus's highest priorities was recruitment of Fairbanks sportsmen. His particular target was the organization that represented interior Alaskan hunters and fishermen, the Tanana Valley Sportsmens Association. Collins had done little to enlist the support of this well-organized group, probably because as a Park Service employee and a nonhunter, he would have been at a loss to gain its members' confidence. But Murie, in Collins's words, "was masterful in getting the ear of the shooter-type conservationist."[97]

Consistent with his evolutionary perspective of the human-nature relation, Murie viewed hunting as a part of the species' heritage, a "race-bred instinct that clings through many generations."[98] Appropriately pursued, and "away from reliance on the gadgets of the machine age," he believed hunting provided a wholesome means of connecting to the natural world. Although he was no longer a hunter, his reputation as one continued. His exploits of the 1920s had earned him an honorary membership in the fraternal organization the Pioneers of Alaska. No one else could have as credibly assured the Sportsmens Association that in the wilderness "hunting is by no means barred" and that the proposed area would provide "the kind of hunting and fishing the true sportsman enjoys in a wilderness environment, in the tradition of the highest form of the sport."[99]

Although Murie had the respect of the Sportsmens Association, he was also apprehensive about recruiting it. Formed in 1936, the organization sought to enhance hunting opportunities both by promoting the introduction of nonindigenous species such as elk, pheasants, and capercaillie grouse and by lobbying for predator control. The group was highly critical of McKinley Park's recent discontinuation of wolf killing.

While these positions conflicted with Murie's view of hunting as a means of participating in the natural order, he knew the potential contribution of the group's support, and the political costs of incurring its opposition. Keeping the focus on the quality of hunting and fishing experiences a wilderness area would provide, and diverting attention from the game-stocking and predator programs it would preclude, would surely test his diplomatic skills and strain his desire to be forthright with all concerned.

But while opportunities to harvest fish and game were the chief concerns of the Sportsmens Association, wilderness values more central to Murie's philosophy were not entirely absent. In July the organization's secretary, Joel Smith, wrote to Murie, thanking him for his Alaska conservation work, including his efforts to preserve wilderness areas. "The value of these areas," Smith wrote, cannot be measured in monetary terms any more than can value of religious institutions. Spiritual values reside in the spirit and it is of utmost importance that those few sources of spiritual inspiration which are provided by wilderness areas be preserved from desecration.[100]

On November 21 Murie wrote to Collins, saying that he was feeling better than he had for many years. That same day he wrote Osborn's organizations to describe the expedition arrangements he was making and to identify the people he had selected to accompany him and Mardy.

Four organizations cosponsored and participated in the expedition. The Wilderness Society, the New York Zoological Society, and the Conservation Foundation were the original sponsors, whose intent was to establish some form of wilderness withdrawal. Joining sponsorship was the University of Alaska, whose new president, Ernest Patty, was an old friend of the Muries. Mardy in particular had close ties to the university. She had grown up in Fairbanks and held the distinction of being the institution's first woman graduate. Patty was eager to support the project's biological research; whether he, a former mining engineer, also supported its main purpose is doubtful. Although William Pruitt, John Buckley, and other faculty already supported the Arctic proposal by this time and played important roles in the campaign, opposition was developing in the mining and geology departments. The university itself would remain neutral on the establishment issue.

The university sponsored one of the five expedition participants. Brina Kessel was a young associate professor who would later become Alaska's leading ornithologist. Kessel's primary role was to document the distribution of birds and plants and to study their ecological relationship to the area's various habitats.

Murie also selected Bob Krear, a family friend who had fought in Europe during the war with Murie's son Martin. Krear was a doctoral student in zoology with research experience in Alaska and Canada. More important, Krear was an experienced filmmaker and photographer; he was to visually document the area and the group's experience of it. He would go on to become a professor of biology and a noted national park naturalist.

Finally, Murie chose a young student who had written two years earlier, offering to work for no compensation beyond the experience. George Schaller would assist the others in field studies and take care of much of the camp work. He would continue an association with the Zoological Society and become one of the world's leading conservation biologists. The first of his many acclaimed books, *The Mountain Gorilla*, would be dedicated to Olaus.

Mardy would be the camp manager and chief cook. She would also provide physical and emotional support for Olaus, who was still recovering from his bout with meningitis. She planned to write articles, and anticipated helping Olaus write the book on the area that he was planning. But his *Journeys to the Far North* would be published posthumously, twelve years after the campaign. Mardy's journal and eloquent magazine accounts of the expedition became part of her now classic book, *Two in the Far North.*

Shortly before the Muries left for Alaska, they received word that the battle to protect Dinosaur Monument had been won. On 11 April 1956 President Eisenhower signed legislation prohibiting construction of dams in any part of the national park system. "The wilderness movement had its finest hour to that date," Roderick Nash writes. The hard-earned victory "gave preservationists the momentum necessary to launch a campaign for a national policy of wilderness preservation."[101] The milestone demonstrated an encouraging level of public support for protecting natural areas. It affirmed the effectiveness of the arguments and many of the tactics that would be used in the concurrent campaigns to protect northeast Alaska and pass a wilderness act. In fact, on the day of the victory, Howard Zahniser wrote several congressmen requesting sponsorship of his wilderness bill. The outcome of the Dinosaur conflict affirmed what Zahniser referred to as "the sanctity of dedicated areas"—the increased likelihood that once designated, conservation areas would be permanently protected.[102]

4

The 1956 Sheenjek Expedition

Here we found Nature's freedom.

—Olaus Murie[1]

Science, Adventure, and Inspiration

In mid-May 1956, the five expedition members assembled at the University of Alaska. While the other four packed, Olaus met with a variety of organizations in Fairbanks and Anchorage to talk about the Arctic proposal and to make arrangements for meetings and presentations of the expedition's findings upon their return in the fall.

Olaus and Mardy had decided that the expedition would thoroughly explore one area of the proposal, as opposed to gaining a less intimate understanding of the entire region. George Collins had recommended the Sheenjek River Valley. The Muries wrote that they selected it because it was centrally located

◀ FIGURE 28. The 1956 Sheenjek Expedition camp at Last Lake. *Photo by George Schaller.*

within the boundaries Collins and Sumner had proposed and because it was among the least-known areas in the region.

After a send-off party by Virginia Wood and other Fairbanks conservationists, the group flew to Fort Yukon. The 1954 plan had been to hire Indians to boat them into the region. Instead, they chartered a Cessna 180 to fly them to a frozen lake near where the Sheenjek River flows out of the mountains. They named it Lobo Lake in honor of a large wolf that trotted across the ice before them. Keith Harrington, the bush pilot who ferried the group in and resupplied them throughout the summer, recalls a comment his Native helper made as they loaded Olaus, Mardy, and their gear into the plane. Noticing the couple were elderly and had no gun, he remarked to Harrington, "I wonder if these guys know what they're doin'?" The pilot knew nothing of those he was taking into the "unforgiving country" in which an adventurer he had dropped off the previous summer had perished. But his passengers' backcountry expertise later became apparent, and over the summer he came to appreciate that, in fact, "they were *very* good at what they were doing."[2]

A month later Harrington moved their camp twenty miles upriver to the lake well into the mountains where Collins and Sumner had camped. Harrington told them it was the northernmost lake in the valley large enough for a floatplane. They gave it the name Last Lake.

In his report to the expedition's sponsors, Olaus summarized the research tasks he had assigned each member. Beyond the scientific purposes, he reported that he "had emphasized also that one of the main objectives of the trip would be for each member of the party to have a rich experience from it! In a way, this was to be a 'sample adventure' in wilderness experience."[3]

Brina Kessel remembers their first morning, June 1, when "at breakfast, Olaus gave our work papers so to speak: 'I want you to get the best that you can out of your experience here this summer.' And that was our assignment."[4] Bob Krear recalled that "Olaus and Mardy and all of us wanted the feeling of peace that could come only by being totally isolated from what was going on in the world ... just to be surrounded for three months by that great, pristine arctic beauty." That feeling would require more than remoteness. They knew that the circumstances they imposed upon themselves, including what to bring and what to leave behind, would shape their experience. Hence, they refused—twice, Krear remembers—offers for the loan of two-way radios.[5] George Schaller recalled their purpose as two-fold: "to study not only the natural history but also to gather impressions of the 'precious intangible values' as Olaus phrased it, with the hope that this knowledge will lead to protection of the area." Within a few days of their arrival, Schaller recalls, "We all knew that it must be preserved as an original fragment of our past, a last opportunity to protect part of this continent as it once was."[6]

They came as humble guests of a landscape they considered to have intrinsic value. "And this attitude of consideration, and reverence," Mardy later wrote, "is an integral part of an attitude toward the still evocative places on our planet." Such was the "spirit of the place" in which their scientific work would be conducted and their impressions recorded.[7]

The natural history information collected that summer was less important for its scientific value than for its contribution to descriptive and impressionistic portrayals of the area. To convey the values of this remote area to the conservation-minded public was, of course, the primary purpose of the expedition.

Olaus and Mardy would publish prolifically on their summer's experiences. Feature articles would appear in the *Alaska Sportsman, Animal Kingdom, Audubon, Living Wilderness, National Parks*, and *Outdoor America* magazines, as well as in various newspapers. Mardy's articles would be incorporated in her book, *Two in the Far North*. Schaller would appeal to sportsmen's interests in an *Outdoor Life* feature the magazine titled "New Area for Hunters."[8] Their experiences were described by other writers as well, including a visiting columnist from the *Seattle Post-Intelligencer* who, Olaus said, "wrote a good plea for wilderness." The group's Sheenjek experiences also provided material for letters they and others would write to potential supporters, legislators, and key government officials.

Three years earlier, during the Dinosaur campaign, the Sierra Club had pioneered the use of short movies as a means of publicizing preservation initiatives. Its *Wilderness River Trail* was a model for the two 16-mm motion pictures Krear filmed for distribution to organizations and schools. He narrated the twenty-one-minute *Arctic Wildlife Range*, produced by Thorne Films. The Alaska Conservation Society *News Bulletin* described it as a "moving ecological portrayal of the plant, animal, and bird life of the tundra world of the Brooks Range." It provided "graphic proof of the need to give this area permanent protection and status so that generations to come will always have an area with an arctic environment, unchanged by man." The nine-minute *Letter from the Brooks Range* was produced by Fairfield Osborn's Conservation Foundation. Narrated by Olaus and Mardy, it was a more personal plea for the area's protection. Reflecting the purpose of both films, the *News Bulletin* reported, "It's a wonderful film and has stirred up a great deal of interest, and will result in letters to congressmen."[9]

Probably the single most effective product was the slide show Olaus developed and presented to a variety of Alaska and lower-forty-eight

audiences, including the secretary of the interior during the final days of
the Arctic campaign.

In late July, Supreme Court Justice William O. Douglas and his wife,
Mercedes, joined the expedition. The acclaimed conservationist and controversial jurist was the most publicly recognized of those who would use their
Sheenjek experiences to extol the area's values. Douglas "could attract publicity
for conservation simply by casting a fly or going for a hike."[10] George L. Collins,
who came to confer with Olaus on campaign strategy at the time of Douglas's
visit, referred to him as "that goofy bird from the Supreme Court whose name
on anything in our kind of conservation was sterling, and magic."[11] Among
his contributions to the campaign, Douglas featured his Sheenjek trip as the
opening chapter of his book *My Wilderness: The Pacific West*.[12]

As a scientific expedition, the project had an eminently qualified leader. In
addition to his pioneering study of caribou, Olaus had recently published two
highly regarded books, *The Elk of North America* and *A Field Guide to Animal
Tracks*.[13] His approach to investigating the area was more in the tradition of
natural history than today's biological research. He was little interested in
what understanding could be gleaned from numbers. He eschewed intrusive
techniques and the use of airplanes for surveys. As Mardy wrote, "Olaus has a
strong belief that valuable scientific data are accumulated *on the ground*, afoot,
with eyes and ears alert, notebook and camera ready."[14] Also ready was a bag
of plaster of Paris, which, since early in his field career, had a permanent place
in Olaus's knapsack. Animal tracks fascinated Olaus and he could hardly pass
up the opportunity to cast a good one.

The introduction to Schaller's comprehensive report on the expedition's
findings lends further insight into its leader's approach. Dr. Murie, he wrote,

> taught me in his quiet way to observe and to appreciate many aspects of
> wilderness which I had formerly overlooked. Untiringly he roamed the
> valleys and mountains collecting scats, sketching, and taking copious
> notes on everything which came to his attentive eyes.[15]

An "earnest disciple" of this approach to the landscape, Schaller later recalled
an incident that characterized Olaus's search for "the wholeness of it." While
hiking across the muskeg tundra, the two came across "a big pile of very
soggy grizzly bear droppings." Schaller recalled,

> One would be tempted to ignore them . . . but Olaus kneeled down and
> cupped the wet droppings in his hands. And with a great big grin, he
> looked at them and dissected them to see what the bear had eaten. That

became just another small fact that cumulatively gave us some insights into what went on in the ecology of the area.[16]

Regarding the ecological insights Olaus sought, two points should be made. First, he was interested in the interrelatedness of all life forms, not just that of the large charismatic mammals. As he emphasized in an *Outdoor America* article on the expedition, "Not all the creatures of this country are fascinating because of sheer size." No less important to the area were "the diverse manifestations of its life."[17] Mice and sparrows received their full attention, as did invertebrates—they cataloged no fewer than 23 species of spiders. They identified 138 species of flowering plants and, as interested in the most primitive plant forms, they collected 40 species of lichen.[18] Each species formed a part of the "whole assemblage of living things which go to make up the rich life of that piece of country we saw and studied and learned to admire."[19]

Murie's appreciation of "the whole ecological ensemble" was grounded in an overarching interest in the large-scale process of evolution. In "The Grizzly Bear and the Wilderness," published soon after the expedition, Olaus emphasized one of the great values of northeast Alaska as a wilderness area:

FIGURE 29. Olaus Murie making a plaster cast of an animal track, 1956. *Courtesy of George B. Schaller.*

Here the scientist, especially the ecologist, be he professional or amateur, has the opportunity to study the interrelationships of plants and
animals, to see how Nature proceeds with evolutionary processes.[20]

Evolution to Murie represented the transcendental idea of the interrelatedness of all life and provided time depth to ecological perception—"that
incredible sweep of millennia," in the words of his friend Aldo Leopold.[21]
Evolution related the area's ecology to its genesis; it was for Murie the scientific
story of creation, connecting all species to a common mysterious past and an
unknown future. Evolution placed humanity within the timeless continuity
of natural processes.

So central was this creative process to Olaus's thinking that he had recently
concluded a *Journal of Wildlife Management* article by telling wildlife profes-
sionals, "We need to look up from our technical study at times and look at the
horizon. Evolution is our employer."[22] In this vein, he characterized the Arctic
campaign as a "basic effort to save a part of nature as evolution has produced
it."[23] Though not scientifically oriented, Mardy, too, saw the area's wildlife
in the context of an ageless dynamic process. Part of the feeling of adventure,
she said, was "wondering what life there was long ago."[24]

Caribou and Wolves

Collins, Sumner, and others had established the caribou as one of the area's
keystone species and, more important, as a symbol of the area's untrammeled
ecological and evolutionary processes. For expedition members, the caribou's
unbounded wanderings also served as an evocative representation of these
unseen forces. In Schaller's words:

> The animals dominate the landscape wherever they are, a river of life,
> always moving, moving toward the ridge beyond, not only defin-
> ing this Arctic ecosystem, but also symbolizing the freedom of its
> wilderness.[25]

Mardy's writings repeatedly presented the caribou in terms more descriptive
of an essence than a species. "Here was the living, moving, warm-blooded life
of the Arctic," she wrote, "out of some far valley in the west of this region, into
some far valley to the east." Evoking primeval associations, she described this
force as flowing "with the wisdom of the ages." These nomads were "needing all these valleys and mountains in which to live." In the context of her
advocacy for preservation, she skillfully led readers to question the potential
consequences of not protecting the caribou's entire range. What might happen

to their ageless movements, she implied, the unbroken connection to their evolutionary past?[26]

But more than the caribou, expedition writings portrayed the wolf as the main carrier of the ideological significance of a landscape and its life forms which were to be left free of human alteration, control, and subjugation. It was probably no coincidence that they named the lake at which they first camped Lobo—the name of the noble wolf-pack leader who was relentlessly pursued by ranchers and bounty hunters in one of Olaus's favorite childhood books, Seton's *Wild Animals I Have Known*.

Shortly after returning from the expedition, Olaus wrote a cover story for *Audubon Magazine* titled "Wolf," the animal whose "serenade of the dawn stands out as one of the high points in our experience." The wolf, he said, "symbolizes all those original natural values so important for us," especially "the concept of wilderness itself."[27]

Although Olaus was soft-spoken and restrained, he had, according to his son Donald, "a core of steel when aroused," and probably nothing roused him more than the treatment of wolves, which violated his concept of wilderness.[28] As he had throughout his career, Olaus reserved his strongest language to protest the work of "government poison squads," conducted "to the accompaniment of lurid hate-propaganda." In "Wolf" he argued that the wolves' killing of caribou was part of the natural cycle of life and balance of nature. Predators, he pointed out, prevented the numbers of caribou from increasing beyond what the habitat would support. Further, because wolves can most readily take the old, diseased, or crippled animals, they serve as an evolutionary force keeping the herd healthy. "Do we dare to get ecological facts?" he asked.[29]

The iconic wolf echoes the area's sublimity in Justice Douglas's *My Wilderness*. His sighting of a wolf loping across a tundra hillside was "as moving as a symphony." But more important than the excitement of the encounter, the animal's wild presence contributed meaning to the area. "His very being," he wrote, "puts life in new dimensions." Emphasizing its vulnerability "in this our last great sanctuary," Douglas also decried the practice of aerial wolf hunting and the bounty that subsidized it. After citing Olaus's research on wolf–prey relationships, Douglas pronounced, "This is—and must forever remain—a roadless primitive area where all food chains are unbroken, where the ancient ecological balance provided by nature is maintained."[30]

To emphasize the need to establish northeast Alaska as an inviolate sanctuary, expedition writings combined long-established romantic conventions with visceral images of the wolf's vulnerability to humans with antiquated attitudes toward predators. The authors employed the wolf to illustrate the potential contributions of "the new science of Ecology" to advance what Murie optimistically believed to be "the recent evolution in human thinking … a greater sensitivity … the wholesome impulse of generosity toward our fellow creatures."[31]

Foregrounding the symbolic significance of the wolf is the hopeful question Mardy posed to readers in the concluding sentence of *Two in the Far North*: "Do I dare to believe," she asked, "that one of my great grandchildren may someday journey to the Sheenjek and still find the gray wolf trotting across the ice of Lobo Lake?"[32]

In addition to collecting observations of flora and fauna, the group established study plots to more systematically describe species composition, phenology, and ecological associations. Two scientific reports resulted from the expedition. *Birds of the Upper Sheenjek Valley, Northeastern Alaska*, was coauthored by Kessel and Schaller and published in 1960. Written in standard biological form and parlance, it described eighty-six species of birds and their habitats.

Schaller's *Arctic Valley: A Report on the 1956 Murie Brooks Range, Alaska Expedition* was more inclusive of mammal, fish, and invertebrate observations. It concluded that the chief value of the expedition's scientific findings lay in the context of wildness: the fact that "the area has been left undisturbed by man—a vast natural laboratory in which plants and animals live as they always lived."[33] Emphasizing this value, Schaller went on to quote, as many others would, one of Collins and Sumner's statements from the "Last Great Wilderness":

> The region offers science probably the best opportunity of any place in Alaska, if not in the whole of North America, for studying the processes by which … Arctic animals maintain their numbers through natural checks and balances of climate, food supply, and predation.[34]

As predicted, the expedition's documentation of the valley's natural history, the earliest such comprehensive study in the Brooks Range, has become increasingly important as a baseline for understanding environmental change. Forty years later, some sixty years after Aldo Leopold first espoused this scientific value of wilderness, the Fish and Wildlife Service established a long-term ecological monitoring site next to Last Lake. "Fulfilling the Vision," the introduction to the Arctic Refuge's ecological monitoring plan, recognizes the "distinctive function" the early Arctic proponents thought the area should serve and explains how that vision "compels the Fish and Wildlife Service to think beyond the traditional mission of refuges."

The plan cites Olaus in support of the idea that this was "to be a place embodying values that transcend its boundaries," where "scientific understandings found here might someday serve on a global scale." Such places, Murie had emphasized in one of his Arctic range writings,

> should be kept for basic scientific study, for observation, as a help to us for our understanding of the natural processes in the universe. . . . We have only begun to understand the basic energies which through the ages have made this planet habitable. If we are wise, we will cherish what we have left of such places in our land.

Further recognizing the early proponents' vision and idealism, the plan cites Sumner's hope that the area would be granted the "freedom to continue . . . the particular story of Planet Earth unfolding here . . . the majestic story of evolution . . . the intricate and inscrutable unfolding of the Earth's destiny."[35]

"This Wondrous Mingling of Weariness and Triumph"

Schaller acknowledged the scientific value of the expedition's findings in his *Arctic Valley* report, but emphasized the group's "hope that the long range effect may culminate in the ultimate setting aside of this last and greatest remaining wilderness."[36] His 1,000-plus miles of day hikes and lengthy solo treks—during which he wore out two pairs of L.L. Bean boots—led him to laud the group's "life of rugged adventure and high spiritual reward." Schaller contrasted the adventurous experiences available here with life in postwar society and its "modern reach for ease and gadgets." Living in peace and harmony with the land, he wrote, "dispelled the uneasiness of body and soul which seems to accompany our life in civilization in the cities."[37]

Even Olaus and Mardy went off for a five-day exploratory trek, although their main motivation for ascending the headwaters of the Sheenjek may have been more, as Krear recalled, "to recapture the memories of their honeymoon together," when, thirty-four years earlier, they boated and mushed 550 miles through the Central Brooks Range.[38] But Olaus was sixty-seven now and still weak from his bout with tuberculosis. He struggled across the tussocks, and both he and Mardy questioned their store of endurance. "Our patience and strength were pushed to the limit," he wrote in one account. "Several times on this afternoon, loaded as I was with a pack, I lost my footing and fell—and just wanted to lie there." But like sojourners of the ancient journey quest, they found satisfaction in having persevered in the face of hardship, a benefit more fully realized after the return. "As we look upon the experience," Olaus wrote, "it was surely enhanced by our struggle to achieve it."[39]

Olaus would prescribe a management approach to recreation that would ensure perpetuation of the engaging opportunities the group experienced. This area, he wrote,

> should be reserved for those who crave a true wilderness experience, those who can stand weather, who have the stamina to deal with the vicissitudes of camp life, and still enjoy the experience.... Those who want wilderness should have the privilege to go there and find it undisturbed.... [S]o far as possible it should be left alone ... capable of satisfying an important human urge, the use of wilderness as wilderness, and not as make-believe.[40]

This prescription reflects Olaus's belief that the nation needed places that do more than "bring the out-of-doors to the tourist in convenient form." More important, he said, "Americans need a more virile recreation, a form of enjoyment earned through effort."[41] This area, he believed, might provide experiences in rugged outdoor living in the tradition "of that precious frontier atmosphere which helps build a strong civilization."[42]

As previously noted, the notion that preserving wilderness might help perpetuate the conditions that had shaped American character and affirm the nation's distinctive frontier-forged identity was a common theme of the back-to-nature literature popular at the turn of the century. These ideas had been espoused by Theodore Roosevelt, who argued that

> no nation facing the unhealthy softening and relaxation of fiber that tends to accompany civilization can afford to neglect anything that will develop hardihood, resolution, and the scorn of discomfort and danger.[43]

This idea of wilderness adventuring grounds serving to cultivate and enhance one's heartiness and, at a societal level, affirm the nation's identity was, of course, a prominent theme of Ernest Thompson Seton and the other woodcraft-tradition writers of Olaus's youth. These heritage values had been furthered by Leopold, brought to the Brooks Range by Marshall, and associated with the Arctic proposal by the frontier references of Collins and Sumner. In that tradition, Olaus believed this area would provide a setting for challenging, self-reliant, "virile" engagements with nature that might enhance one's physical strength and personal character.

Up to the time of the expedition, accounts celebrating the benefits of encountering adventure and challenge in the wilderness were almost exclusively written by men. The social and cultural changes that would encourage women to venture into the wilderness and then speak for it were still more than a decade away. But since their marriage, Mardy had been Olaus's partner on many of his extended and arduous expeditions. She knew both the joys and rigors of wilderness life, and she knew how to write.

Mardy's writings about their summer celebrated the cathartic effects of their treks. She did not need the masculine rhetoric of frontierism to provide a sense of how endurance and struggle gave rise to "this wondrous mingling of weariness and triumph."[44] Readers of the era's nature literature were often warned of the psychological and social ills accompanying the demographic shift from country to urban living. They were advised that experiences in nature could provide an antidote. In that genre, Mardy wrote that the vast, challenging Arctic wilderness offered "the greatest reservoir of that kind of medicine for mankind."[45] Reflecting upon their experiences in light of contemporary trends in American civilization, she predicted that

> [t]here are going to be increasing numbers of young people, and older ones, who will need and crave and benefit from the experience of travel in far places, untouched places, under their own power. For those who are willing to exert themselves for this experience, there is a great gift to be won in places like the Arctic Wildlife Range, a gift to be had nowadays in very few remaining parts of our plundered planet—the gift of personal satisfaction, the personal well-being purchased by striving—by lifting and setting down your legs, over and over, through the muskeg, up the slopes, gaining the summit.[46]

Noteworthy is Mardy's reference to "our plundered planet." Undoubtedly it was intended to bring to mind the postwar concerns highlighted by Fairfield Osborn's popular apocalyptic book, *Our Plundered Planet*. Osborn, the expedition's primary sponsor, had warned of the ecological and human threats posed by seemingly unrestrained technological progress. For the Muries and many other Arctic proponents, the preservation effort was, at the same time, an antimodernist reaction against what seemed to be the national imperative to adopt new technologies without adequately weighing their consequences—personal and social as well as environmental. Thus Mardy preceded her statement with the warning that present trends could result "in turning the children of the near future into robots and automatons and weaklings."[47] Worse, she feared that man would "destroy himself through his idolatry of the machine."[48] Olaus referenced one of the worst "ills that now beset us … the creation of that Sword of Damocles that hangs over us all, the atom bomb and the missile to deliver it."[49]

"Look, Where Are We Going?"

For many conservationists the nuclear peril was emblematic of the threat posed by advancing technology. Environmental historian Donald Worster traces the American "Age of Ecology" to July 16, 1945, when the first atomic bomb was exploded. By the mid-1950s the national press was regularly reporting the development of more powerful bombs, and a few weeks after the group arrived at the Sheenjek River, both *Time* and *Newsweek* reported on troubling findings concerning radioactive fallout. Under the threat of the atomic bomb, Worster writes, "a new moral consciousness called environmentalism began to take form, whose purpose was to use the insights of ecology to restrain the use of modern science-based power over nature."[50]

For the Muries and other early proponents of ecological thinking, recent insights into evolution contributed to the fear of disastrous consequences if humans do not accept the need to restrain technology and live within the limits of the biosphere. By the early 1900s, most of the naturalists and scientists with leading roles in the wilderness movement believed in evolution, their acceptance eased by the assumption that the process was progressive and following a predestined direction. During their formative years proponents had been influenced by writers such as John Muir, who wrote that nature follows a course of "law, order, creative intelligence, loving design."[51]

By mid-century, however, advances in paleontology, zoology, physiology, and population genetics were eroding the comforting notion of a directed cosmic order. Natural selection, the mechanism of evolution, was now seen as a random process—unconscious, disorderly, and lacking in design. "We know now what was unknown to all the preceding caravan of generations," Aldo Leopold had recently concluded in *A Sand County Almanac*, "men are only fellow-voyagers with other creatures in the odyssey of evolution."[52] By implication, man was not the pinnacle of evolution. Human progress was not inevitable.

For many, optimism that science would inevitably improve the human condition was giving way to the pessimism associated with the technologies of war and resource exploitation. For them, there was an ever greater need for a symbol of their species' capacity to cultivate, as Howard Zahniser wrote that year, "the humility to know ourselves as dependent members of a great community of life."[53]

PLATE 1. *The Muries in Alaska.* A painting of the Muries overlooking the Sheenjek River valley by C. Rusty Heurlin, 1963. *Courtesy of the University of Alaska Museum of the North.*

PLATE 2. Left to right: Robert Krear, Olaus Murie, Noel Wien, Mercedes and Justice William O. Douglas, Mardy Murie, and George Collins at Last Lake, August 1956. Pioneer bush pilot Noel Wien had just flown George Collins in to confer with the Muries on campaign strategy. *Photo by George B. Schaller.*

PLATE 3. Last Lake camp, July 1956. From left to right: Olaus Murie, George Schaller, Robert Krear, Mardy Murie. *Photo by Brina Kessel; courtesy of the Murie Center.*

PLATE 4. Robert Krear gets a haircut from Don MacLeod, Olaus's physician, who visited for two weeks in June 1956. *Courtesy of Robert Krear.*

PLATE 5. Mardy Murie recording her observations along Big Creek near Last Lake, July 1956. *Photo by George B. Schaller.*

PLATE 6. Brina Kessel and Margaret Murie watch caribou from their camp at Lobo Lake, June 1956. *Photo by Robert Krear.*

PLATE 7. Last Lake and the Sheenjek River valley. *Photo by Wilbur Mills.*

PLATE 8. Nichenthraw Mountain reflected in an unnamed lake in the Chandalar River valley. *Photo by Subhankar Banerjee.*

PLATE 9. The Porcupine caribou herd along the Niguanak River. An estimated 60,000 caribou were in this aggregation in July 1986. *Photo by Fran Mauer.*

PLATE 10. Midnight on the Kongakut River, where it flows out of the northern foothills and onto the coastal plain. *Photo by Subhankar Banerjee.*

PLATE 11. The Kongakut River valley, looking south to the Romanzof Mountains.
Photo by Wilbur Mills.

PLATE 12. Summer storm over Marsh Creek, south of Camden Bay, 1998.
Photo by Roy Corral.

PLATE 13. Sojourners before Mount Weller, Sadlerochit Mountains, 1998.
Photo by Roy Corral.

PLATE 14. *Gates of the Valley*, by Bill Brody, was painted on location on the Marsh Fork of the Canning River in 1993. Brody is a member of Artists of the Arctic Refuge, a group that continues the tradition of creating images that expand public awareness of the refuge's wilderness character.
Courtesy of Bill Brody.

The Muries' writings exemplified the long-established wilderness literary practice of disparaging trends in modern civilization. By their time, the concerns ranged from the softening of citified youth to fears of nuclear Armageddon. But at least since the time of Thoreau, the leading wilderness philosophers, who tended to be among the more educated of their society, believed that wilderness also complemented civilization and helped strengthen it. As in the ancient journey quest, their periodic escapes to the wilderness enabled them to return stronger and better prepared to deal with civilization's deficiencies. Further, sojourners returned more appreciative of civilization's benefits. As Zahniser had just written, wilderness "is not a disparagement of our civilization ... rather an admiration of it to the point of perpetuating it."[54] And as Olaus wrote upon returning from a trip to the Arctic, wilderness preservation was part of a broader effort "to try to improve our culture."[55] Wilderness experience, they believed, provided a historic, even prehistoric, perspective from which to understand the modern order—enhancing appreciation of its benefits and increasing understanding of its shortcomings that might be rectified.

By the mid-1950s many wilderness advocates had come to believe that the technological imperative was so embedded in American culture that people could no longer grasp its impact on them. Thus, Mardy bemoaned Americans having "learned to need all the comforts and refinements and things and gadgets all the technology has presented to us." "In all this complexity of *things*," she went on, "where is the voice to say: Look, where are we going?"[56] Wilderness was seen as providing the distance from technology necessary to understand the values underlying its use and the worldview built into its various forms.

The couple thought deeply about which characteristics of the environment contributed to, as Mardy expressed it, the experiential "gift" available in northeast Alaska. One was the area's scenic beauty, regularly and effusively described in their writings. But it is noteworthy that they, like Aldo Leopold, used the word *aesthetic* more often than *scenic*. Aesthetic perception arose from a melding of the visual qualities of the surface with the unseen values associated with the area. As Olaus said, "A deeper beauty lies in an understanding of the significance of a landscape."[57] That significance derived in part from their knowing it was wild, whole, and that the ageless processes that formed and shaped what is seen continued. "This is the value of this piece of wilderness," Mardy wrote.[58]

The "landscape" Olaus referred to was, of course, more than the objective, physical environment they saw. This was also a place becoming infused with subjective meanings. Seen through the filter of the wilderness ideology, the Sheenjek region was a conduit for symbolic associations expedition members brought to it. Attaining the "gift," they recognized, required a perceptual readiness—that is, a knowledge and appreciation of the values embodied in the wilderness concept. Moreover, the "gift" depended upon arriving with an expectation for experiencing the benefits associated with these imbued values. As Olaus had asked, "What would happen if the people who plan a wilderness sojourn would prepare the mind for the experience?" He suggested prospective visitors read a book on ecology like John Storer's recently published, now-classic book, *The Web of Life*. If they arrived with an awareness of the unseen beauty of ecological integrity and evolutionary process, Olaus believed, "a whole new world of understanding could open up for them."[59]

An Evolutionary Heritage

But while Olaus felt the attitude and knowledge one brings would help catalyze a connection—or reconnection—to the natural world, he also believed one arrives with an innate predisposition for finding it. He surely would have agreed with the thesis of *Coming Home to the Pleistocene*, a book later written by his friend and fellow Arctic proponent Paul Shepard, who argued that humans' short history of civilization had not erased the memory of the millions of years of wilderness wandering that had programmed their genes.[60] "Before discussing the Arctic Range," Olaus began a science conference presentation, "let me first consider how it happens that we want wild country. We came by this urge through evolution."[61]

Murie believed that people who want to experience wilderness do so because of an innate urge—often obscured by modern culture—for relatedness with the natural world of their origin, later described as biophilia.[62] And beyond this primal affinity, he felt that wild country and this Arctic wilderness in particular might serve an impulse the psychological literature was then beginning to describe as the "exploratory drive."[63]

Olaus noted that throughout history, many people "have had the strong urge to go places, to explore ... to discover, to find out."[64] Indeed, the explorer's anticipation figured prominently in the group's experiences. It was the Arctic's "call to adventure" for Justice Douglas: "a call that is compelling. The distant mountains make one want to go on and on and on over the next ridge and over the one beyond."[65] Adding an element of intrigue to Kessel's hikes was "just knowing that we were in an area that hadn't been mapped."[66] In words reminiscent of Bob Marshall, Schaller experienced "the atavistic pleasure of seemingly being an explorer."[67] Lending meaning to the group's explorations was Olaus's belief that for both the Arctic's human visitors and its indigenous life forms, "Exploring is a fundamental impulse.... So the instinct to go into far places, to learn and achieve, is something we have inherited from our early sources. Life itself, evolution, is exploratory."[68] The same impulse that drove the caribou's wanderlust, Olaus believed, had become part of the human psychological makeup and continued to serve in our species' evolution. Because "this urge has come down to us from the earliest time," he wrote, "we must not ignore it if we believe in progress of the human spirit."[69]

Contributing to this effect was the area's sheer vastness. A sensation of immensity pervades the group's landscape descriptions. "The mountain world here is multiplied," Mardy wrote, "mountain and valley, mountain and valley...all reaching back against more mountains, far into the distance." She also captured the more elusive sense of mystery and unknown that the area held for the party, the stimulus for those joyful explorations and discoveries. "Each valley," she wrote, "made you wonder what was at the head of it; what was on the other side."[70] Schaller shared her enthusiasm for the region's mystique: "Those ridges—those valleys—you just want to go on and on!"[71]

The area's remoteness provided both a physical separation and a psychological distance from civilization that the group found conducive to the emergence of what Krear described as "a balanced perspective on life."[72] The idea of wilderness as a setting for transformative experience, where the freedom of the wild facilitated mental freedom, was a long-established theme of the transcendental and romantic literature. Like Thoreau, whose Walden sojourn left him "free to adventure upon the real concerns of life," they found their separation from the inventions and conventions of the modern world conducive to expanding their awareness. Krear found himself contemplating basic life questions that had never occurred to him at home. In one discussion of the Arctic range, Olaus referred to experiencing "moments that illuminate the mind." Human ideals, he explained, "may be engendered in moments of relaxation within the frame of physical recreation in areas of natural wonders when the mind is free."[73]

From the high perspective of the Brooks Range divide, sitting on the ridgeline separating the Hulahula River's flow to the Arctic Ocean, and the Sheenjek River's course toward the Yukon basin, Schaller came to experience the state his mentor spoke of. "At the convergence of mountains and sky," he wrote,

> I am alone at a place without roads or people, not even trails except those trodden by wild sheep and caribou, with nothing to violate the

FIGURE 30. George B. Schaller, 1956. *Courtesy of Robert Krear.*

peace, with mountains still unaffected by humankind. Here one can recapture the rhythm of life and the feeling of belonging to the natural world.[74]

Justice Douglas felt a similar connection in a less dramatic setting, on the edge of a series of quiet pools hidden in a stand of tall spruce. "It was indeed a temple in the glades," he wrote. Yet even in this "beautiful, delicate alcove in the remoteness of the Sheenjek Valley," Douglas could not find escape from his concerns about the technological age. "Here were pools never touched by man," he mused, "except perhaps by the awful fall-out from the atomic bombs that is slowly poisoning the whole earth."[75]

Douglas's visit, like most wilderness trips, had been a journey toward one way of being and away from another, both a search and an escape. Perhaps the single week of his visit was insufficient to loosen the grasp of outside world concerns. From her summer-long perspective, Mardy found that "it was easy here to forget the world of man, to relax into this world of nature. It was a world that compelled all our interest and concentration and put everything else out of mind."[76]

Mardy had entered what psychologists have since termed a "flow state," so named because those immersed in such an experience describe it as analogous to being on a river, carried away by the flow.[77] Repeatedly she referred to being "completely absorbed." Her diary describes how "the whole environment . . . soaks into one's being."[78] With time no longer segmented by the clock or fragmented by the calendar, and thousands of miles from the pressures of conformity and everyday distractions that get in the way of an unmediated response to the natural world, she was able to, as Thoreau had said, "cast off the baggage of civilization."

A Spiritual Dimension

Olaus and Mardy sought to connect this area to a foundational concept of the wilderness movement—the notion that retreat to the wilds is conducive to attaining a sense of an ultimate value beyond the self that enhances the meaning of one's life.

Mardy "felt real 'participation'" in the landscape, yet she described herself as merely a visiting observer. An attitude of humility pervades her descriptions of the place she came to as a "privileged guest." She conveyed the notion that one of the area's greatest benefits to visitors emerges from their coming to the perspective that its highest purpose is not to provide benefits to them. "The environment is not tailored to man," she wrote, "it is itself, for itself." While Collins had also said a primary purpose of the area should be to be there for itself, Mardy published accounts that conveyed a sense of the experiential benefit of that function. "Fitting in, living in it," she wrote, "carries challenge, exhilaration, and peace."[79] Olaus, too, experienced a unitive state. His journal contains several references to a blurring of the boundaries between his self and the encompassing natural world. As he wrote in a late-season entry, "I don't know when in my life I felt closer to the earth and all that is on it."[80] This sense of connection is what Olaus would refer to three years later when, in concluding his Senate testimony on the range proposal, he stated that we long for "something that has a mental, spiritual impact on us . . . we must give serious attention to our mental and spiritual needs—hard to define but of greatest importance."[81]

Olaus never specifically defined the spiritual needs that wilderness or this area in particular might serve. But his writings suggest that chief among them was the ennobling effect he believed accrued from yielding one's uses and conveniences to a place dedicated to maintaining nature's primacy. Like a church or cathedral to which it was so often compared, wilderness to him was a place symbolically set apart from the dominant utilitarian orientation of society. Assuming a role as a guest of the landscape, not the purpose of it, served to instill a sense of connection to an ultimate reality larger than the self—the universal core of spiritual experience and, since the times of Emerson, Thoreau, and Muir, a permanent theme of the wilderness literary tradition.[82]

Thus Olaus wrote of the value of saving some natural places, not just for the direct benefits they may provide, but also for their existence value, simply remaining natural, "unchanged as nature made them or, if you prefer, as God made them."[83] But although he occasionally accompanied Mardy to church, Olaus didn't believe in God. His spirituality was secular, unlike that of his Presbyterian friend Justice Douglas, who, from his temple in the glades, had exclaimed, "Never, I believe, had God worked more wondrously."[84]

Olaus was guided by the belief that modern humans are possessed of "a latent sense of kinship with nature."[85] The thin veneer of civilization, he believed, had not erased an innate predisposition for connection to the force that relates man to the natural world and all species, the common origin of all life, the timeless, encompassing process of evolution. While Olaus considered the source of spirituality more earthly and Douglas more celestial, each interpreted their insights in terms of the notion of transcendence. Immersion in unaltered nature, they believed, lifted one from the narrow confines of the self. It was conducive to opening one to something inside the self that seeks relatedness to an ultimate reality beyond—however conceived.

FIGURE 31. Justice William O. Douglas at Last Lake, 1956. *Courtesy of George B. Schaller.*

Collins, Sumner, and others had extended this early wilderness precept to the Arctic proposal in an abstract sense. Expedition writings conveyed a sense of how it might be experienced—how one's discovery of a sense of proportion in the larger scheme of things might lead to a self perceived more through the context of relationships and connections, and less through the individualistic perspective they believed pervaded 1950s American culture. The well-established notion of wilderness as a setting for transformative experience finds succinct expression in the conclusion of Douglas's chapter on the Sheenjek in *My Wilderness*. With rhetoric reminiscent of Muir, he wrote, "This is the place for man turned scientist and explorer, poet and artist. Here he can experience a new reverence for life that is outside his own and yet a vital and joyous part of it."[86]

A Place of Restraint

Olaus expressed the fervent hope that others could enjoy the kind of "spiritual uplift" the group experienced here. To ensure the perpetuation of this opportunity, he said, "We human beings need to muster the wisdom to leave a few places on the earth strictly alone."[87] Such wisdom, to Murie, meant a national willingness to administratively and symbolically set some places apart from the dominant cultural imperative to alter nature to serve human purposes. For visitors it would require arriving with an attitude of respect, reverence, and, especially, restraint. Subordinating their uses and conveniences to nature's primacy, Murie knew, would be necessary to protect the easy to scar but slow to heal Arctic environment. At the same time, the visitors' act of yielding themselves to a larger purpose would open them to the implicit message of wilderness—that we need to share this Earth with other creatures and people of the future.

The Muries described the types and levels of recreational use they felt were consistent with the special promise of this area. While they encouraged recreational use, they believed the area should not be altered to facilitate access. Roads were absolutely unacceptable. Trail construction was unnecessary. Although Olaus had opposed the use of aircraft in non-Alaska wilderness areas, he felt planes were appropriate—or a necessary compromise—for access here. But he opposed the construction of airstrips. Although often less convenient, he believed only natural, unaltered landing surfaces, such as lakes and gravel bars, should be used by planes.

Olaus believed that hunting, as a means of participating in the natural order, was appropriate. In fact, when the group first arrived, he encouraged Krear to shoot a caribou for camp meat. Kessel, however, reminded them that hunting season was closed. Krear later wrote that considering the remote circumstances, if he and Olaus had been alone, "we would have been eating venison."[88] But while supporting hunting, Olaus strongly believed that hunts needed to be nonmechanized, conducted in the spirit of fair chase, and "in the tradition of the highest form of sport."[89]

Seeking to minimize the cutting of live trees for tent poles, as was common practice, the group searched about for dead timber. Envisioning a precedent scarcely imaginable to the era's wildland recreation managers, they believed the entire nine million acres must remain void of recreational "improvements"—campgrounds, shelters, trails, and signs. The country must be left, as both Muries repeatedly wrote, "untouched." Thus Olaus wrote that before departing, "we destroyed every trace of our presence."[90] Mardy described leaving "with every possible sign of our short occupancy obliterated."[91]

The Muries were advocating an approach to recreation that in the 1970s became the widely accepted minimum-impact camping ethic, supplanted in the early 1990s by today's "Leave No Trace" standard of wilderness travel. But this was 1956—the ax was the dominant symbol of camping, and wilderness guidebooks taught the art of making shelters from felled trees and stripping evergreens of their boughs for bed padding. Although Lowell Sumner and Richard Leonard had written groundbreaking articles advocating limits to recreational use in wilderness, few at the time understood the need to limit the activities and numbers of wilderness visitors.[92]

Recognizing that large groups would impact the fragile tundra and disturb wildlife, Olaus recommended visitors come "a few at a time."[93] Mardy went further, specifying "never a party larger than six."[94] This was at a time when group size limits were practically unheard of and even the Sierra Club was routinely leading parties of twenty, thirty, and even more people into the alpine areas of western parks.[95] "The idea, not yet understood by all," Olaus wrote, "was to protect permanently another portion of our planet for sensitive people to go to get acquainted with themselves, to enjoy untouched nature, and to leave the lovely, unmarked country as they find it."[96]

While they wanted the area to be left untouched for the benefit of visitors like themselves, the group was motivated by other beliefs as well. This was to be a bequest to future generations who, as heirs to an increasingly mechanized and regimented world, would be in even greater need of the experiential benefits that an ultimate wilderness could provide. "I feel so sure that, if we are big enough to save this bit of loveliness on our earth," Mardy would tell a Senate committee, "the future citizens of Alaska and of all the world will be deeply grateful. This is a time for a long look ahead."[97]

But the long look also included the belief that the area should remain, as Olaus said, "a little portion of our planet left alone" for reasons independent of any recreational use. "Man, for all his ego, is not the only creature," Mardy wrote. "Other species have some rights too." Wilderness itself, she said, has a right to continue. "Do we have enough reverence for life to concede Wilderness this right?"[98]

Her statement alludes to a deeper motivation for preserving the area. To many (though not all) proponents, the Arctic campaign represented a countercurrent in the postwar flow of industrial progress. Many were coming to believe that the area would serve the nation not only by providing important uses, but also through its use as a symbol. Northeast Alaska was becoming a point of reference for those aware of their species' dependence on the larger community of life and of their obligation to it and to future generations. Establishment would be an act of national contrition and provide a much-needed legacy of restraint that would serve beyond the area's boundaries. "This idealism, more than anything else," Olaus would testify, "will set us apart as a nation striving for something worthwhile in the universe."[99]

An Emerging Sense of Place

Two books published at the time of the expedition expanded public awareness of the area and understanding of its varied values and functions.

Although not specific to the Arctic proposal, *Arctic Wilderness* contributed to supporters' perceptions of the kind of values it held. It was an account of Bob Marshall's explorations of the Central Brooks Range, based on trip journals edited by his brother George Marshall. The book was widely read and cited in the statements and testimony of proponents. Combining Marshall's romantic descriptions of the Brooks Range with his notion of the opportunity it afforded "to search in wild places for what is basic in life," the book became a definitive statement of the entire region's experiential values. George's introduction reminded readers of his brother's 1938 proposal for a vast Arctic wilderness, and the text's effusive descriptions of "mental adventure and physical adventure" offered a plethora of reasons for supporting it.[100]

In his review of the book, Justice Douglas wrote, "It tells why this great area should be preserved in perpetuity as a wilderness area." Presumably George published it at this point in the campaign to serve this purpose for the Arctic proposal. Undoubtedly it did, as Douglas predicted, "help marshal public opinion to preserve the Brooks Range as a wilderness, keeping it forever free of roads, lodges, and filling stations."[101]

Olaus was so optimistic about the potential of *Arctic Wilderness* to sway public opinion that he had George Marshall send a copy to Walt Disney, with whom he had been corresponding regarding the producer's True-Life nature films. In a letter to Disney, Olaus explained how his summer in the Arctic "brought home to me more strongly than ever the value to us of the wilderness concept." He told Disney that publicity on the book, possibly through incorporating its theme into the *White Wilderness* documentary Herb and Lois Crisler were filming for him, would "further the general cause." Murie's emphasis on the wilderness concept and the general cause is indicative of his hope that the Arctic campaign would also expand support for the wilderness preservation movement and further the new conservation ideas it was coming to represent.[102]

Also published in 1956 was Frank Fraser Darling's book, *Pelican in the Wilderness: A Naturalist's Odyssey in North America*. Darling recounted his and Starker Leopold's work with Collins and Sumner at Schrader Lake while exploring the area as a potential "Arctic Wilderness Area." The region, he wrote, is "the grandest piece of wildlife country in the north." But the Scottish ecologist suggested that more than just an American wildlife sanctuary was at risk. "Try exploitation or some such idiocy as what is called development," he told readers, "and the planet will lose forever one of her most glorious pristine places."[103]

As intended, the writings, films, photographs, drawings, and slide presentations that resulted from the expedition, along with these books and the earlier writings by Collins, Sumner, and others, shaped conservationists' image of the area as a last great wilderness and inspired them to work for its protection. A set of recurring "values" or arguments for preserving the area was becoming apparent. They included tangible characteristics of the area and its wildlife, the personal and societal benefits it was thought to provide, and symbolic associations. The values that were forwarded as purposes for establishing the area can be summarized as: (1) a place for wildlife in an ecological context; (2) a place for recreation, and related psychological benefits; (3) a place of scientific values; (4) a remnant of American cultural heritage; and (5) a bequest to the future.

The Conservationists' Indian

As noted, the set of wilderness values that underpinned the Arctic campaign were rooted in a convergence of social movements, ideologies, ecological developments, and postwar concerns held by a discrete, perhaps elite, group of Americans. For the most part, they were not within the experience of the region's indigenous inhabitants. Not having been exposed to the urbanization, industrialization, loss of natural areas, economic security, and education that have historically preceded and preconditioned development of a wilderness ethic, the region's Gwich'in Indians and Inupiaq Eskimos would have found most tenets of the Arctic campaign foreign to their worldview. This fact did not, however, significantly interfere with the expedition's interpretation of the area's Native history in terms that supported the wilderness perspective they brought to these peoples' homeland.

Throughout the Sheenjek Valley, expedition members encountered historic and prehistoric artifacts and campsites. They enjoyed their discoveries of ancient arrowheads and more recently abandoned toboggan and snowshoe parts, fish traps, and graves. This evidence of indigenous occupancy added meaning to the landscape, increasing its capacity to connect the group to a venerated, if somewhat mythologized, past. Musing upon an old Indian grave, Olaus wrote in his journal that it served an urge to "look backward in history, to view the origin of things, an instinctive urge to trace our route of travel."[104] But his urge was probably less archetypal than learned. In fact, it represented a common literary convention of the early back-to-nature writers: romantic primitivism. Romantic primitivism idealized the assumed simpler and happier life of prehistoric people. It also idealized contemporary primitive cultures, presuming them to be relatively free of the ills of modern civilization.[105]

Murie was of the generation of conservationists for whom a formative influence had been Ernest Seton's popular series of children's books. Much in the primitivist genre, Seton's books prescribed to children like Murie an "outdoor life" because healthy lives were most common among those "who live nearest to the ground, that is, who live the simple life of primitive times."[106] Murie's favorite was Seton's *Two Little Savages*, a romanticized tale of two white boys who adopted an Indian lifestyle. The book shaped his childhood enamoration with Indian lore. Murie's biographical article "Boyhood Wilderness" pictures him and his face-painted friends camping in a tipi and following their "hunting instincts" with bows and arrows. "We were virtually Indians," he recalled.[107]

But Murie's perceived image of Indians represented what the era's conservationists wanted them to be. The "noble savage" served to validate their precept of an organic connection between human nature and wild nature, supporting efforts to preserve areas where this connection could be re-experienced. Zahniser had recently expressed this common sentiment, stating that wilderness preserves "a piece of the long ago we still have with us." In the Indian, one could see that part of the original self that had been obscured—but not erased—by modern culture.

This was a benefit derived from what Zahniser had gone on to describe as "the opportunity to relive the lives of ancestors," and it paralleled the "base datum of normality" scientific function of wilderness that Aldo Leopold had espoused.[108] Just as the ecological effects of environmental modification could best be understood by comparing altered areas to unaltered ones, the psychological effects of living in an industrial, urban, and materialistic society could best be understood by comparison to those who lived free of it. Uncorrupted by the ills of modern civilization, Indians were thought to provide a picture of the human condition that had prevailed for the 99 percent of history during which humankind's relationship with the natural world was focused on harmony rather than control.

More important than showing what had been lost, Indians were thought to reveal a part of one's self that might be regained in the wilderness. These

FIGURE 32. Peter Tritt from Arctic Village, hunting for wolves and wolf dens, July 1956. *Courtesy of George B. Schaller.*

models of man's presumed Paleolithic wise stewardship might stimulate one, as Murie wrote, to "give thought to our ancestors and feel humbly grateful for the beginnings of thoughtful regard and enjoyment of our land."[109]

But the Indians of 1956 were not exemplars of man's idealized past. In mid-July the group made the acquaintance of three Gwich'in Indians from Arctic Village. Ambrose Williams, David Peter, and Peter Tritt were hunting wolves and wolf pups for the fifty-dollar bounty offered by the territory. Accounts from both parties indicate that their interactions were friendly and enjoyable. The expedition gained some traditional knowledge of the area and their visitors left with packs of foodstuffs. Expedition members did not appreciate the Indians' bounty hunting, though Mardy rationalized that they would rather have the money go to the Natives than "to some white hunter flipping around in an airplane for the 'sport' of it."[110]

In his accounts of his early encounters with Canadian and Alaskan Indians and Eskimos, Olaus expressed a strong affinity with and admiration for Native people. In a journal entry at the time of the Indians' visit, he lamented that "the Indian has lost his own traditions, his pride in accomplishment in the wilderness." Further, "Our visitor had even forgotten some of the birds in his own language."[111]

Murie attributed the plight of the visiting bounty hunters to newly found ambitions, "much as we have festering in the heart of modern civilization." Expressing the underlying cause in terms of antimodernist sentiment, he concluded that "they have been taught the white man's appetites and need the white man's dollar to exist."[112] Succumbing to materialistic temptations, the Indians were falling from the Edenic state of harmony with nature that endeared Native people to conservationists.

Olaus explained the expedition's major purpose, but it is doubtful that their Gwich'in-speaking visitors understood well. Their limited English and lack of experience with conservation withdrawals would have made communication about a wilderness reserve difficult. Pilot Keith Harrington, who flew several Arctic Villagers in to visit when he delivered the group's mail, doubts his passengers had any idea that the Muries were seeking a wilderness reserve, although in his opinion, they would have been supportive.[113] Margaret Sam, a young woman from Arctic Village who visited three times, has fond memories of her visits. She recalls thinking that the expedition's purpose was "to look at the animals." Spending a summer in pursuit of such a nonutilitarian end seemed a bit odd, but at the time she was little interested in their purpose. What stands out in her memory is Schaller stuffing small mammal specimens, Olaus's animal sketches, and Mardy's cooking.[114]

"And what of the future for these people?" Olaus wrote in his journal. No answer was forthcoming. While not mentioning bounty hunting, he would often state that the Arctic proposal would accommodate Natives' traditional activities. He wrote that these visitors "fit in with wilderness living, and our system of wilderness areas does not intend to interfere with hunting and trapping by such people."[115]

Undoubtedly, the Muries, like Collins and Marshall before them, presumed that wilderness protection would be in the best interest of the region's indigenous people. But would preservation of the Natives' ancestral homeland as wilderness serve to perpetuate aspects of their history that they, themselves, wished to continue? Neither the Muries, nor any Arctic proponents or involved agencies, would meet with the communities of Arctic Village, Fort Yukon, or Kaktovik to explain the proposal and gain their input. This was, of course, the 1950s. Given the limited political influence of Natives in that era, proponents may have believed that attaining local support or endorsement for their goal would not be worth their effort. The same could later be said of opponents, including Alaska's political leaders, who made no contact with local people. As Fort Yukon leader Richard Carroll recalls, "Nobody asked me. Back then everybody thought the government knew what was best for Natives. They'd go to the BIA and ask them."[116]

But a generation later, the visitors' descendants would play a major role in the battle to prevent oil development in the Arctic Refuge. The Gwich'in people's argument that wilderness protection for the caribou calving grounds is essential to their well-being would come to carry significant political weight. And conservationists, sometimes drawing on the romantic precepts of their early predecessors, would promote preservation of Native tradition and culture as a primary reason for protecting the refuge's wilderness qualities. But during the 1950s campaign, this benefit was not among the major purposes forwarded for withdrawing the area.

Alaskan Support

"I never left anyplace with more reluctance." So Olaus wrote after the group's August departure from the Sheenjek Valley.[117] Now armed with a collection of photographs, he and Mardy went directly on to Anchorage to begin an intensive sixteen-day effort to gain Alaskan support for the proposal. They met with the media, various organizations, the Territorial Land Commission, and many individuals to describe their experience of the area and ideas for its future.

In Juneau the Muries met with several federal and territorial agencies and the local sportsmen's group, the Territorial Sportsmen. Returning to Fairbanks, they had radio, television, and newspaper interviews; conferences with university officials; meetings with the military, Fish and Wildlife Service scientists, civic groups, and garden clubs. Morva Hoover was with the Fairbanks Garden Club when it hosted the Muries at the home of prominent businessman Leslie Nerland. She recalls the Muries as great people who fascinated them with their slides of the Sheenjek country. The thirty-some members in attendance unanimously decided to support the proposal. "There wasn't any debate," she said.[118]

The most important Fairbanks contact was with the Tanana Valley Sportsmens Association, which hosted them at a meeting of seventy people. Olaus's slide presentation must have been effective because, as he later wrote, "afterward several came to me and fervently promised their support, and greatly surprised me by giving me an honorary life membership in their organization."[119]

Arthur Hayr, a member of the Alaska Fish and Game Board, was among those present. In his 1959 Senate committee testimony three years later, he discussed Murie's eloquent portrayal of the area that evening and noted that none present spoke against his persuasive proposal for its withdrawal. "I very definitely understood that he was seeking an inviolate wilderness area," Hayr testified, adding that "I very definitely had some reservations." Likely others did as well. But no one spoke against Murie's proposal, probably because, as Hayr stated,

> on that evening there would have been just as much sense for me to get up and express an opinion opposite that offered Dr. Murie as it would now to stand and say that I am in favor of sin and against motherhood. Believe me, it was just that rough.[120]

Murie's personal qualities were critical to obtaining Alaskan support, which was essential to the campaign's success. Contributing to his effectiveness was his humble and sensitive demeanor. Charles Gray, the aerial wolf hunter, was a member of the Sportsmens Association. As he remembers, Murie was effective because "he was a mild-mannered fella; he was sincere and had facts."[121] No doubt, Murie's effort to understand the concerns of his opponents was sincere, as was his disarming empathy with their perspectives. As he wrote to Howard Zahniser, "a lot of psychological progress will have to be made before enough Alaskans favor any further federal reserves, that is a phobia in Alaska." The less patient Zahniser responded by asking, "Will the wilderness disappear while we are waiting to be good psychologists?"[122]

Murie further explained his approach to obtaining Alaskan support in a letter to Collins, who was both impatient and doubtful that a significant number of Alaskans could be convinced to accept a wilderness reserve.

> George, in this whole project I have adopted a go-easy method. As an oldtimer up north said to me once: "Easy does it." I met with many people, from Fort Yukon to Juneau, and I can't remember a time when I came right out and said: "Support this wilderness proposal." I told them what our experience was, and I sincerely wanted them to make up their own minds. Without the sincere backing of people, who have thought the thing through, I feel we can get nowhere.[123]

Another significant contribution to Murie's effectiveness was the fact that, unlike Collins, Sumner, Darling, and Leopold, who first began promoting the proposal, he was not seen as an outside expert. Although not currently residents, he and Mardy retained some standing as Alaskans. His genuine affinity with the old-timers that Alaskans so respected was apparent. In fact, he had received an honorary membership in the Pioneers of Alaska, which he described as "one of my most valuable treasures." Furthering local support, Murie wrote that if the area were designated as a wilderness, "I would urge that this area be dedicated, in all sincerity, to the Pioneers of Alaska, in recognition of the kind of life they enjoyed."[124]

As important as Murie's insight into the territory's culture was his understanding of its politics. More so than in the lower forty-eight states, success here would require local support, and not just among the small conservation and scientific communities. The five-hundred-member Sportsmens Association, he knew, was likely the most influential outdoors organization in Alaska. This was undoubtedly the primary reason that Murie focused on recruiting it into the effort. That said, it is also true that he believed that "a wilderness type of hunting" was appropriate here. This would be a place, he wrote, for those "who want to hunt in the highest sense of the sport, that is, by their own efforts."[125] Wilderness, Murie believed, would serve members' interests by enhancing the quality and elevating the ethics of hunting.

Toward the end of 1956, Murie was considering potential rules and policies for the as-yet-unnamed wilderness proposal. Among his most important tasks was to obtain agreement among supporters on the issue of hunting. A few believed it should be prohibited. That, and the unresolved possibility of national park status, made many hunters leery. Starker Leopold and Sigurd Olson Jr. were among those who wrote Murie supporting his position that hunting should be allowed. Olson said he could not agree with those who "want it as an area to serve science only."[126] His letter reflects a growing recognition of political reality; establishment of a wilderness area would require some compromise in the idealism of the campaign's beginnings.

But there were also those such as Lois Crisler, whose articles and soon-to-be-published book *Arctic Wild* would further a wilderness-oriented appreciation of the Brooks Range wilderness and, in particular, the preservation of its wolves. She wrote a long letter to Murie criticizing the "hunting syndrome." She reminded Murie of his recent article in *Audubon Magazine* advocating the cultivation of a "wholesome impulse of generosity toward our fellow creatures." She cited a psychiatrist's diagnosis of hunting as "neurotic behavior because it is no longer rooted in the demands of reality."[127]

Murie's response is unknown. Considering his view of hunting as a vestige of humankind's evolutionary heritage, he must have disagreed with Crisler's analysis of the hunting impulse. But he must have agreed with her appreciation for predators, as well as her disdain for "professional wolf haters" and "Clarence Rhode's phobia against wolves."[128]

Murie knew that most members of the Sportsmens Association favored the Fish and Wildlife Service wolf-control program, which Rhode administered. He knew they would not support, and would be likely to oppose, any proposal that threatened to preclude it. Thus, he told Fairfield Osborn, "we should not bring into this wilderness project the controversial wolf question."[129] For the most part, proponents would accept this political necessity and not specifically oppose wolf control. Many would, however, continue to argue that natural processes should be maintained here, a situation that would preclude the control, management, or manipulation of any species.

In December 1956, the concern that the wildlife and ecological values of the Arctic proposal were increasingly at risk from the postwar march of progress was heightened by another article Lowell Sumner published in the *Sierra Club Bulletin*. In a foreword to Sumner's "Your Stake in Alaska's Wildlife and Wilderness," University of Alaska professor John Buckley revealed that a winter road for tractor-trailer trucks had been bulldozed from the Yukon River to the Arctic coast, traversing a southern section of the proposal.[130]

"If man is going to remain boss of his machines," Sumner warned, "thinking on conservation problems will have to keep up with the technological speed-up."[130] Citing the government-sponsored Hackett Report, *Alaska's Vanishing Frontier*, he argued that Alaskans should identify and hold on to the landscape attributes that made Alaska unique.

Stressing the Arctic's ecological vulnerability, Sumner pointed to the caribou, the "classic symbol of the old frontier abundance." A half-century earlier, he said, Alaska's herds were comparable to the buffalo that once swarmed the American plains, but due to human activities, many herds had shrunk.

Looking ahead fifty years, Sumner predicted that the Arctic proposal might offer "the only opportunity for maintaining a pure wilderness large enough for the indefinite preservation of the caribou and other space requiring animals." The undiminished ecological condition of the Arctic proposal, he wrote, would make the area indispensable as a "control" area needed for comparison with "the remainder of the Territory where man is altering 'the balance of nature' for industrial purposes."

As was common in Arctic proposal writings, Sumner also drew upon "primeval" associations and "intangible" and "immeasurable" values to elicit support. He further told readers that wildlife

> still have an unquestioned right to be in their wilderness world, to live and die there. Man can change all this, but need not. He may do it by mistake if he does not consider what is there, and the meaning of it.[132]

FIGURE 33. Lois Crisler with wolf pup in the Central Brooks Range, 1953. Crisler's writings and her and her husband's Disney documentary brought national attention to Arctic Alaska's wolves and wildness.

Photo by Herb Crisler, with permission of HarperCollins Publishers.

Not long after, Lois Crisler highlighted the larger meaning of the preservation effort with an article in *Living Wilderness* magazine. Now a member of the Wilderness Society's governing council, she and her husband Herb had recently returned from eighteen months in the Central Brooks Range where they completed their Walt Disney–sponsored filming of wolves begun in McKinley Park. Describing the social life and ecological interactions of wolves, "Where Wilderness Is Complete" eloquently conveyed the hope for an untrammeled Arctic that had motivated the campaign's leaders. Furthering understanding of their Thoreauvian belief in the enlightening and cathartic effect of experiencing a humble, nonmanipulative relationship with nature, Crisler wrote that the Brooks Range was practically "the only authentic living wilderness left for humans to learn from—to learn something more important than scientific knowledge; to learn the feel of a full response to a total situation involving other lives."[133]

Also emphasizing the Arctic's vulnerability, she described aerial wolf hunting. And reminding readers of the attitude toward nature that the wilderness concept stood counter to, she denounced the hunter's "great fun as the plane circles the small furred animal veering and running beyond what the heart of flesh and blood can endure." Crisler added a sense of urgency and fear to the technological threat to which Sumner had alluded. "Tomorrow," she warned, might bring "that final sportsmen's weapon, the jet helicopter with silencer.... Here in the Brooks Range," she continued,

the biggest of all historical movements, man against nature, meets actual living wilderness making its last stand.... So far, man has always won; living wilderness has always perished into desert or mere scenery.[134]

Alluding to the emerging environmental perspective, she expressed hope that the "new mind toward nature" would reverse the outcome in the Brooks Range. Preservation efforts here, she suggested, represented a larger test of the national will. Following her article was a quotation from Leopold's *A Sand County Almanac*. It succinctly captured what for many was the overarching issue symbolized by the Arctic controversy: "Now we face the question whether a still higher 'standard of living' is worth its cost in things natural, wild, and free."[135]

5

Wilderness, Wildlife Range, or Both?

*We are only emulating ostriches if we think that even Alaska
can long remain immune from the pressure of civilization.*

—Virginia Wood[1]

1957: Political Action

By early 1957, the concept of an Arctic wilderness had attained considerable public support. Now Murie and other proponents needed to focus on the politics of establishment.

One means of establishment was through an executive order. Under the auspices of the Antiquities Act of 1906, the president had the authority to withdraw lands for conservation purposes by proclamation. Although the act was intended to protect relatively small areas of historic and prehistoric interest, Theodore Roosevelt had used it to withdraw many areas that would become

◄ FIGURE 34. Tundra pond near the Kongakut River, 1953. *Photo by Lowell Sumner; courtesy of the National Park Service.*

national parks, forests, and refuges. Roosevelt's actions set two significant precedents. The act became a means of preserving sizable tracts of land, and for designating areas where historic values were actually secondary to scenic, scientific, wildlife, or recreational values. Both advocates and critics of the Arctic proposal recognized that executive withdrawal was a viable possibility, as the precedent had been extended to Alaska by proclamations establishing the Katmai National Monument in 1918, Glacier Bay National Park in 1925, and the Kenai National Moose Range in 1941.

Regarding mining, there were only two options for areas established under this presidential authority: An area could either be open to mining under the existing mineral leasing laws or it could be completely closed to it. Existing mining laws permitted claims to be patented. Since the time that Arctic proponents had first proposed the mining compromise, they were insistent that it not include provision for claims to become privately owned inholdings. Their concerns were twofold. First, they feared that legitimate mining interests would sell surface rights after completing their work, and that the subsequent uses might be incompatible with conservation purposes. Their second concern, as one Arctic proponent expressed it, related to "one of the biggest land grabs in the West ... the scratching of the ground with a pick and a shovel and establishing a claim to huge timber or surface resources, or just a place to build a fine country home."[2] Legislation was introduced in Congress that would allow mining rights to be obtained without surface ownership of the claims, but mining interests found the measure unacceptable and succeeded in blocking it.

The alternative, an executive order that prohibited mining, would surely lead opponents to press for a proclamation to be overturned. There were precedents for such a consequence as well, including one in the territory. Jim King, a young game agent working for Clarence Rhode at the time, recalled that proponents discussed how the Yukon Delta Refuge had been established by Theodore Roosevelt, then later abolished by Warren Harding. Proponents knew that "with the same flick of the wrist," a subsequent administration could abolish an Arctic withdrawal. Thus, many believed that although an executive order might be quicker and easier, establishment through the drawnout process of legislation was preferable because it would increase the likelihood of permanence.[3]

Further, advocates for legislation knew Alaskans would long resent an area established through a means widely considered undemocratic and that they would be less likely to support good management provisions for it. As Olaus told Fairfield Osborn, "The area will be safer for all time if Alaskans themselves are behind it. That is why I am so concerned over developing this general Alaskan attitude."[4]

Establishment opponents knew their chances of eventually overturning an administrative withdrawal were greater, but they feared that the management provisions of an area established without the guidelines of congressional intent would become more restrictive over time. As Alaska's commissioner of natural resources would testify, "any withdrawal of this classification can be automatically put into the wilderness concept."[5]

Many proponents remained ambivalent about the administrative versus the legislative process question. In either case, they agreed with Murie that establishment would most likely be successful if sponsored by an Alaska organization. In either case, prospective sponsors would require the resolution of two long-standing questions: What title should the area have, and which agency should administer it?

Resolution, for most proponents, came on Sunday, March 17, at the Fairmont Hotel in San Francisco. During the preceding two days, four hundred conservationists had convened for the Sierra Club's Fifth Biennial Wilderness Conference, chaired in 1957 by George Collins. Participating this year were the heads of each of the four federal land management agencies. Their involvement reflects the increasing likelihood that a wilderness bill—limiting their discretionary authority—might pass. They were coming to realize that they could not afford to ignore the growing movement.

More so than the previous wilderness conferences, this gathering highlighted the ecological aspects of wilderness preservation. The first presentations in particular, by leaders of the Arctic campaign, reflected the postwar concerns underlying the efforts to establish the Arctic Range and enact a Wilderness Act. Lowell Sumner's opening presentation, "The Pressures of Civilization," began with reference to the 1955 report "Man's Role in Changing the Face of the Earth." "Staggering evidence" revealed that human activities were profoundly affecting the earth, thus "the urgency of protecting our relatively wild areas while there is still time." Increasing population threatened humankind's physical and mental health. As the stress of civilization continued to increase, Sumner predicted, "the therapeutic benefits of wilderness and natural areas, the philosophy, understanding and serenity derived from contact with them, will be more and more needed by everyone."[6]

Starker Leopold followed with "Wilderness and Culture"—an expression of hope that history would see the twentieth century as "a time of outstanding advance in man's feeling of responsibility to the earth." Beginning with our species' earliest relationship with wild nature, Leopold traced the emergence of the sense of "obligation to preserve untrammeled some remnants of the natural scene." He concluded with the observation that the force motivating wilderness preservation was "the moral conviction that it is right, that somehow we owe it to ourselves and to the good earth that supports us to curb our avarice to the extent of leaving some spots untouched and unexploited."[7]

In that spirit the conference unanimously voted to support two resolutions. One endorsed the "Wilderness Bill" authored by Zahniser and recently introduced in both the House and Senate. The other resolution recommended that "the Bureau of Land Management formally designate and administer [the Arctic proposal] as an Arctic Wilderness." Emphasizing the area's "primeval" and "primitive" conditions, the resolution specified "the paramount objective of maintaining unimpaired the ecological conditions within the area."[8]

For reasons unknown, those at the convention who drafted the Arctic Wilderness resolution were unaware of what Zahniser and Murie had learned from previous meetings with Bureau of Land Management officials. As Murie had written to Osborn, the BLM "would not be eager to maintain wilderness as a permanent policy, under their own bureau." The bureau's director, Edward Woozley, supported the proposal and was willing to release nine million acres of his domain to an agency better suited to its wilderness purpose. The bureau was, according to Murie, willing to withdraw the area as a wilderness, but only "pending the ultimate disposition."[9]

On March 17, the day following the conference, there occurred, in Collins's words, "a momentous gathering" of Arctic proponents to decide what that ultimate disposition was to be. Representing the National Park Service were Collins, Sumner, and the agency's director, Conrad Wirth. Representing the Fish and Wildlife Service were its director, Dan Janzen, who the day before had made a strong pro-wilderness presentation, and Alaska regional director Clarence Rhode. Bureau of Land Management director Edward Woozley was present. Olaus and Mardy Murie and Howard Zahniser represented the Wilderness Society, and Richard and Doris Leonard represented the Sierra Club.

Also present was the president of the National Parks Association, Sigurd Olson. The author of the recently published bestseller, *Singing Wilderness* (1956), Olson was well on his way to becoming one of the century's most prominent wilderness writers. Like Marshall, Leopold, Murie, and others who had influenced the ideological orientation of the campaign, Olson was a biologist by training. His master's degree, the first scientific study of wolves, and his popular writings supported campaign leaders' efforts to enhance appreciation of the wolf's ecological and symbolic role in wilderness. Also like them, he had come to realize that "the intangible values of wilderness are what really matter." Olson thought in terms of ecological and evolutionary processes, and this led him to appreciate "the timeless and majestic rhythms of those parts of the world [man] has not ravished."[10]

Olson believed that wilderness, as both a place and a concept, provided man the physical and psychological distance necessary to rediscover the "sense of close animal relationship, belonging, and animal oneness that once sustained him." Olson's "wilderness theology," as his biographer describes it, undoubtedly placed him closer to those who argued for selecting a land status that would be most consistent with the campaign's ideological roots.[11]

Most important, Olson brought to the campaign a friendship with the recently appointed secretary of the interior, Fred Seaton, for whom he would soon serve as a consultant. Olson's involvement in Alaska had begun only six years earlier when his son moved to the territory to work as a biologist for the Fish and Wildlife Service. While he had not been a key player in the Arctic campaign, Olson would come to play a significant role—perhaps a crucial role—in its outcome.

Having accepted that neither the Bureau of Land Management nor the Forest Service were possible custodians, the group had to decide whether the area should be administered by the Park Service as a national park or by the Fish and Wildlife Service as either a wildlife refuge or a range. The group

FIGURE 35. Sigurd Olson at Old John Lake. *Courtesy of the Robert K. Olson family.*

concluded, in Collins's words, "that wildlife range status would be the best, the simplest, the least controversial." But significantly, he added that the range "would still be generically a park-type thing."[12] International status was considered, but to avoid adding to the controversy, the group decided to limit the proposal to Alaska.

Collins later regretted that notes were not taken at that pivotal meeting, but in a detailed letter written in 1985, and in subsequent interviews, he recalled some of the factors that led to the range decision. A national park, with no provision for allowing hunting or mining, would face far greater political obstacles. Although not a significant political factor, another consideration was that a park probably could not accommodate the hunting and trapping activities of the area's Natives.

Most of those present at the meeting feared that a park would result in facility development and worse—road construction. The remarks of Park Service director Wirth the day before accentuated the concern. During his presentation Wirth opined that building a "wilderness road" to Wonder Lake in Mount McKinley National Park did not mean the area was no longer wilderness. Undoubtedly intending to invite comparison to the Fish and Wildlife Service and its wildlife refuges, he stated that building a road into wilderness may be "far less destructive of the natural character" than allowing hunting and predator control.

In contrast, Dan Janzen, the Fish and Wildlife Service's director, had emphasized that "easy access to a wild area is often akin to killing the goose that laid the golden egg." Reflecting his agency's different primary constituency, he spoke of the value of maintaining areas "accessible only by trail or canoe" in terms of furnishing "very high quality hunting and fishing for those who are willing to earn it."[13] While hunting and fishing were not significant interests of most of those attending the conference, Janzen's statement resonated with those concerned about Wirth's Mission 66 program and the loss of opportunities for challenging and adventurous experiences in parks.

Another deciding factor was that the Fish and Wildlife Service, which had not been interested in acquiring the area, now wanted it. This recent development was probably not the result of a newfound recognition of its wildlife values. Statehood was becoming increasingly certain. Much of the agency's authority to protect nonmigratory wildlife outside federal withdrawals would be transferred to the new state, which, many believed, would have less commitment or ability to restrain development of wildlife habitat. The agency had a sufficient organizational structure in Alaska to administer a vast reserve. And it had Clarence Rhode, who was politically connected and well liked in the territory, factors that would increase the likelihood of success.

There is no record of why the title "Wildlife Range" was selected over the similar category "Wildlife Refuge." Wildlife ranges were more associated with big game animals. As the assistant secretary of the interior would later clarify in Senate testimony, a refuge "is set aside primarily as a sanctuary for wildlife," while a larger proportion of wildlife ranges are open to hunting. The word *sanctuary* would be more threatening to hunters. Further, mineral leasing was more of a possibility in a range, and that might lessen opposition from the mining industry.[14]

"The majority favored wildlife range designation, so we made it unanimous," Collins wrote. "The main thing was to get agreement on *something*." Collins was chief among those of the minority opinion. "I felt, and still do," he wrote in 1985, "that in the long run national park and international park status would be the best. That country is one of the finest, sometimes I think the very finest national park prospect I have ever seen."[15] Although most proponents accepted what was considered a compromise in the Arctic proposal's original purposes, and most organizations would thereafter refer to the proposal as a Wildlife Range, some continued to support more protective status. Among them, William Pruitt "most emphatically" did not think the Fish and Wildlife Service should administer the area. It was too oriented toward "management," which he feared would result in manipulation of game animal and predator populations. Soon after establishment he would argue for the "re-classification and upgrading of the status of the region to that of full wilderness area."[16]

Clarence Rhode, Fish and Wildlife Service Proponent

The group's decision, Collins wrote, now placed responsibility for official action on the Fish and Wildlife Service and Clarence Rhode, "with, of course, all the help we could provide—nothing official, of course."[17] From that day until his fatal plane crash while on a reconnaissance flight in the vicinity of the proposed range sixteen months later, Rhode would be second only to Murie as the most visible proponent of the proposal. In spite of their disagreement on predator control, Collins described him as a close friend, and as one of the campaign's staunchest supporters. He attributed Interior Secretary Seaton's initial support for the range to aerial tours that Rhode had provided to Seaton and his assistant secretary.[18]

Rhode began working with the agency in 1935 as a dog-team-driving game warden. Dedication to wildlife protection and exceptional organizational abilities led to his appointment as the Fish and Wildlife Service's Alaska regional director in 1947. By all accounts the self-educated Rhode was a committed conservationist. But he was not a preservationist. His philosophical

FIGURE 36. Alaska game agent Clarence Rhode on patrol, late 1930s.
Photo courtesy of the NCTC Archives.

distance from the others is suggested by a statement made before the Alaska Sportsmen's Council. "Raising a big moose crop," he told the assembly, "is farming the land exactly as if it raised Hereford cattle."[19]

This commodity approach to the land was the basis of the predator control program Rhode administered. It was popular with Alaskans and especially sportsmen's groups. Rhode, a public relations expert, knew that to a large degree, compliance with game laws, cooperation with other programs, and support for proposed wildlife refuges depended on the goodwill of sportsmen. The wolf killing that had so irritated Collins, Sumner, and others was, at least in part, a function of fulfilling popular demand to maintain public support for the agency's overall conservation mission.

Whether or to what degree Rhode came to personally believe northeast Alaska should be maintained as a wilderness without manipulation of wildlife populations is unclear. In contrast to the campaign leaders he was joining, Rhode was not inclined to write philosophically about the values the Arctic proposal held for him. His early correspondence does not reveal whether he thought manipulative management practices would be appropriate here. But in his annual report on the agency's Alaska programs, submitted two months before his death in August 1958, Rhode stated that management of the Arctic Range "would be directed toward preservation of wilderness recreational values and maintenance of undisturbed ecological conditions for scientific research."[20] Perhaps by this point Rhode, like Murie and Aldo Leopold before him, was undergoing a personal evolution in his thinking about the role of predators in such areas. In an article published a year after Rhode's death, Murie wrote that Rhode "assured me that he was planning to replace wolf-killing with much-needed research on the caribou." Murie further indicated that Rhode wanted conservationists' support for the change.[21]

Rhode's energy and his standing among Alaska outdoorsmen were immediately pressed into service. He agreed with the strategy Murie had devised at least two years earlier: After settling on a designation that most Alaskans, particularly hunters, could accept, they would convince one or more Alaska organizations to officially sponsor the proposal. Rhode's first action was to contact Professor John Buckley, an active member of the Tanana Valley Sportsmens Association, to arrange for the organization to invite Murie to Fairbanks to discuss the Arctic Wildlife Range proposal. With a designation finally agreed upon, Murie was eager to return to Alaska and garner support. Invitations from the Tanana Valley Sportsmens Association, as well as the university and the Fairbanks Garden Club, soon arrived.

Olaus and Mardy landed in Alaska on May 10 for an intense month of lobbying in Anchorage, Fairbanks, and Juneau. Anchorage was a particularly strategic target this trip because, as Rhode had recently advised, it would be the proposal's greatest source of opposition. "They oppose everything around here except immediate Statehood," Rhode told Olaus. Most residents, he said, "feel we should get on immediately with complete exploitation and the papers there keep this theme before the public."[22]

"This trip was evangelism, not adventure," Mardy wrote. "Olaus was speaking and showing slides of the north country before every possible organization."[23] Sportsmen's and conservation groups, agencies and elected officials, Boy and Girl Scouts, university groups, chambers of commerce, women's and garden clubs, Soroptimists and Rotary clubs, four television appearances, numerous newspaper and radio interviews—"our calendar was full every day," Olaus wrote in his report to Osborn's Conservation Foundation, which financed the trip.[24]

The Sportsmen's Proposal

The most important meeting, Olaus knew, would be with the Tanana Valley Sportsmens Association in Fairbanks, which he hoped would not only endorse the proposal, but also serve as the first Alaska organization to formally request Interior Department action on it.[25] On the evening of May 14, Olaus met with association members at their rustic log clubhouse. After Olaus's slide presentation, which avoided the wolf issue, president James Lake introduced a two-part resolution. The first part described the area and its "unique and necessary opportunities of recreational use…impaired by uncontrolled exploitation." It stated that the area "contains comparatively small amounts of known mineral resources the development of which would conflict with recreational use." The association resolved to urge the Fish and Wildlife Service to institute establishment of an Arctic Wildlife Range to preserve these recreational values.[26]

Second, the resolution stated that the area should be administered according to the policies outlined on an attached "Suggested Plan of Administration and Regulations."[27] The plan contained language and provisions considerably more representative of Collins's "park-type" area than of a wildlife range. It specified that recreation and scientific programs be subject to "the maintenance of undisturbed ecological conditions" and to "the preservation of wilderness conditions essentially unimpaired through the entire area." The plan referenced perpetuation of the region's "primeval features" and its "unique qualities of primeval wildlife and wilderness scenery, and its Arctic frontier flavor."

"Legitimate" prospecting and mining would be allowed, subject to restrictions on access and nonmining use of the surface estate. However, in light of the plan's preservationist language, such restrictions could only be viewed as substantially limiting mining operations. Hunting, fishing, and trapping were to be allowed, but use of aircraft for these and other recreational activities would be "prohibited except as permitted by the administrative agency." The use of helicopters, a potential threat brought to popular awareness by the abuses of some high-ranking military hunters, would be prohibited.

Although the Sportsmens Association claimed to have prepared the suggested plan, the content and wording leave no doubt that Olaus and probably others at the Wilderness Society had a major hand in it.[28] Before the Sheenjek expedition, Zahniser had discussed with Olaus the need to develop such specific provisions, which could be incorporated into establishing legislation. Governing Council member George Marshall, Bob's brother, had recently corresponded with Murie about the Arctic proposal and provisions to "protect wilderness as wilderness." Marshall argued that all mechanical means of transportation, including airplanes, should be excluded to provide "true wilderness... for what it can do for people as wilderness." He felt there should be some wilderness areas "in which one really must travel at least a greater part of a month to penetrate its heart." Marshall acknowledged that many would consider this position impractical, but, reminding Murie of his own values, he added, "[A]fter all, what can be more impractical than wilderness itself, or any of the sensitive and higher values of life?"[29] Murie did not need to be reminded that the Arctic proposal represented their best chance to perpetuate opportunities for the adventurous experience and the wilderness ideals Bob Marshall had extolled.

The resolution and suggested regulations generated heated discussion at the sportsmen's meeting. Miner Joe Vogler was among the most outspoken of those who opposed the motion. He would become one of the proposal's most virulent critics and later, as the Alaska Independence party's gubernatorial candidate, a foremost critic of the environmental values that had underlain the campaign.

The promise of frontier freedom had brought Vogler up from Texas in 1942. He arrived equipped with a law degree and multiple talents, which he put to work homesteading, mining, logging, road building, and later politicking—"just plain raising hell about what's happening to Alaska."

Unwilling to concede that the era of limitless opportunity and unstifled access to resources was, or should be, a thing of the past, Vogler's philosophy exemplified what one historian described as the foundation of Alaska political life: Alaskans were victims of distant forces—the federal government and outside conservationists chief among them—that obstructed progress.[30] In a later interview, Vogler said he opposed "this pristinity nonsense" because it conflicted with what made America great: "freedom to own the land, freedom to use it the way you want, freedom to make something of it, freedom from regulation." Those freedoms had made Americans a hardy stock of people, he said. "The inheritors of those genes need a place to keep that spirit alive."[31]

Vogler believed the proposed regulations on mining were as potentially restrictive as those in Glacier Bay National Monument. While open to mining, the monument was resented by the industry because regulations effectively precluded most operations. Vogler was also suspicious because members supporting the proposal had said that "the only means of transportation which should be allowed in there is by foot." He felt the sportsmen's association was "being used" by the Wilderness Society or the Sierra Club.[32]

Association member Ivan Thorall, an oil exploration company foreman at the time, was unconvinced by Murie's pitch. "He made the area sound so wonderful, beautiful—I thought he was living in a dream world," he recalled in an interview. Like Vogler, Thorall doubted mining would be practicably allowed in an area established to preserve the kind of values Murie espoused. Murie's rhetoric, he said, made him suspicious that proponents would not remain satisfied with the proposal as presented. Self-described as a practical conservationist, Thorall was convinced that "*those* kind of conservationists always wanted to grab more."[33]

Nevertheless, the resolution readily passed on a ballot vote, with forty-three members voting in favor, five against, and seven nonmembers supporting.[34] Disgusted, Vogler quit the Sportsmens Association and vowed never to enter the clubhouse again.

The day after Murie's meeting with the association, President Lake sent Clarence Rhode a copy of the resolution and the "Suggested Plan of Administration and Regulations." His transmittal letter requested that Rhode immediately initiate official action to establish the Arctic Range. This stimulated the first governmental action to withdraw the area. The request would subsequently be referred to by Murie and others as the "initial" proposal for an Arctic Wildlife Range. (Though technically correct, most of the provisions sought for the range had been part of the earlier National Park Service and conservation organizations' proposals for a wilderness area here.)

Also on May 15 Murie again met with the Fairbanks Garden Club and showed his slides from the Sheenjek. That day, the president of the club, Mrs. Paul Haggland, sent Rhode a similar resolution, including the "Suggested Plan of Administration and Regulations." Mrs. Earl Cook was the club's publicity chairperson. "I was quite carried away by Dr. Murie's presentation," she recalled, "and wrote considerably for the local newspaper in favor of it." Later, however, she came to feel that they had heard "merely one side" of the issue, and concerns about the proposal's effect on mining and other factors led her to withdraw her support.[35] Soon after, another sportsmen's organization, the Anchorage chapter of the Izaak Walton League, sent Rhode a letter endorsing both the range proposal and the plan of administration.[36] That was followed by a letter of endorsement from the Fairbanks Women's Club.

The Letter-Writing Campaign

The next step was to convince Interior Secretary Seaton to take action on the requests. The year before, President Dwight Eisenhower selected Seaton to replace Douglas McKay, nicknamed "Giveaway" McKay, in an effort to improve public perception of his administration's regressive conservation policies. Although he hadn't come to the job as a conservationist, or even as an outdoorsman, Seaton was open-minded and became a strong supporter of Zahniser's early wilderness bills. However, his boss, Ike, was a conservative Republican who favored business interests and embodied the nation's widespread contentment with its expanding development and growing prosperity. Eisenhower had run on a platform advocating "restoration of the traditional Republican lands policy."[37] Conservationists considered his lands policy of freedom from federal interference abysmal and thought it imperative that Seaton be shown that there was wide support for the proposal. Rhode and Murie agreed that it was time to launch a letter-writing campaign. Murie contacted many groups and individuals, urging them to write to Seaton's

FIGURE 37. Secretary of the Interior Fred Seaton. *Photo by the National Park Service; courtesy of the Dwight D. Eisenhower Library.*

assistant secretary, Ross Leffler. "These individual letters from Alaskans mean so much," he wrote, adding that writers should "be sincere and give the right reasons."[38]

The letters came from Alaska as well as from around the country. An index of supporters' sentiment, they offered a variety of reasons for establishing the area, most of which went well beyond the purposes normally associated with wildlife ranges. The Hamilton Acres Garden Club of Fairbanks sent a letter endorsing the Sportsmens Association resolution and became one of many groups forwarding the restrictive "Suggested Plan of Administration and Regulations" as their notion of how the area should be managed and according to what values.

Citing the "scientific, philosophical, and recreational value of wilderness," the American Society of Mammalogists overlooked the decision to go for a wildlife range and urged the secretary and other officials to "do all within their power to aid in the establishment of a wilderness area."[39] Ira Gabrielson, president of the Wildlife Management Institute and former director of the Fish and Wildlife Service, urged action because there were so few places left "where wildlife and ecological relationships have been undisturbed."[40] Writing on behalf of Hawaii's Bureau of Game, Richard Warner said creating the range would be "lauded by conservationists throughout the Territory."[41] Noting that "[s]omehow every time a few conservationists get together, the subject of the Arctic Wildlife Range comes up," American Nature Association president Richard Westwood argued for the preservation of the area's various wilderness-associated species.[42] Territorial doctor Phillip Moore had visited the proposed range and urged establishment "because the public has found out about the area and because of the ease with which airplanes can land in a good share of the area, may severely damage it in a short time."[43] Some, like Mary Harris, who had never been to the area, made the point more strongly. Stimulated by Lois Crisler's writings, she urged action because "the wolves and other wildlife are fast being wiped out by torturers from airplanes. The whole ecology of the region and the balance of nature is being destroyed so fast that action should be swift to save what is left."[44]

While the letters were coming in, Rhode wrote Murie a letter marked "confidential" advising him of the many endorsements being received, some by "substantial people." "I think we can detect your interest in them," he noted. But Rhode's main reason for writing was to express concern that establishment of the Arctic Range not be considered a substitute for the Kuskokwim refuge proposal he had been working on for several years. Located in southwestern Alaska, this rich waterfowl breeding ground, Rhode feared, might be jeopardized by oil exploration if not safeguarded as a refuge.[45] Murie, who had pioneered waterfowl research there in 1924, fully agreed. Months earlier he had written Secretary Seaton urging establishment of both the Kuskokwim and Izembek Bay areas as refuges. In the shadow of the campaign to establish the 14,000-square-mile Arctic Range, the effort to withdraw these 2,924- and 680-square-mile refuges quietly continued. They would be established concurrently with the Arctic Range.

By mid-1957, sportsmen's organizations were becoming increasingly influential sources of support. On the national level, Charles Callison of the National Wildlife Federation wrote to Assistant Secretary Leffler endorsing the range proposal. Representing several hundred local hunting and fishing clubs, the federation claimed to be the largest conservation organization in the world. Probably at his friend Olaus's suggestion, Callison copied his letter to all the federation's affiliated clubs, encouraging them to write. Thus, groups as distant and diverse as the Ohio Fin and Wing Club and a New York muzzle-loading rifle club came to endorse the proposal.

Callison delegated responsibility for the range issue to the federation's young conservation director, Stewart Brandborg, and that decision was indeed fortuitous for the campaign. A former big-game biologist with the Idaho and Montana fish and game departments, Brandborg had become an effective lobbyist, with a particular interest in advancing the federation's support for the recently introduced Wilderness Bill. Brandborg was among the conservation leaders of the era who, as a child, had been an avid reader of Ernest Thompson Seton's nature books. (Today the complete set has a prominent place in his living room.) By the mid-1950s he "had fallen under the influence" of Howard Zahniser and Olaus Murie, and they arranged for his appointment to the Wilderness Society's Governing Council. Their philosophy, Brandborg recalled, "crystallized my thinking about the rich experience I had had in the backcountry … gave a framework for something that was deep in my psyche, my life." Much of Brandborg's outdoor experience had come from hunting, and hunters were the federation's primary constituency. But "[w]hile I had to represent the interests of the hunting community and recognize appropriateness of hunting in specific places, I didn't feel in my heart that this was the function of the Arctic." Brandborg felt this should be a place "set apart," a repository of evolutionary processes and symbolic and spiritual values. Using the language of his mentors, he described his opinion of its greatest function in terms of

> the immensity of this evolutionary creation and being humbled by it, coming down to appreciation of what we as human beings are, or perhaps more importantly, what this place represents if we leave it as it is.[46]

FIGURE 38. Stewart Brandborg, 1950s. After Howard Zahniser's death in 1964, "Brandy" became director of the Wilderness Society. He would play important roles in passage of the Wilderness Act and the Alaska National Interest Lands Conservation Act of 1980.
Courtesy of Stewart M. Brandborg.

A specialist in legislation, Brandborg would be most influential when bills in the House and Senate were being considered. Although his organization joined the campaign later than did the Wilderness Society, Sierra Club, and Conservation Foundation, Brandborg matched their leaders' eloquence and idealism. At a time when each of those organizations had relatively small memberships, Brandborg would command attention when he testified representing many of the federation's million-plus conservation-minded members.[47]

In Alaska, the Tanana Valley Sportsmens Association resolution was quickly adopted by the Alaska Sportsmen's Council, an umbrella organization of thirteen territorial clubs affiliated with the National Wildlife Federation. The council represented about twenty-five hundred Alaska hunters and anglers. One of the council's major purposes was to "prevent repetition of the many mistakes in resource management" that had occurred in the lower forty-eight states.[48] Bud Boddy was the council's energetic executive director and also president of Territorial Sportsmen Inc., the group based in his hometown of

Juneau, the territorial capital. A civic leader, Boddy had considerable standing there. He was also a good friend of Clarence Rhode, who headed the Alaska region of the Fish and Wildlife Service from Juneau. Boddy actively solicited support from Alaska sportsmen and made the interior secretary's office aware of that support. He undoubtedly strategized with Rhode who, because of his government position, was limited in his role as an advocate.

That Boddy's motivation transcended maintenance of wildlife populations and opportunities for hunting and fishing would become apparent in his Senate testimony on the range proposal. With passing reference to these, he emphasized the "moral obligation" the proposal represented. "The Arctic Wildlife Range is unique," he said; "only here in Alaska has the United States a chance to preserve for future generations a substantial piece of Arctic country essentially undisturbed." Citing the area's unique scientific, ecological, recreational, and aesthetic values, he compared the shortsightedness of the proposal's opponents to those who had been unable to foresee the values of Yellowstone Park. Responding to criticism that "outsiders" had too much influence in Alaska affairs, he stated that "we, as Alaskans, should recognize our obligation to the citizens of the United States as a whole and support the setting aside of this area of national concern."[49]

The main values Boddy expressed and his use of words such as "preserve" and "undisturbed" were associated more with wilderness than with wildlife refuges and ranges. In fact, at the time, management of Fish and Wildlife Service areas was little informed by either ecology or wilderness considerations. Most of the agency's areas were disturbed—altered and manipulated—to attract or increase production of favored species, particularly those of interest to hunters, the agency's main constituency.

But it is noteworthy that at both the national and territorial levels, the main representatives of hunting organizations spoke more from the perspective of the emerging ecology-based environmental perspective than from the dominant conservation-of-resources paradigm. Ironically, their letters and testimony in support of the range proposal tended to affirm one of the main arguments that opponents used against it. As the proposal's most powerful critic, Alaska Senator Bob Bartlett put it: "Many proponents actually want a true wilderness area, not a wildlife range."[50]

Interior Department Leadership

In July 1957, Seaton's assistant secretary of the interior for fish and wildlife, Ross Leffler, visited Alaska and was given an impressive aerial tour of the proposed range by Rhode. The following day Leffler met with reporters from the *Fairbanks Daily News-Miner* and made the first official Interior Department endorsement of the proposal. "ARCTIC WILDLIFE AREA IS PROPOSED" was the July 13 headline. "Interior to Press for Reserve in Alaska's Northeast Corner" read the subtitle. The article reported Leffler's assurance that the area would be open to mineral leasing and mining, as well as to hunting and fishing. To further assure Alaskans, he stated that the establishment of a wildlife area was "preferable to incorporating the remote section into the [proposed] national wilderness area system as has been discussed."[51]

In a report on the occasion to his boss, Fish and Wildlife Service director Dan Janzen, Rhode reported that Leffler had advised Service employees that they were now free to openly support establishment of the area. Rhode mentioned discussing strategy with Leffler and reported that they had agreed that legislative establishment was preferable to an executive order. If designated by Congress, he told Janzen, the area would continue to have the public's active support and would be more likely to remain permanent. Rhode added that following the announcement, there had not been a single adverse public comment and reminded the director of the many endorsements that had been received. Further, he offered the opinion that Congress would act favorably.

Leffler's visit signaled two important developments: the beginning of the political process and the transfer of official leadership of the campaign to the government, through officials of both the Interior Department and the Fish and Wildlife Service. This shift was more significant than it might seem today because in the 1950s, federal officials enjoyed greater respect, their recommendations had greater influence, and their actions were less subject to public scrutiny. Until the final days of the campaign, legislative establishment would be the goal of department and agency officials.

Proponents were pleased by this progress, though certainly many agreed with Dick Whittaker of the *Anchorage Times* newspaper, who, in his congratulatory letter to Olaus and Mardy, offered the sympathetic acknowledgment that "there is a world of difference between what you wish as a wilderness area and a wildlife refuge."[52] While this was undoubtedly true, the Muries knew the realities of Alaska politics, and they realized that the less restrictive classification, Fish and Wildlife Service leadership, and Clarence Rhode's support were essential to attaining something close to their true goal. Throughout the campaign they fully supported range status. They would, however, work for the adoption of protective provisions intended to result in a wildlife range that was a de facto wilderness.

Proponents' efforts now shifted to informing, encouraging, and supporting those in the administration who would bring the range proposal to Congress. Rhode recognized that the secretary's legal counsel and special assistant would play a key role and recommended that Ted Stevens be prepared. Soon thereafter, Washington-based Zahniser provided Stevens with the Wilderness Society's information on the proposal and their recommendations for its management. John Buckley sent a copy of the "Last Great Wilderness" article to Stevens, along with a description of how the initiative had progressed from that beginning.

Harvard-trained and already politically savvy, Stevens was Seaton's trusted advisor. He knew Alaska, too, having been a Fairbanks district attorney and legal advisor to the *News-Miner*, which would soon assume a prominent role in the campaign. Although decades later as a senior senator Stevens would arguably become the most powerful foe of wilderness protection for the Arctic Refuge's coastal plain, in the late 1950s he was among the most effective of those who defended the proposal against its most powerful critic, Alaska's U.S. Senator Bob Bartlett.

November 1957, the busiest month of the campaign to date, began with the first formal step toward establishment. Fish and Wildlife Service director Janzen sent a letter to the secretary of the interior requesting that the area be withdrawn from all forms of public appropriation for purposes stated in an accompanying justification entitled "Establishment of Arctic Wildlife Range."[53]

The justification outlined the official rationale for establishment, with descriptions that were repeated through agency and Interior Department announcements and documents. Though signed by director Janzen, the

FIGURE 39. Ted Stevens (right) with Ernest Gruening, circa 1962. *Courtesy of the Archives, Alaska and Polar Regions Department, University of Alaska Fairbanks, acc. no. 76-21-526.*

rationale and wording suggest contributions by the Wilderness Society, most likely authored by Murie and provided by Zahniser. Notably, the term "preserve" and the phrase "wildlife and wilderness frontiers," both uncharacteristic of Fish and Wildlife Service parlance, recur throughout the document. Quoting the 1951 Hackett report's finding that the Alaska frontier "is rapidly vanishing under the impact of progress," the letter stressed the importance of wild areas to the territory's increasingly important recreation industry. "For the wilderness explorer," it stated, the area will "offer a wilderness experience not duplicated elsewhere."

Paraphrasing one of Sumner's articles, the justification stated that in "looking ahead 50 years at the unfolding story of Alaska's development," it was clear that this area provided the only "feasible opportunity for maintaining a wilderness frontier large enough for the preservation" of large, wide-roaming Arctic animals. The letter also proposed reintroduction of the musk ox, which had been extirpated from northern Alaska. It concluded with a statement, borrowed from Collins and Sumner, that touched on their notion that ecological wholeness was the context within which the area's wildlife and other values were found. The statement would be quoted and paraphrased by officials and conservationists throughout the campaign, and in the decades to come: "The proposed Arctic Wildlife Range offers an ideal opportunity, and the only one in Alaska, to preserve an undisturbed portion of the Arctic large enough to be biologically self-sufficient."[54]

At Leffler's invitation, Olaus Murie went to Washington in mid-November to make a presentation on the proposed range before Seaton and his Interior Department Advisory Committee on Fish and Wildlife. He showed his slides from the 1956 expedition and presented plans for the area's preservation. The committee, of which Howard Zahniser and Sigurd Olson were members, noted "with grave concern the receding wildlife and wilderness frontiers in Alaska." They voted to support the proposal.[55]

The next week, on the morning of November 20, Seaton held a press conference to make two closely related announcements. In the company of Alaska Governor Mike Stepovich, Ted Stevens, and other department officials, he began by announcing his directive for the department to publish a *Federal Register* notice of intent "to go forward with the establishment of this wildlife range." Following a brief mention of wildlife values, Seaton's statement made clear that the area would be open to mineral leasing, though subject to regulations and a permit system. Seaton referenced pending legislation that would enable federal agencies to grant mining claims without the right of surface patent. But no one could have missed the threat implicit in his following comment: If Congress did not provide such authorization, "we will have to reconsider the opening of this area to mining activities." A permit system, with unspecified regulations and no opportunity for surface patents—these conditions were unacceptable to the mining industry, whose opposition was becoming a formidable obstacle to range establishment.

But for Alaska's governor and many other territorial leaders, the threat to mineral development that these provisions represented was small compared to the importance of Seaton's second, compensating announcement that morning: "Also, I have just signed a notice of intent to modify Public Land Order 82."[56] The linkage of this action to the range proposal tempered some Alaskan opposition. It was a pivotal development in the campaign.

Public Land Order (PLO) 82 was a 1943 executive proclamation by Franklin Roosevelt. It had withdrawn all land north of the crest of the Brooks Range from all forms of civilian appropriation and development for use by the military "in prosecution of the war." The forty-nine-million-acre reservation included the preexisting twenty-three-million-acre Naval Petroleum Reserve No. 4. By the mid-1950s the military no longer needed the withdrawn lands outside the naval reserve, and Alaskan interests lobbied for revocation of this much-disliked obstacle to economic development. Senators Gruening and Bartlett had cosponsored a bill to abolish the reserve. Their efforts were unsuccessful, in large part because, as Stevens would remind Bartlett during Senate range hearings, "there were conservation people who realized that the order... while it was promulgated for one purpose, had the effect of protecting the area."[57]

As Stevens would explain to Bartlett, if the Arctic Range were established, "the conservationist interests throughout the United States would be more eager to help" in modifying the land order. But perhaps hunting-guide proponent Martin Vorys more accurately portrayed the situation with his statement that "the conservationists, who from a practical standpoint are a highly-potent factor, would be more inclined to ease off their opposition to the land restoration if they were sure that a specific area had been set aside to preserve the natural arctic state."[58]

The Tradeoff

The national conservation organizations would withdraw their opposition to modifying the land order if they could have the Arctic Range. Bartlett spoke for many of his constituents when he described the trade as "blackmail." "I believe it is basically wrong," he later protested, "to connect the one with the other because if this land isn't needed in prosecution of the war effort any longer it ought to be put back in the public domain, whether or not a wildlife range is under contemplation."⁵⁹ Dr. Robert L. Rausch did not deny the political strategy connecting the Arctic Range and the land order modification. And he spoke for many of his fellow proponents when he acknowledged to Bartlett, "Well, perhaps some of us feel that almost any length is reasonable to establish some of these things before the opportunity is lost."⁶⁰ Looking back, Rausch recalled thinking that such trades were a normal part of the political process and that the range, while large, was half the size of the area conservationists were "giving up." They had already compromised a great deal, he believed, when they decided to work for a wildlife range rather than a national park, which he preferred.⁶¹

The prospect that twenty million acres of north slope land would be opened for oil and gas development and, after (impending) statehood, would be available for state selection delighted many Fairbanks businessmen—and no one more so than C. W. "Bill" Snedden, president and publisher of the *Fairbanks Daily News-Miner.* The day of the announcements he ran a special 144-page edition with the banner headline "SEATON OPENS ARCTIC GAS, OIL." While it carried the subtitle "Part of PLO 82 Area Set Aside for Wildlife Refuge," the significance of that action lay in its relation to the new possibilities for oil and gas development. Beneath the headline, a large photo captioned "MAKING ALASKA HISTORY" showed the smiling Governor Stepovich watching Seaton sign the statement of intent to modify PLO 82. Snedden also placed his glowing editorial on the front page, declaring that Seaton's action "opening up the untold riches lying to the north of us should launch a new era of progress for the territory."⁶² Much of this optimism was actually based on the belief that the presumed huge Gubik gas field, adjacent to the naval reserve, would bolster the Fairbanks economy. As it turned out, Gubik, which had been featured on a front-page map, proved uneconomical. But the discovery of oil, eleven years later, at the state-selected Prudhoe Bay area would more than justify boosters' enthusiasm.

The *News-Miner* in distant Fairbanks was able to print an amazing amount of information on the very day the announcement took place. As reporter Michael Carey has documented, Snedden had connections; he knew the story was coming and when. He and Seaton were good friends. They were working on the statehood issue together, and it was Snedden who had recommended Stevens for his position under Seaton. In October Snedden had written Seaton, requesting that the announcement be made on November 20, the planned publication date of the special edition. Seaton complied. The five-hour time difference between Washington and Fairbanks enabled timely transmission of the expected material.⁶³

Soon after, the governing board of the Fairbanks Chamber of Commerce unanimously voted to endorse the range proposal, contingent upon mining being permitted. It also presumed the area had little economic potential, but wanted the area managed under the multiple-use principle in case the area was found to hold valuable mineral or oil deposits.[64]

Although Seaton's action of November 20 did not establish the range, his statement of intent to withdraw the area for that purpose and his expression of strong administration support were mistakenly considered by many supporters to be the equivalent. He soon received thank-you notes. "God bless you, Mr. Secretary!" a Mrs. Mae Morris wrote. "I am seventy-three years old, and this action you have taken has brightened my shortening day."[65]

The Muries received many congratulatory letters. One was from George Schaller, who, believing that they had "finally achieved this goal," penned a large "HURRAH."[66] Fairfield Osborn wrote of the "grand news… concerning the creation of the Arctic Wildlife Range."[67] Even George L. Collins got

FIGURE 40. The November 20, 1957, *News-Miner* headline actually reports the secretary's intent to modify PLO 82, thereby enabling oil and gas development on the Arctic coastal plain west of the proposed Arctic Wildlife Range.

caught up in the overly optimistic interpretation of the secretary's action. The "successful outcome," he wrote, "made the memory we have of Bob Marshall...more meaningful than ever."[68] Lowell Sumner was "electrified" to hear Seaton had designated the range, though because of that status, he acknowledged that "much remains to be done to keep this area safe."[69]

Olaus Murie, however, was more realistic. As he replied to Sumner, Seaton's action "does not finish the whole story." Murie realized that the action was only "the necessary first step."[70] Indeed, much remained to be done, more than even Murie realized at the time. While Seaton's announcement had bolstered conservationists, it also galvanized mining interests, and their formidable opposition prolonged the effort for three years and nearly reversed its outcome.

In December 1957 News-Miner reporter John Thomson began his involvement in the campaign by publishing the first of two accounts describing his and Geological Survey engineer Pete Isto's challenging first ascent of 9,020-foot Mount Michelson, the highest peak in northeast Alaska. Thomson had served in the Eighth Air Force during the war. Haunting memories of his role in the bombings brought him to the conviction that "some of the world should be immune to destruction and exploitation." He had found inspiration in the works of Thoreau, Muir, and others, but when he discovered Bob Marshall's 1938 proposal for a vast Arctic wilderness, he said, "I found a hero and the germ of my conservation thinking." Thomson moved to Fairbanks in 1955, intent on experiencing the wilderness and adventure Marshall had so effusively described in Arctic Village. His three trips to the proposed Arctic Range area led to Marshallesque descriptions of the "remoteness and grandeur" of this "last Frontier for those who love to conquer mountains."[71] At the same time, ecological writings reinforced his belief that "some of our little planet needs to be kept for all the other creatures."[72] These writings and his revulsion toward the territorial and federal governments' aerial shooting and poisoning of wolves furthered his conviction that nothing less than an inviolate sanctuary was acceptable.

1958: The Mining Industry Aroused

On 14 January 1958 the Fish and Wildlife Service filed the withdrawal notice Seaton had promised. A week later it was published in the Federal Register and a sixty-day comment period began. The purpose of the withdrawal, the document stated, was "for the preservation of the wildlife and wilderness resources of northeast Alaska."[73] While the words "preservation" and "wilderness" surely pleased proponents, they undoubtedly heightened industry fears that the unspecified provisions of the proposed mining permit system and regulations would run counter to their interests.

Industry objection was based on three uncertainties. First, the mineral potential of the little-explored area was poorly known. The U.S. Geological Survey's limited work in the region had not revealed any significant quantities of commercially valuable minerals. However, the survey had noted the presence of rocks and geological structures often associated with ore deposits, and this was probably the industry's main source of optimism. The presence of some oil seeps on the north slope had been noted, but the possibility of oil and gas reserves received little attention compared to the area's mineral potential. A few prospectors had made brief excursions into the area and proposal critic Ed Owens had been living year-round and prospecting in the upper Coleen River region for nearly forty years. They variously reported discovering or finding indications of gold, copper, manganese, phosphate, nickel, zinc, and platinum. But even Owens, whose often-cited reports helped fuel the optimism, had yet to find a prospect worth developing. It was nevertheless true, as some in the industry pointed out, that more recently developed exploration techniques might locate profitable deposits that had been missed by decades of traditional foot prospecting.[74] Thus the industry believed that several years of exploration should precede any consideration of a conservation withdrawal.

Second, although the secretary and many proponents offered assurances that prospecting would be allowed, many doubted that tools more intrusive than a pick, shovel, and gold pan would be permitted. Contemporary exploration often involved drilling, trenching, and blasting, and was often supported by track vehicles—sure to conflict with the purposes of the withdrawal. Industry representatives pointed to what they felt were gross inconsistencies between the prospecting provisions of the laws establishing Glacier Bay National Monument and Mount McKinley National Park and the restrictive regulations later promulgated. Many in the industry, including the director of the Alaska Division of Mines and Minerals, cited a section of the law creating Mount McKinley Park that guaranteed that no citizen "shall be denied entrance to the park for the purpose of prospecting or mining." But James Williams pointed out that the park prohibited the landing of airplanes and helicopters and that prospectors had been denied entry to the park because they had planned to use these forms of transportation, now considered necessary for modern prospecting.

Even more doubtful was the likelihood that the Fish and Wildlife Service would allow—practically—the extraction of minerals that might be discovered. Many mining operations caused considerable surface disturbance and, worse, required track vehicles or roads for access. As Williams stated, Congress might establish the range with the intent that it be open to mineral entry, but it might not work out that way because the "bureaucratic urge to keep an area under its jurisdiction closed to all but its own functions is too strong."[75] Warning that "the bureaucrats prescribe the regulations," miner Douglas Colp said that it was his "duty as a citizen to object strenuously" to the "preposterous fantasy" of the Arctic proposal.[76] Many in the industry shared their suspicions regarding how the Fish and Wildlife Service would choose to interpret and implement mining provisions. Even more were concerned with the underlying intentions and political influence of the advocates for a preserve that was, in the words of the Alaska Miners Association vice president, "being forced on us by conservation groups in the States." Summarizing the concern, Harold Strandberg declared that eliminating mining

> is the intent of those dedicated souls who are trying to set this aside; they feel that they cannot get this through without allowing mining, petroleum operation, and they are willing to go along full well knowing that impossible regulations placed on the mining industry would…serve their purposes; they would have what they want—the area put in the deep freeze.[77]

On January 29 the *Fairbanks Daily News-Miner* published the first of its innumerable editorials strongly supporting establishment of the range—"one of the most magnificent wildlife and wilderness areas in North America…undisturbed as God made it." The potential economic benefits of tourism to the area had been a relatively minor justification for the Arctic proposal until editor Snedden seized upon it. "During the coming years," he predicted, "thousands of tourists with cameras and fishing gear will leave many millions of dollars in Alaska on trips to visit the Arctic Wildlife Range, the only one of its kind in the world."

Addressing the main reason that the withdrawal "riled" many Alaskans, Snedden noted that no mines had been established in the area prior to Public Land Order 82. He suggested that the proposed permit system would accommodate legitimate mining interests. But the main reason for his enthusiasm was the fact that the Interior Department had decided to release twenty million acres of the potentially oil-rich PLO 82 reserve, a decision "closely related" to the creation of the much smaller wildlife range. "Without the latter," Snedden wrote, "it is unlikely we would get the former." Chiding range opponents, he said, "We think the complaint of those opposing [the range] is akin to that of a small boy who has just been given a pie much larger than he can eat but who cries anyway when someone tries to cut a small sliver out of it."[78]

Concern that restrictions would effectively preclude mining was the reason that both the Anchorage and Juneau chambers of commerce went on record opposing the range withdrawal. The Fairbanks-based Fourth Division

Democratic Committee sent the Republican Seaton notice that it "emphatically opposes" the withdrawal. Their letter noted that the Democratic Party had historically and consistently opposed such "indiscriminate" withdrawals, emphasizing the effect on "the peoples' right" to prospect, mine, and drill for oil and gas.[79] In March the Bureau of Land Management completed a categorical analysis of the fifty-seven comments its Fairbanks office received in response to the withdrawal notice. Most were submitted by mining or related business interests; all but two opposed the withdrawal.[80]

The most lengthy protest came from long-time miner Ernest Wolff. After summarizing the mining industry's contribution to the territory's economy, Wolff explained that the proposed provision for mineral leasing without surface patent would "only result in killing any prospecting or mining." Evoking the image of the venerable frontier prospector, he stated that because of the isolated nature of mineral deposits "they must be sought out by individuals who often walk the country for years." Such individuals, he said, lacked the financial resources to develop a mine. Without the possibility of obtaining a surface patent, which could be sold or leased to a mining company, prospectors would not be sufficiently motivated to thoroughly explore such a vast area. Wolff went on to argue that there was no need for a wildlife range because the wildlife could be "controlled" through regulated hunting and wolf poisoning. The real reason behind the withdrawal request, he said, was "agitation by an extremely small group for the establishment of a 'wilderness area.'" This group, he warned, advocated that such areas "be preserved as 'exhibits' of primeval conditions."[81]

In a detailed letter also printed in *Jessen's Weekly* newspaper, Chandalar Gold Mines Inc. president Eskil Anderson complained about the area being removed "from all possibilities of productive [mining] use." He predicted that if established, the remote, roadless reserve would only be available to a few wealthy hunters and nature lovers. But Anderson's most strongly stated objection had to do with what he believed to be the primary motivation of proponents: reservation of the area "for the preservation and propagation of predatory animals." The protection of predators, and particularly the symbolic wolf and its role in the ecosystem, was an early and continuing concern of proponents. And Anderson was at least partially correct in stating that in an effort to prevent a presumed "slaughter" of caribou, "wolves have been poisoned and shot from airplanes by fish and wildlife agents and by civilians for the large bounty offered." He pointed out that the program was conducted by "the same Fish and Wildlife Service now requesting this withdrawal"—an inconsistency noted by Collins but avoided by Murie and others throughout the campaign. Echoing popular criticisms of McKinley Park's termination of predator control, Anderson warned that what was being proposed is "an enormous breeding ground for wolves from which sanctuary they would be able to raid neighboring areas destroying the caribou herds there after those on the withdrawal area itself had been decimated."[82]

The comments of fifty-some conservation organizations and individual supporters of the withdrawal were not included in BLM's analysis because Murie and Alaska Sportsmen's Council director Bud Boddy, and probably Clarence Rhode as well, had urged conservationists to write to Washington instead.[83] Among them, Virginia Wood, her husband Morton, and Celia Hunter wrote BLM director Woozley, stating, "We don't want all of Alaska to become a carbon copy of what we left behind in the States." Borrowing from Collins's first article, they asserted that "[t]his is the last great wilderness left under the American flag, almost the world." "Our children and their children," they said, "deserve to find some of it as wild, unspoiled, as unique, and as exciting as we have found it." Adding a novel twist to the bequest argument, they made the point that "[e]ven if no mining were allowed ... future generations might rejoice that some minerals had been kept in a 'mineral bank' for their use rather than all the oil and ore being extracted by our generation."[84]

James Lake of the Tanana Valley Sportsmens Association drew upon the territory's "last frontier" image in writing for "preservation of a portion of that frontier in its natural state." He accused the mining industry of being "selfish and shortsighted."[85] George Schaller likewise accused mining interests of being "notoriously dollar-minded" and expressed the widespread concern about their "powerful lobby" that had in the past "pushed through legislation of great detriment to all concerned."[86]

Scientific reasons for preservation continued in proponents' letters to Washington, coming from both scientists and nonscientists. Rosella McCune, Secretary of the Mt. St. Helens Club, wrote that the area is "practically all we have left of untouched wilderness and should be kept that way as a natural scientific laboratory." Reflecting the cold-war-era emphasis on science, she concluded that "[m]any millions of public money is spent on laboratories for research; let us save this natural one."[87]

Lois and Herb Crisler wrote Seaton urging preservation of "the only place left on this continent where great, authentic wilderness can yet be reserved." The Crislers, like many others, extolled the area's value as wildlife habitat. But they were not among those willing to compromise the "inviolate" concept. Echoing Stewart Brandborg's belief that this should be a place "set apart," they emphasized a deeper philosophical value at risk through administering the area under the utilitarian conservation paradigm:

We have the Midas touch: what we touch, we have touched. "Otherness" vanishes; technical environment supersedes. Please save a wilderness with "otherness." One vast enough to be a great wilderness.[88]

The third week of March was National Wildlife Week and the theme in 1957 was "Our Public Lands." Snedden took advantage of the occasion to publish a lengthy editorial by that title, which digressed from the values of wildlife to the benefits of preserving wilderness. While the range proposal was not specifically mentioned, Snedden's main argument—that wilderness is the root of American cultural heritage—so closely paralleled the frontier arguments of range proponents that the connection could hardly be missed. He pointed out that even during the pioneering westward migration, the nation's forefathers had had the wisdom to establish Yellowstone National Park. More than a connection to Alaska's venerated frontier past, he said, "Wilderness areas are an expression of American determination to hang on to the invigorating pioneer spirit that is good for any civilization." Perhaps seeking to counter claims of some range opponents that wilderness preservation was a disparagement of civilization, Snedden made the case that wilderness provides a touchstone to qualities central to the American character. Cold-war anxieties were probably in mind as he told readers,

It is from the land that we will draw much of the strength to perpetuate the freedom that we cherish and the leadership that the world calls upon us to provide. It remains for us now … to protect and preserve this national heritage for the America and the Alaska of tomorrow.[89]

Also in March, territorial commissioner of mines Phil Holdsworth let loose with what the Associated Press described as "a 3000 word blast" attacking the creation of "an Arctic playground at the expense of future mineral development."[90] Published as a Territorial Department of Mines Bulletin, "THAT 9,000,000 ACRE WITHDRAWAL," would be repeatedly cited by mining interests and other opponents. After recounting the venerable history of mining in Alaska, Holdsworth launched into a detailed synopsis of why, because of the proposed permit requirement, "the area will not be open to mining…in a real and practical sense."

Holdsworth also argued that mines caused less impact than many believed. "One thing that mines interfere with very little," he said, "is wilderness." In fact, by bringing roads and providing public access, he argued, they actually improve the wilderness. Making the point that "the Stateside national parks are overrun," he argued that the problem "is not going to be helped by the creation of a nine-million-acre wilderness area "way up there where the people cannot get to it."[90]

In a March 7 editorial response aimed at Holdsworth, the *News-Miner* expounded upon why it supported the proposed range. "How much do mining men like Mr. Holdsworth have to have to be satisfied?" it asked. "The answer is easy. They have to have everything." Surely antagonizing miners, the editorial compared many of them to those who had eradicated the musk ox and decimated Alaska's fish stocks and fur seal and sea otter populations. Citing the overexploitation of some salmon stocks by the commercial fishing industry, the article asserted that "some mining men possess the same kind of frenzy for self destruction." The recreation industry, it said, was more important to the Alaska economy than mining, and unlike mining, recreation provided "benefits not just once but year after year forever." Mining, the article continued, "is a one-shot proposition," but the Arctic Range would "leave as heritage to the future something besides tin cans, dilapidated buildings, rust and an assortment of holes in the ground."[92]

Predictably, the editorial stimulated a critical response from miners and their supporters. A subsequent editorial affirmed the paper's support for the range proposal and complained that the letters to the editor the paper had received had been "abusive enough, terming our comments misleading, untrue, and dilapidated," and calling the editor a "wet blanket, joy-killer, one-track-mind ... pencil pusher, and a poor one at that."[93]

Among the critics, a Mr. H. Francis complained of the *News-Miner*'s "low blow" to the mining industry. He took issue with its statement regarding the proposed range's potential contribution to the territory's promising recreation industry. "The proposed reserve is of no use as a tourist attraction," he declared, adding that "[i]f some one will go in and turn a few creeks bottom up, bury the mosquitoes and niggerheads and put the gravel on top a few tourists might venture in."[94]

Champion of frontier abundance and freedom Joe Vogler agreed. "It would take quite a salesman to book a tourist to the area in question," he said, suggesting that someone should put in a dude mining camp. "Let's go back to the American subject of free and open competition and opportunity," he told the editor.[95]

Central Brooks Range miner and trapper Alfred Withrow wrote "for the purpose of arousing interest to counteract the movement." Appropriating the preservationists' often repeated "forever" theme, he warned that the area would be "forever closed to prospecting and mining. Yes, forever!" Wasn't the withdrawal, he asked, "a means of withdrawing from the common people the right to search the land for riches it may hold? OIL? GAS? URANIUM? GOLD?"[96]

Turning the paper's characterization of miners around, C. M. Kinyon described proponents as "some short-sighted individuals [who] think only in their interests." Like many, he felt the allegation that mining would significantly injure this remote area was "a far-fetched fantasy." Kinyon accused the *News-Miner* of being inconsistent for criticizing mining while at the same time promoting statehood and using the mining industry as an example of the potential state's economic stability. "You speak with two tongues," he said.[97]

Fabian Carey agreed. He was not a mining proponent and had concerns about some of the industry's practices, but Carey was more concerned with the principle involved in acquiescing to the feds. "How can you possibly advocate Statehood in one breath and land giveaways [in] the other?" he asked. "After watching the bureaucrats grab off all the choice slices of Alaska for the past so many years," Carey wrote, "I fail to see how you can condone this phony land grab on any basis."[98]

Stanley Samuelson was among the letter writers who focused on the statehood implications of the range proposal. The paper's editorial stance, he said, "amounts to betraying Alaska's future" because admitting that the federal government could control this part of Alaska better than Alaskans would be an admission that it could better control the whole territory. "The whole idea of becoming a state is to get released from absentee control," he wrote, "and now you want to hand over a fourth of Alaska to that same control."[99] (Following Samuelson's letter, an editorial note pointed out that the range proposal would total less than one-fifteenth of Alaska's land area, not a fourth.)

Some letter writers asked the paper to print the entire text of Holdsworth's article, which it did a week later—along with another editorial highly critical of its author.[100] "The Mischief Good Men Do" restated publisher Snedden's support for the range proposal. "We favor it on the grounds that some few sections of Alaska should be preserved for posterity just as God made them," he stated. He went on to note, however, that this particular area was appropriate for preservation because of its "being remote and unpromising as far as commercial and industrial development is concerned." Snedden added that Holdsworth's diatribe posed another danger: "that Alaska might again incur the powerful opposition of conservation organizations in the States who maintain that Alaskans have no stability when confronted by small pressure groups." Emphasizing the influence of the national groups in Washington, he warned that opposition could jeopardize the revocation of Public Land Order 82, and even attainment of statehood.[101]

Charles Gray worked for Snedden at the time and later succeeded him as publisher. He believes that Snedden had little personal interest in preserving wild places. He attributes Snedden's advocacy to his friendship with

Seaton and his belief that range establishment would serve as a "payoff to the conservationists for not objecting to statehood."[102] One of the territory's foremost statehood proponents, Snedden had good reason to mollify conservationists. Their concern that diminished federal control would result in less resource protection in the Arctic and elsewhere had figured in the opposition expressed during statehood hearings earlier in the year.[103] In fact, as reported in his newspaper's article, "Wildlife Group Throws Block in Alaska Statehood Hearing," the influential National Wildlife Federation's threat that it might oppose statehood brought a congressional statehood hearing to an abrupt end.[104]

Commissioner Holdsworth soon received a critical response to his article from Clarence Rhode, emphasizing the "obligation to future generations" theme of the campaign. Rhode also sought to undermine Holdsworth's argument about the importance of mining. Drawing upon data supplied to him by the Izaak Walton League, he stated that mining contributed less than one percent of taxes collected in the territory. He said that sportsmen, who supported the range, contributed more than five times that in license fees. Further, while only two thousand Alaskans were engaged in mining, sixty thousand hunted and fished, contributing more than $17 million to the economy. In a rather strong statement for a public servant, Rhode said that in opposing the range, "the mining and oil industries would be acting for selfish reasons rather than the public good."[105]

The mining fray brought Virginia Wood back to the editorial pages, advocating establishment of the range "for the perpetuation of wildlife, ecological research, and for wilderness recreation for all for generations to come." Like Rhode, she attacked mining proponents "who don't really care about the country or the rest of the people as long as they can make their fortune and get out." But unlike Rhode, who as usual came from the more narrow perspective of wildlife and sportsmen's interests, Wood argued from the perspective of the campaign's founding ideals. "The wilderness that we have conquered and squandered," she wrote, "has produced the traditions of the frontier that we want to think still prevail—freedom, opportunities, adventure, and resourceful, rugged individualists." Preservation of these American virtues, she argued, depended on preserving places like northeast Alaska.

Her letter exemplified conservationists' concerns about the postwar order, concerns that were among the underpinnings of the Arctic campaign and the emerging environmental perspective from which it developed. She bemoaned "the price we have paid for our high standard of living and unparalleled industrial leadership." Areas such as the Arctic Range, she said, would become increasingly important for relief from the pressures of expanding civilization and increasing population, "if we don't blast ourselves off this planet with atomic bombs or start regressing to something subhuman by merely testing them." Using language that may have been borrowed from her Bob Marshall readings, she argued that wilderness experience was an alternative to finding "relief with tranquilizers or the psychiatrist's couch."[106] Like many in the movement, Wood shared the hope David Brower expressed in that month's *Sierra Club Bulletin*, that "man will soon discover his least-exploited resource, Restraint."[107]

Exacerbating the mining industry's distrust of the range proposal was an article the secretary of the interior wrote for the distinctly preservationist venue, *National Parks Magazine*. In "America's Largest Wildlife Area," Seaton made the surprising statement that "no substantial mining or mineral values exist in the Wildlife Range." While stating that "parts of it" could be opened to mineral leasing, he made it clear that any development would be in accordance with regulations "which will protect and preserve the wildlife and the primitive character of the land."

The values the secretary thought existed were clear from his wilderness-oriented characterization of the area and his description of the recreational opportunities it would provide. This was a place, Seaton wrote, where "the 'mountain men' will spend their time in the 6,000 to 9,000 foot altitudes"; "where the mountain climber can face the challenge"; "where the riverman will find white water which will test the highest courage"; "where the naturalist can watch the tree sparrow or the polar bear, or glory in caribou"; "where the person who 'just wants to look' can see vast expanses...and marvel at the land of wild and natural beauty."[108]

As the mining industry feared, values more associated with the preservationist national park origins of the proposal than with a wildlife range remained central to the campaign. Such values were reinforced with the publication of Lois Crisler's book, *Arctic Wild*, based on her and her husband's filming of wolves for the Disney documentary *White Wilderness*. An expansion of the preservationist themes forwarded in her article "Where Wilderness Is Complete," the book was widely read and cited by proponents. Zahniser recommended it as descriptive of the kind of experiences the Arctic proponents were seeking to preserve.[109] Pruitt probably further agitated miners by publishing a review (later paraphrased in his Senate testimony) declaring the book's insights to be "of more value to the human race than all the gold mines in the north."[110]

Early in 1958 Secretary Seaton received a letter from a surprising source criticizing his withdrawal action. National Park Service director Conrad Wirth claimed that prior to the announcement, his agency was unaware that the department was planning to withdraw the area for a wildlife range. He provided a three-page justification for establishing the area as an "Arctic Wilderness National Park" instead. He described and attached copies of "Northeast Arctic: The Last Great Wilderness" and other articles by Collins and Sumner to emphasize that the proposal was initiated by his agency. Wirth claimed that because of mounting opposition, the Park Service had held back on recommending a park, but intended to do so at a more opportune time. He noted that the wildlife, wilderness, and scientific purposes associated with the range proposal were more appropriately park values. Wirth stated that the Interior Department should not place the Fish and Wildlife Service "in the park conservation field, as the proposed Arctic game range appears to do." He stated that as a wilderness park the area could also accommodate mining. However, "the provision for hunting and trapping of fur-bearing animals in the proposed Arctic game range falls short," he said, "of the complete protection of both plants and animals that would be afforded by national park or monument status." Wirth added, however, that hunting and trapping would be allowed by the Natives "for their own needs."[111]

Seaton's response, if any, is unknown. Wirth copied the memo to the Fish and Wildlife Service, and soon after Clarence Rhode wrote to his boss, Director Janzen, stating he was "puzzled" as to how Wirth could profess surprise at the secretary's action toward a wildlife range. He noted that Wirth and Collins were among the Park Service employees at the March 17 San Francisco meeting where it was decided that a wildlife range, not a park, would be sought.[112]

Wirth, in fact, had never shown much interest in the Arctic proposal. Although he had made reference to it, there is no previous record of his signing correspondence approaching the length or detail of this letter. This had been George Collins's project, and he wanted a park, and probably more so now that Wirth had apparently agreed that the Park Service could accommodate some Native hunting and trapping. It is possible that Wirth suddenly became concerned about the rival Fish and Wildlife Service gaining nine million acres of park-quality land. More likely, Collins was so bolstered by Seaton's withdrawal action and the park-associated values the secretary espoused that he was able to persuade Wirth to make one last attempt to go for a park.

Nothing came of the revived park proposal—except for worry about a backlash on the part of most leading range proponents. In March 1958, fourteen of them gathered in St. Louis to discuss the range proposal and, according to the notes taken by Mardy Murie, "to scuttle any rumors regarding its being proposed as a national park." The Muries, Starker Leopold, Sigurd Olson, Bud Boddy, and John Buckley were among those present.

David Brower, executive director of the Sierra Club and a strident wilderness advocate, also attended. Collins and Sumner had drawn him into the Arctic project early on. But beyond Brower's self-described role as the "ringleader" of its advocacy at the annual North American Wildlife and Conservation conferences, he had not played a visible role. Collins, Sumner, and other leaders had not encouraged more involvement, probably because they feared that his ill opinion of hunting and general unwillingness to compromise might jeopardize the effort.

Lowell Sumner attended, but he was either silent or his comments—likely critical of the range compromise—were not recorded. Significantly absent was George Collins. After noting the opposition a park proposal would face and agreeing that further consideration of it might jeopardize the whole project, the group reaffirmed the proposal for a Fish and Wildlife Service wildlife range. That action apparently ended discussion of a park proposal by conservation organizations.[113]

A week later Olaus received a letter from John Boswell, current president of the Tanana Valley Sportsmens Association and an officer of the Alaska Miners Association. Boswell attached a copy of Phil Holdsworth's Territorial Department of Mines Bulletin attack on the range proposal and expressed the worry that "this is only the fore-runner to further opposition that will eventually extend to more powerful lobbies in the United States." He was also concerned that Seaton's statements on mining might cause the Fairbanks Chamber of Commerce to withdraw its support. The chamber, along with the Sportsmens Association and several other Alaska groups, had endorsed the proposal with the understanding that the area would be practicably open to legitimate mining. Boswell reminded Murie that proponents had a "moral responsibility" to ensure that the range would be open as they had assured.[114]

Murie immediately responded to Boswell and, significantly, copied his letter to Holdsworth, the Fairbanks Chamber of Commerce, Senator Bartlett, and several others. He used the occasion to describe the outcome of the St. Louis meeting, and to assure them that range proponents recognized both "a moral obligation to stick by the plan that was endorsed by the many Alaskan groups" and the need to "be fair to legitimate mining activities."[115] Although Olaus left no record of how he felt about the mining compromise, he surely disliked it. Robert Krear later documented an evening discussion on the Sheenjek River during which Olaus and the others had agreed that preventing mining "would be of utmost importance."[116]

A few days later Murie wrote to Fairfield Osborn describing the St. Louis meeting, the status of the establishment legislation that the Interior Department would send to Congress, and his sense of the futility of trying to appease the proposal's chief opponent, the Territorial Department of Mines. That department, he wrote, was "always and continually and for any reason and no reason, opposed to any withdrawal of any kind." The best strategy for the moment, he concluded, was "to keep quiet and not stir things up until the bill gets into Congress."[117]

Things remained quiet on the range issue through the summer and into the fall as proponents waited for a bill to be introduced. On 20 August 1958, Clarence Rhode, game agent Stanley Fredericksen, and Rhode's twenty-two-year-old son Jack took off from Fairbanks in a twin-engine Grumman Goose aircraft headed for the proposed range. It was to be a routine hunting-season law-enforcement patrol, although a secondary purpose was to locate groups of caribou to show some national conservation leaders who wanted to see the area.[118] They flew to Peters–Schrader Lakes, then, according to some geologists camped there, they headed west.

With a referendum on statehood just a week away, things were anything but quiet in Fairbanks when they left. President Eisenhower had signed the Alaska statehood act into law on July 7, but the bill required the approval of Alaska voters. While most Alaskans desired statehood, controversy surrounded several provisions of the act. Of relevance to the range issue was a provision retaining the much-resented federal jurisdiction over Alaska's fish and wildlife resources pending certification by the secretary that the state legislature had made adequate provision for their management and conservation "in the broad national interest." Representative of these concerns was a letter to the editor in that day's News-Miner by local homesteader and future state legislator Niilo Koponen. He said he opposed statehood because "I cannot vote away our rights to the northern and western portions of Alaska" and because of the "humiliating paternalism" inherent in federal control of Alaska's fish and wildlife.[119]

Also in that day's News-Miner was a front-page article describing a meeting the Tanana Valley Sportsmens Association had scheduled with eighteen top officials of federal and territorial fish and game agencies and conservation groups. They hoped to develop a proposal for fish and game management that would satisfy the statehood act and facilitate timely transfer of authority to the new state. Two of those invited, Charles Callison of the National Wildlife Federation and C. R. Gutermuth of the Wildlife Management Institute, were prominent Arctic Range proponents and widely considered to be statehood opponents. Gutermuth had been visiting Clarence Rhode and planned to discuss the Arctic Range proposal with him later that week. The article, reinforcing the view of many Alaskans toward national conservation organizations, reported that Gutermuth had testified at a statehood hearing that Alaskans "were politically immature and had demonstrated that they could not manage their own resources which … belonged as much to the rest of the country as to Alaska." Sportsmens Association president Boswell denied accusations that an "anti-statehood maneuver" would result from the meeting scheduled for that Saturday. Diverse interests were invited, he said, to find common ground and develop a wildlife management proposal that would be acceptable to all. Undoubtedly the association recognized that national conservation groups would have considerable influence on the secretary's decision to relinquish wildlife management authority to the new state.[120]

The following day, Thursday, August 21, a party of hunters saw Rhode's plane over Chandler Lake, heading west. Along with election articles in the day's paper was a notice that Secretary Seaton would arrive on Saturday. He had been invited to dedicate a monument to the late Judge James Wickersham, who had introduced the first Alaska statehood bill in 1916. Probably the strongest statehood supporter in the Eisenhower administration, Seaton took full advantage of his visit to promote the benefits of statehood.[121]

On Monday, August 25, the *News-Miner* ran two headlines: "Seaton Urges Full Vote on Statehood" and "Record Vote Expected Tuesday." Sharing the front page with election articles was a short notice: "FWS Men Overdue on Flight." It reported that Clarence Rhode, his son Jack, and Agent Fredericksen had not returned Saturday as planned. Six planes had begun a search and military aircraft would be joining the effort.[123]

Above Tuesday's headline, "Alaskans Casting Record Vote," ran the banner "Arctic Air Search Continues for FWS Plane." The Air Force, it was reported, had taken charge of the search, which now involved a dozen military, agency, and private planes. Fog in the mountains hampered the search and a magnetic storm blocked communications from the area.[122]

On Wednesday, the *News-Miner* headline proclaimed "Statehood Wins 5-to-1 Victory." Alaska would have representatives in the House and Senate by the time an Arctic Range bill was up for a vote, and that did not bode well for the campaign. Also bad news was the report that poor weather and an atmospheric radio blackout continued to impede the search for Rhode's plane. Volunteer pilots from as far as Kodiak Island were arriving to try to find the popular Rhode, bringing the number of planes available to more than twenty. Also arriving was Frank Armstrong, top general of the Alaska Command, who personally flew a four-engine C-131 to Fairbanks to help in the search.

On Thursday, August 28, *News-Miner* reporter Jack De Yonge joined the massive search and provided firsthand accounts of the effort, which now included several large Air Force C-54 and SA-16 aircraft. But while the fleet grew, so did the size of the search area. False leads and the possibility that

Rhode's long-range Goose might have gone as far as the west end of the Brooks Range led to an expansion of the search area to more than 100,000 square miles. De Yonge told readers how the vast country "stupefies and over-powers" the observer. He also noted its "impartiality to humans." Conveying the sense of urgency that pervaded the mission, and perhaps a creeping sense of pessimism, he wrote that each day the three remained unfound "means one less chance that they may survive."[124]

In late September planes began dropping out of the search. In November the Air Force withdrew from the effort. On December 3, Rhode's acting replacement Dan Ralston wrote to the Rhode family:

> Winter overtook us two weeks ago but we have continued the search despite 30 to 45 degrees below zero temperatures, icing conditions, and snow. However I can no longer expect or ask the boys to continue flying under these hazardous conditions, I just can't risk their lives.

More than 260 people had participated in the search and as many as twenty-eight planes were involved at one time, flying a total of more than two

FIGURE 41. Clarence Rhode in a Grumman Goose. *Courtesy of the NCTC Archives.*

thousand hours. As Ralston told the family, "Without question it has been the largest, most thorough and longest search ever conducted in Alaska."[125]

The fate of the "last patrol" remained a mystery until August 1979, when two backpackers discovered the charred wreckage of Grumman Goose N-720. Investigators surmised that the accident was caused by bad weather. The wreckage remains high on a mountainside above the Ivishak River, within what is now the Arctic National Wildlife Refuge.[126]

6

Finally, Legislation Introduced

A Bill ... to preserve, in the public interest, a magnificent

wildlife and wilderness area in the State of Alaska.

—Senate Bill 1899

1959: The Name Issue

Soon after Rhode's disappearance, several of his friends began to
advocate for changing the name of the Arctic proposal to the "Clarence
J. Rhode Wildlife Range." The controversy that followed reaches into
some of the deepest philosophical and psychological underpinnings of the
Arctic campaign. The geological metaphor "outcroppings" helps reveal
why the opponents of the name change believed that without causing any
tangible impact, affixing a person's name to a wilderness would change how
it was perceived and the meaning it held.[1] As geophysicist Keith Echelmeyer
explained, rock outcroppings on the tundra surface may appear insignificant,

---

◄ FIGURE 42. McCall Glacier and Romanzof Mountains. *Photo by Subhankar Banerjee.*

but they reveal the underlying structure of the landscape. Similarly, people's response to affixing a name to a place can serve as an outward manifestation of underlying values it holds for them. The name issue reveals some of the belief structures that lay beneath the surface of the preservation effort.

In April 1959, Rhode's old boss, former Fish and Wildlife Service director Albert Day, initiated the controversy by sending letters soliciting support for naming the area after Rhode. That month's issue of *Conservation News* favorably reported his proposal, and soon after *Nature Magazine* did as well. Letters of support from individuals and a few conservation groups, citing Rhode's dedication, accomplishments, reputation, and ultimate sacrifice, poured into Seaton's office. Ironically, even Senator Ernest Gruening, who the next year would help to block passage of the establishment bill, wrote that Rhode's accomplishments spoke "for naming of that beautiful area in his memory."[2]

Seaton received just as many letters opposing the name change. Many writers thought like Allston Jenkens, president of Philadelphia Conservationists, who wrote that "the drama and beauty and expanse of the Range should be reflected in its name."[3] Robert Krear, who had discussed the issue of naming the region's features with the Muries and Justice Douglas on the Sheenjek River, told the secretary of "that intangible appeal of a great natural area that suffers a loss of dignity when a human place name is given the area." He believed that namelessness contributed to the area's aura of mystery and enhanced the recreational experience. For him, names were intended to influence how an area or feature was perceived, thereby lessening the visitor's independent, unmediated response to the environment. "The sensation of being in an area so remote, untouched, and unspoiled," he told the secretary, was enhanced by "the fact that many of the natural features were unnamed."[4]

All the letters of opposition expressed respect for Rhode and regret over his loss, and all but one opposing letter expressed the view that the range should not be known by any person's name. Wilbur Libby, the exception, thought it should perhaps be named for Olaus Murie.[5]

No one would have been more opposed to such an action than Olaus himself. His son Martin recalls overhearing his father's refusal to allow a mountain to be named after him, and particularly "the vehemence with which he absolutely refused."[6] After Olaus's death, the U.S. Board of Geographic Place Names proposed to name a mountain in the Brooks Range in his honor. Mardy immediately wrote the board's executive secretary, explaining that "Olaus had always been opposed, in principle, to the naming of any natural object after a human being." Because she and their children knew Olaus felt so strongly about the issue, she said that "it would be a betrayal on our part if we allowed such a naming to take place." She even suggested that if the proposal were not recalled, she might have to "make a public outcry about it."[7]

Olaus sent a letter to Seaton, and unlike previous advocacy, he wrote "this time to urge you not to do something." He told the secretary that the 1956 Sheenjek expedition party had discussed the issue and members were unanimous in their feeling that landscape features should not be named after any person. Geographic names happened to be an issue at the time because that year the U.S. Geological Survey had initiated a project to fly throughout northern Alaska to identify the existing names of the region's major features or develop names for those that were nameless. Approximately twenty-five hundred new geographic names were processed during the operation.[8] The Geological Survey crew visited the Murie camp at Last Lake, and that November Olaus wrote to Gerald FitzGerald, a noted survey explorer and one of the place-name project's supervisors. What Murie said is unknown, but FitzGerald's response references "your prejudice against naming features after people."[9]

Murie went on to tell Seaton that he preferred Native names because they were descriptive of the country and "give the dignity that geographic places deserve." He stated that Clarence Rhode himself, with whom he had discussed the issue, had agreed. While stating he would not go into further detail in this correspondence, he emphasized that "important principles" were involved.[10]

Murie elaborated on those principles in a more detailed letter to *Nature Magazine* editor Richard Westwood. Again, he noted that Alaska Natives had not named places after people. "They were humble, and looked upon nature with respect." Citing their example, he told Westwood, "Let us give nature, the natural beauty that such a place has to offer us, the dignity and respect of at least naming it in accordance with its own characteristics." After one of his typically lyrical descriptions of the area and its wildlife, he wrote that the whole ensemble was

> nature's own sanctuary of nature's beauty. It can be for our pleasure and inspiration just as soon as we let ourselves become understanding and responsive to such a benign influence.[11]

The concluding sentence reveals the ideological significance of the name issue. Consistent with Murie's wilderness philosophy, it makes the point that people may realize the fullest value of this area only when they come to understand what its preservation represents symbolically. The act of establishing the area as a sanctuary, Murie believed, would represent society's recognition of the need for a sense of environmental humility. In contrast, affixing a person's name to this landscape would be an act of human pretension to dominate a place whose essential symbolic value derives from its being left free from human domination. Imposing an anthropocentric name would deny the area's inherent autonomy and diminish its capacity to carry meaning as a place set apart from modern society's rush to alter and subjugate nature.

The name controversy highlights the fact that to Murie and others, the Arctic campaign was not just about protecting this particular environment's biophysical qualities. Coming to recognize the symbolism inherent in the name by which it would be known, they believed, might open a person to one of the effort's underlying purposes—to further understanding of those ideas about man and nature embodied in the wilderness concept.

Seaton responded to both supporters and opponents of the Clarence Rhode name proposal with generic letters acknowledging the public interest in the issue and advising writers that "we shall be glad to keep your views in mind when final action is taken."[12] But no action was forthcoming. Public interest faded and the Interior Department continued to refer to—and finally established the area as—the Arctic National Wildlife Range. It remained the area's title until 29 February 1980 when the name issue resurfaced.

Wilderness champion and Supreme Court justice William O. Douglas died on 19 January 1980, at the height of the contentious Alaska National Interest Lands Conservation Act (ANILCA) debate, which at year's end culminated in the establishment of 104 million acres of new conservation areas in the state. President Jimmy Carter admired Douglas for his work on both environmental and civil rights issues. At a White House ceremony the following month, to the surprise of both the act's proponents and opponents, he issued Proclamation 4729 "to memorialize this great American with one of America's most remarkable places." Reflecting Douglas's humanitarian interests and his philosophical orientation toward the area, the document stated that the justice cared for the range's wildlife "as he cared for all whose life and liberty were threatened by forces larger than themselves." It noted that he "took strength from the refuge that nature and wilderness give the human soul." Succinctly encapsulating Douglas's hope for the area, the proclamation cited his book's pronouncement that "this last American wilderness must remain sacrosanct."[13]

But some of the range's supporters felt that even Douglas's name violated the sanctity of this area. Robert Krear wrote to President Carter, saying,

> I sincerely urge you to retract this proclamation! It offends all of those who worked so hard to save this great area from human exploitation, and I can assure you that it would offend Bill Douglas!

Krear referenced an evening discussion on the question of place-names that he and the other Sheenjek expedition members had gotten into with Douglas.

A human name on wilderness, they had agreed, would "degrade the area and detract from its intended significance." Krear acknowledged the name change was well intended, but insisted that "there is nothing Bill Douglas would have wished less, and he would be even more dismayed than I."[14]

Krear received no response from Carter. The president's proclamation that the Wildlife Range "shall henceforth be known as the William O. Douglas Arctic Wildlife Range" remained in effect—but only for nine months. Ted Stevens, now Alaska's senior senator and arguably the most powerful opponent of ANILCA, was even more dismayed than Krear, though for quite different reasons. Stevens despised Douglas, who was perhaps as far to the left of the political spectrum as Stevens was to the right. Bill Reffalt, the Fish and Wildlife Service's chief of Alaska planning at the time, recalls hearings and meetings during which Stevens expressed "extreme bitterness and anger" over the fact that an area in his state carried Douglas's name. Stevens vowed that ANILCA would not be passed with Douglas's name on the Arctic Refuge, and it was dropped from the final Senate bill.[15]

Statehood

On 3 January 1959, President Eisenhower signed the proclamation officially admitting Alaska into the Union as the forty-ninth state. The new state's House and Senate wasted no time in taking a position on the Arctic proposal. During their first session that March, they passed House Joint Memorial No. 23, a resolution that "urges that all possible action be taken to discourage the establishment of the arctic wildlife refuge in northeast Alaska." Addressed to Secretary Seaton, Alaska's new U.S. senators, Bob Bartlett and Ernest Gruening, new congressman Ralph Rivers, and others, it complained that "this gigantic withdrawal from the public domain would discourage industrial and mineral development of the area," and alleged that "maintenance of a pristine, untouched Arctic area would actually attract few residents and tourists due to inaccessibility."[16]

Letters from both sides continued to arrive at Seaton's office and, with increasing frequency, at the Washington offices of the new state's congressional delegation. Only one new argument was forwarded; for the most part proponents and opponents restated their positions, often doing so with greater emotion and in terms more disparaging of their opponents' intentions.

The chairman of the Alaska Soil Conservation District repeated the argument that "no known good" would result from the withdrawal and that the area should remain open to mineral development. But Henry Gettinger brought up a concern that until this point had received little attention beyond a brief mention by George L. Collins and Olaus Murie. "It is obvious," he wrote, "that no thought had been given to the possible rights of the natives and Eskimos."[17] (In this and several other documents of the time, the word *native* referred specifically to Indian people.) Acting Alaska Fish and Wildlife Service director Urban Nelson, Clarence Rhode's replacement, responded to Gettinger and, in regard to this point, simply stated that the proposed withdrawal did make provision for them. However, the *Federal Register* notice only stated that hunting and trapping would be allowed according to the Alaska game laws and made no mention of indigenous people or any of their practices that were outside of those laws.

The Northwest Mining Association complained to Seaton about the "powerful political body bent upon retarding the advance of civilization by preserving in status quo large areas of public lands." Like many range opponents, the association professed that it was "ardently in support of conservation," but it clarified that "it is not conservation but waste to preserve public lands in their natural condition."[18]

Supporters such as Douglas Ayres, who represented the New York State Tryon County Muzzle Loaders Club, were in large part motivated to speak for "this last wilderness frontier" out of concern for the bounty killing and commercial trapping of predators. Arguing that "the complexities of its plant and animal inter-relationships may suffer incalculable damage if 'control' measures are introduced," he urged the secretary to "campaign vigorously" for the range. An accompanying letter evoked images of the area's "primeval," "primordial," and "inviolate" condition to argue for closing it to all hunting and trapping "so that throughout the future, as in the past, we may be sure the caribou migration and the predatory wolves will be part and parcel of our American wild life heritage forever."[19]

Anchorage hunting guide Martin Vorys wrote to the secretary to speak for "the mute animals," the "spirit of the buffalo," and the "backwoods breed of Alaskans" and against the "invasion of Alaska by exploiters, the fast buck kind." His frame of reference was "the distant future, a time when you and I will be earth again." Combining notions that the area provided a connection to our evolutionary heritage and served as a bequest to the future, he cited his and the secretary's mutual desire "to see untouched nature from which we both evolved be preserved at least in part for posterity."[20]

Range proponents considered the new congressman, Ralph Rivers, likely to be a foe of wilderness. But unlike his Senate counterparts, he had not been an outspoken opponent, so they wrote to try to enlist his support for the anticipated legislation. Among the writers was William Pruitt. In a March 6 letter he provided his usual wildlife and ecological arguments, but added another concern that was becoming an increasingly significant part of the rationale supporting establishment.

The nation, Pruitt told Rivers, was becoming "closely packed with people." "The population explosion is continuing," he warned; "by 1975 there will be a population increase of 30 million humans in the United States."[21] A decade earlier two popular books—Fairfield Osborn's *Our Plundered Planet* and William Vogt's *The Road to Survival*—had alerted conservationists to the potential environmental and social consequences of the world's growing population.[22] Now the increasingly apparent effects of the postwar baby boom lent a sense of urgency to the effort to save some wilderness areas. The increased emphasis on the population issue at this point in the campaign was undoubtedly related to its prominence in the wilderness legislation being debated in the House and Senate, a copy of which had recently been printed in *Living Wilderness* magazine. The introduction to Wilderness Bill S. 4028 stated:

> The Congress recognizes that an increasing population, accompanied by expanding settlement and growing mechanization, is destined to occupy and modify all areas within the United States, its Territories, and possessions except for those that are designated for preservation and protection in their natural condition.[23]

Still uncompromising, Pruitt also told Rivers he was concerned about how the area would be administered. "I most emphatically do not agree that the U.S. Fish and Wildlife Service should handle it," he wrote. The agency, he said, was too "oriented toward management."[24] No doubt others felt the same, but by this time, Pruitt was the only recognized proponent still arguing against a Fish and Wildlife Service–administered wildlife range.

Pruitt encouraged Olaus to seek Rivers's support, writing that "if he were approached by a good persuader such as yourself he might be won over."[25] Olaus gave it a good try. His letter to Rivers focused less on the primary wilderness arguments and more on the theme of perpetuating Alaska's heritage, which a politician might successfully pitch to the average Alaska constituent. Borrowing from one of poet Robert Service's popular themes, Olaus wrote of how some of the old-timers he had known came for gold, but "began to realize that they had found something more important." Maintaining Alaska's natural heritage, he suggested, was central to "the old-time Alaska spirit"—that "something special, something that is impossible anywhere else." In words reminiscent of Theodore Roosevelt's frontier venerations, Olaus told Rivers that "so much of our country has lost something vital to us as a people." Alaska had a wonderful opportunity, he continued, "just to continue to be Alaska, and not go down the drain like so many other places." Mindful of the range's largest base of political support, Olaus reminded Rivers that "[i]f the place is kept as it is, it will be an ideal place for hunting."[26]

Although Rivers saw more merit in the proposal than did his Senate colleagues, it would soon become apparent that he was not won over. He did, however, respond by telling Olaus that he had "taken a sympathetic attitude toward the idea of a wilderness area in northeast Alaska."[27] His reference to a wilderness area is worth noting because it underscores the fact that many principals in the debate—both for and against—continued to conceive of the proposal more in terms of a wilderness area than a wildlife range.

A few proponents continued to hope that the area would become part of an international wilderness as first proposed by Collins. While Collins took a background role, Sigurd Olson, president of the National Parks Association, took the lead in resuming discussions with Canadian officials. He arranged a Washington meeting between them and U.S. State Department, Interior Department, and Fish and Wildlife Service officials. But the Canadians, still reluctant to move forward with the concept, indicated that they wished to keep international action at the level of "very informal, exploratory talks."[28] Assistant Secretary Leffler continued to correspond with them, sending a copy of the Arctic Range *Federal Register* notice and expressing "the hope that similar action may be taken by your office on adjoining lands in Canada."[29]

On 16 March 1959, Olson wrote to Leffler, advising him of "a most successful meeting" with Canada's deputy minister for northern affairs and national resources, Gordon Robertson. The two had developed wording for a proposed "declaration of intent to preserve the area of the Brooks Range" across both countries. The main provision would be that each country would retain control of the surface and subsurface of lands in the area "in such a way that the ecological character can be preserved."[30] With Olson's editorial assistance, Leffler prepared for State Department review a letter expressing "the sincere wish of the United States that the Dominion of Canada join us in the Establishment of an [international] wilderness game range for the benefit and enjoyment of people of both countries."[31] Interior Department files on the international proposal contain no final draft, nor any evidence that the letter was sent. Perhaps higher-level Canadian officials were less receptive than Robertson hoped or the State Department did not approve. Perhaps Seaton did not want to add more controversy to the range issue. The international proposal received little further attention until after the range was established.

By late March it was nearly a year and a half since Seaton had announced his intent to seek establishing legislation, and conservationists were growing impatient. At the Sixth Biennial Wilderness Conference, Robert Rausch of the Alaska Public Health Service urged conservationists to be more persistent in advocating for action on the range and other wilderness areas. Citing Alaska's "rapidly growing population" and "an ever-increasing demand for unrestricted development," he warned that time was rapidly running out for the establishment of "wilderness reserves inviolate to exploitation."[32] Range advocates such as the Sierra Club's Doris Leonard, Richard Leonard's wife, wrote Seaton expressing "with grave concern the prolonged delay."[33]

On 1 May 1959, the Interior Department issued a news release announcing that the secretary had sent an Arctic Range bill to Congress.[34] Seaton's transmittal letter to Senate president Richard M. Nixon was unmistakably preservationist in tone. The purpose of the legislation, it stated, was "the preservation of wildlife and wilderness values" of the area. It proposed "maintaining a wilderness frontier large enough for the preservation of the caribou, the grizzly, the Dall sheep, the wolverine, and the polar bear." Noticeably absent from the list was the symbolic and controversial wolf. Speaking to the area's scientific values, Seaton repeated the often-stated phrase that the proposal "offers an ideal opportunity, and the only one in Alaska, to preserve an undisturbed portion of the arctic large enough to be biologically self-sufficient." "For the wilderness explorer," the release added, this majestic area would "offer a wilderness experience not duplicated in our country."

As expected, the legislation did not propose an inviolate sanctuary. But it gave even less to mining interests who found a mere two-sentence reference to their concern. The bill, Seaton said, "would permit the Secretary to authorize mineral activity ... while at the same time it would preclude the appropriation of title to the surface of the land."[35]

On May 11, at the secretary's request, Senator Warren G. Magnuson (D-WA), a cosponsor of Zahniser's wilderness bill, introduced S. 1899 into the Senate, where it was referred to the Committee on Interstate and Foreign Commerce. That same day, Representative Herbert Bonner (D-NC) introduced companion bill H.R. 7045 into the House, where it was referred to the Committee on Merchant Marine and Fisheries, of which Bonner was chairman.

The identical bills specified that the purpose of the proposed Arctic Wildlife Range was "to preserve, in the public interest, a magnificent wildlife and wilderness area in the State of Alaska." They delegated to the secretary of the interior the authority to manage and administer the range; to permit hunting, fishing, and trapping according to regulations specified by the secretary; and to enforce such regulations using Interior Department employees. Although much of the secretarial authority to manage wildlife and consumptive uses on federal wildlife ranges and refuges was traditionally delegated to the state game departments, and Assistant Secretary Leffler had indicated that such would be the case here, the bills made no reference to any state involvement or author-ity—a fact that affirmed opponents' fear that Alaskans and their Fish and Game officials would have little influence on management of the area's wildlife.[36]

The bills specified that mining would be allowed subject to existing min-eral leasing laws and "such regulations as may be issued by the Secretary of Interior." The surface of mining claims could be used for purposes "reasonably incident" to mining, but the claims could not be patented, precluding any possibility of surface ownership. The bills contained a provision that national defense activities would not be restricted without the concurrence of the sec-retary of defense.

Opponents responded to the bills immediately. Within a few days, the Alaska Miners Association wrote Bartlett to "protest the creation of a wilder-ness area." Considering Seaton's language, they were well justified in doubt-ing that "mineral development could proceed under the type of withdrawal proposed and regulations we could expect from the Government agency with jurisdiction over [the] refuge."[37] "Gravely concerned," Governor William Egan wrote to provide Seaton his reasons for opposing the proposed "preserve." Among them was his feeling that creating a huge federal wildlife management area subverted the intent of the promised transfer of wildlife jurisdiction to the state.[38]

Then the *News-Miner* went after Egan. In an editorial, "Wildlife Range—Boon to State," publisher Snedden again refuted the mining industry's claims. But now he added another argument: the wildlife "preserve" was needed to protect the area from hunters. The governor ought to be aware, he said, that with the steady growth in the number of people flying, no area was inaccessible. He wrote that "hunters in airplanes—and they are growing more numerous each year—could soon depopulate the game of this area," which he described as more primitive and more beautiful than any national park. Snedden's rheto-ric and arguments began to match those of the most ardent preservationists. "With American population—and world population—growing at an explosive rate," he warned, "the natural pattern of life which has existed in the area since the dawn of time ... its game and primitive scenic beauty—could cease to exist." Presumably lacking confidence in the new state's conservation program, he recommended "taking steps NOW to prevent the destruction and slaughter of game animals tomorrow."[39]

While the aerial shooting of wolves had long been a concern of range pro-ponents, the use of airplanes that Snedden referred to—as a means of access for big-game hunters—had only recently become an issue. The Super Cub bush plane came into general use by private hunters and guides in the early 1950s. By 1959 they were more numerous, and their more powerful engines, larger tires, and other modifications significantly increased the ability of pilot-hunters to locate and land in proximity to game animals. Charles Gray, the *News-Miner* printer, hunting guide, and wolf hunter, owned one and was among those who were growing concerned about the trend. Five years earlier he had written letters opposing the range. Now that it was apparent the area would not become a park, his concerns about "fair chase" hunting and the need to maintain a place "where one can go for a genuine old fashioned hunting trip" led him to change his position and support the range. In fact, he would soon testify that he would also favor a provision to "prohibit the use of aircraft for hunting trips—and thereby preserve the hunting."[40]

Shortly after the *News-Miner* editorial, C. R. Gutermuth of the Wildlife Management Institute told a House subcommittee considering H.R. 7045 that the proliferation of small aircraft presented an immediate threat to the area. Alaska is now "absolutely teeming with small planes," he asserted. "Small planes are going in every direction and in all places." Emphasizing the threat posed by fly-in hunters and fishermen, he urged immediate passage of the bill because "this area is in jeopardy right now."[41]

FIGURE 43. Charles Gray after hand propping his Super Cub, 1955. Oversize balloon tires enabled skilled pilots to land the high-performance bush plane on tundra, gravel bars, and ridgetops. *Courtesy of Charles Gray.*

Wildlife management, not mining, was the subject of the most vociferous statement of objection to the pending legislation. Clarence Anderson, commissioner of the new state's Department of Fish and Game, saw the proposal as depriving the state of fish and wildlife jurisdiction and a violation of the spirit of the U.S. Constitution, which, in his opinion, had delegated control of these resources to the states. Furthermore, he didn't like the Fish and Wildlife Service or Clarence Rhode's policies and was anxious to wrest wildlife management authority from them. One tactic was to boast of his agency's competence; another was to portray the feds as incompetent. On May 21, Anderson wrote Senator Gruening about Senate Bill 1899, stating that it was "incontrovertibly true" that "it will assure wasteful mismanagement of the wildlife resources on the area." It was also true, Anderson asserted, that the bill "will deprive practically all benefits to human beings that this huge 9-million acre area could provide."

One of his stated reasons was that "restrictions on the use of mechanized means of transportation, considered essential by wilderness enthusiasts, would effectively deny public usage." In an argument parallel to the one that had become the staple of mining interests, Anderson suggested that the secretary might well allow hunting and fishing, but considering the likely restrictions, "it would be all but impossible for such activities to be practiced." Not unlike "the pitiful results of inept Federal treatment in the past," he told Gruening that the consequences would be dire: "This will unquestionably leave vast herds of big game to die of starvation, disease, or preditation [*sic*] on the Arctic Wildlife Range, beyond reach of humans who may have vital need for such animals." Anderson went on to summarize why, in his view, there was no need for the proposed range:

> The only real threat to the wildlife and wilderness of the Alaskan Arctic stems from activities of a handful of wilderness extremists and Federal officials. The Arctic is probably in little more peril of being trampled in future years than is the moon, which suggests that a loftier objective might be available to these crusaders.[42]

Anderson's letter would be widely circulated and, as intended, heightened Alaskan opposition. In Senate testimony, Alaska Miners Association representative Charles Herbert would cite the "well esteemed" commissioner's letter as evidence that the range would impede game conservation here and elsewhere in Alaska.[43] Bud Boddy, director of the Alaska Sportsmen's Council, was among those unimpressed. He wrote Ross Leffler, concluding that "the whole damn letter stinks."[44]

After alleging that the legislation "provides for complete removal of all control of fish and game on the Arctic Range from the state," and that "the people of Alaska have long endured complete Federal control of resources," the Alaska Board of Fish and Game passed a resolution opposing creation of the range—unless the state were granted control of wildlife resources. On the national level, both the Western Association of State Fish and Game Commissioners and the International Association of Game, Fish, and Conservation Commissioners passed resolutions supporting Alaska jurisdiction of the area's resident wildlife. Their resolutions, however, did not oppose establishment. Rather, they recommended the legislation be amended to specifically grant state regulatory control over such resources. In fact, to state wildlife officials' disappointment, the International Association recommended the legislation's "immediate passage as so amended."[45]

But while the Interior Department, which had drafted the legislation, supported comanagement of the area's resident wildlife, it insisted that federal authority be supreme. In a letter to the chairman of the Alaska Game Commission, Alaska Fish and Wildlife Service director Urban Nelson indicated that Anderson's "low level attack" did not change that. In explaining why the "national interest" in the Arctic Range precluded relinquishment of wildlife management authority to the state, Nelson asked Forbes Baker to "imagine how the national interest could be protected if Arlington National Cemetery was controlled by Oregon or some other state."[46]

Introduction of the range bills, and the *News-Miner*'s vigorous support of them, stimulated more—and more passionate—letters to the editor. Fabian Carey deplored the paper's support for "the so-called Arctic Wildlife Range ... better named Seaton's Ranch." After listing the state's federal wildlife reserves and parks and an unidentified "wolf refuge," he opined that "we are in fact living in a big zoo." The creation of reserves should be left to the new state, he argued, because it could create or eliminate them as necessary.[47]

John Thomson commended the editor for recognizing that, contrary to what Senator Bartlett was saying, many Alaskans as well as "outsiders" shared the hope that "Alaska in the coming years may still have some reminder of the heritage of its wilderness past." But his reference to the legislation as "the wilderness bill" probably served to reinforce the senator's and others' belief that many proponents did not envision a more multiple-use wildlife area.[48]

Virginia Wood's letter probably did so as well. Citing world population-growth statistics and the "unforeseen consequences of changes man has brought about in the natural order," she argued that no wilderness was safe unless it was "set aside and so designated now." We owe it to future generations, she said, to save some of it. "Let them not say," she concluded, "that in our first blush of statehood we knew the price of everything and the value of nothing."[49]

Since range establishment had become a congressional issue, the influential National Wildlife Federation, representing some two hundred lower-forty-eight and Alaskan sportsmen's groups, began to take a more prominent role. The federation zeroed in on members of the House and Senate committees to which S. 1899 and H.R. 7045 had been referred. Stewart Brandborg, the organization's able point-man on the issue, contacted sportsmen living in those committee members' states and urged them to call, write, or visit their representatives:

> You say, "Here's the Arctic. Here's what it means. Here are the magnificent dimensions of what it represents for wildlife and wilderness." Then you have those people apply words of encouragement and pressure to those who are on that committee.[50]

Heightened activity in faraway Washington, D.C., and increased involvement by outside groups such as the Wildlife Federation prompted the editor of the *Alaska Sportsman* magazine to print a lengthy editorial on the proposed range. In the July issue, Robert Henning acknowledged that he generally supported wilderness preservation. He questioned, however, whether in acquiescing to "this implied 'last' withdrawal of land on the last frontier by a Federal agency," Alaska would be "sacrificing a still greater resource of the American citizen—our basic freedom to rule and not be ruled." Federal rules and regulations, and planned and labeled lands, represented "government interference" with both the state's rights and the individual's basic freedoms. "In Alaska, the frontier American has come to the end of his trail," Henning lamented.[51]

The editorial aroused many states' rights–oriented Alaskans, but it had the unintended effect of activating some of the magazine's preservation-minded national readership. Nancy Camp of Pennsylvania was one. The editorial prompted her to write her state's senators and Seaton urging that the area "be sewed up so tight" that it would never be open to settlement. Drawing on the population issue, which was becoming increasingly prominent in the debate, she told them that "it looks like the present crop of young families are trying to raise the birth rate of this country above that of China and India combined." Thus she argued that future generations would need "lonely places to go to get away from all the pressures of over-civilization and over-population."[52]

Olaus quickly responded to Henning. He pointed out that Alaska was part of a nation where each state was not "for itself alone, with a 'keep out, this is ours' sign." Further, he pointed out that many Alaskan organizations were "determined to hang on to the wholesome aspects of frontier life" and had therefore endorsed the range proposal.[53]

Henning was unconvinced. "I do not like Washington groups deciding my future without my having a larger measure in framing that policy," he responded to Olaus. Connecting the issue to cold-war anxieties, he pointed out that wilderness campaigns seldom begin with the people closest to the area involved. "You certainly cannot blame those local residents for looking askance at the decision of distant groups to move in on 'their' land with the broad assertion that this land is 'ours,'" he stated. "That is socialism."[54]

7

Senate Hearings

The Arctic Wildlife Range can be a symbol
of what Alaska, at its best, can do.

—Olaus Murie[1]

Alaskan Support?

As Robert Henning had said, a federal agency (the National Park Service) and national organizations had launched the Arctic campaign, and with little early involvement by Alaskans. Every major national conservation organization endorsed the proposal, and consequently a majority of supporting letters to the Interior Department came from the lower forty-eight states. But did the majority of Alaskans who were attentive to the issue, as the state's governor, senators, and commissioners of Fish and Game and the Bureau of Mines asserted, oppose establishment of the range? Or had mid-campaign grass-roots organizing by the Muries, Alaskan sportsmen, and

---

◄ FIGURE 44. Rafters on the Hulahula River, 1995. *Photo by Douglas Yates.*

other conservationists brought a majority of interested Alaskans to support the proposal? What did Alaskans have to say? These questions were addressed at the hearings on S. 1899 held in seven Alaskan communities. Two hearings were also held in Washington, D.C.

The Merchant Marine and Fisheries Subcommittee of the Senate Committee on Interstate and Foreign Commerce held the first hearing on 30 June 1959 in Washington. This and all the other hearings were presided over by Alaska Senator Bob Bartlett, a member of the subcommittee.[2] Bartlett was a consummate politician and workaholic whose record of service to Alaska was second only to that of his former mentor and now fellow U.S. senator, Ernest Gruening. Unlike Gruening, who was from the East, polished and urbane, Bartlett grew up in Fairbanks and was plainspoken and folksy. The son of Klondike gold-rush parents, he had mined at the family's claim in the hills north of town and worked as a reporter for the *Fairbanks Daily News-Miner* for nine years. In 1939 President Roosevelt appointed him to serve as secretary of Alaska under then Governor Gruening. Four years later Alaskans elected him as the territory's single nonvoting delegate to Congress, a position to which he was reelected six times until statehood, when he won a seat in the U.S. Senate. His uninterrupted electoral victories can be attributed to many accomplishments, not the least of which was his ability to win passage of bills of interest to Alaskans, especially those that brought federal money.

Arguably no one, not even Gruening, had been more influential in winning passage of the Alaska statehood measure than Bartlett, and he had long argued that residents should control—and develop—Alaska's natural resource wealth. As he emphasized in his keynote speech before the territory's 1955 constitutional convention, residents of the hoped-for state "will not want and above all else do not need a resources policy which will prevent orderly development of the great treasures." The recent Arctic proposal was likely among the threats on his mind when he warned delegates that the state constitution they were to draft must guard against "outside interests" that would "attempt to acquire great areas of Alaska's public lands in order NOT to develop them."[3]

But Bartlett's popularity was also due to what his biographer Claus-M. Naske describes as his "human touch." He identified with the average worker, had warmth and humor, and was sincere. Thus, many whose interests he opposed, including Robert Marshall and Olaus and Mardy Murie, described Bartlett as a good friend.

Assistant Secretary Ross Leffler, assisted by solicitor Ted Stevens and others with the Interior Department, presented the department's position at the first Washington hearing. Testifying in favor of the bill were Stewart Brandborg of the National Wildlife Federation, C. R. Gutermuth of the

Wildlife Management Institute, Joe Penfold of the Izaak Walton League, and Howard Zahniser of the Wilderness Society. Ernest Gruening was the only witness present who opposed it.

Bartlett was polite to the witnesses, but his questioning left no doubt that his fellow senator was the only one he agreed with. Many of his questions were clearly intended to identify or highlight what he considered the bill's disadvantages for Alaska. The hearing record included written statements provided by each of the Muries and four other proponents, and opposing correspondence from Senator Gruening, Governor Egan, and the Alaska Miners Association. Bartlett also entered into the record the Alaska Legislature's opposing resolution of 30 March 1959; Fish and Game commissioner Clarence Anderson's cynical letter of 21 May 1959; and Robert Henning's *Alaska Sportsman* editorial.

The following day, July 1, the House Subcommittee on Fisheries and Wildlife Conservation held a hearing on H.R. 7045. Leaders of five national conservation organizations testified in support of the bill. The only opposing testimony came from Alaska's congressman, Ralph Rivers.[4]

FIGURE 45. Alaska's congressional delegate (1944–1959) then U.S. Senator E. L. Bob Bartlett holding a gold brick at Flat, Alaska, 1950s. *Courtesy of the Archives, Alaska and Polar Regions Department, University of Alaska Fairbanks, acc. no. 90-176-352.*

Bartlett had known most of the Washington testimony would favor the bill; he was more hopeful that a majority of Alaskans would support his position. In October, he presided over hearings in Ketchikan, Juneau, Anchorage, Seward, Cordova, Valdez, and Fairbanks. One hundred forty-one residents testified or submitted written statements to the subcommittee at these hearings; seventy-seven residents were from Fairbanks, where interest was especially keen.

Although Alaskan hearings were held as far away as Ketchikan, nine hundred miles from the proposed range, none were held in the nearby communities of Arctic Village, Fort Yukon, or Kaktovik. Near the end of the hearings Sherman Noyes of Fairbanks asked the committee if it had asked the opinion of any of the Natives who lived near the area. Senator Bartlett answered that the committee "has not had the opportunity to do that," but if Noyes would supply them with some names and addresses, he said, "We'd be glad to get in touch with them and ask them certain questions."[5]

At the final Washington hearing six months later, Assistant Secretary Leffler acknowledged that the only effort to consider the interests of Natives had been to consult with the Bureau of Indian Affairs, which had no objection to the range proposal. It was further noted that no Natives had provided testimony before or during the hearings. Solicitor Ted Stevens stated that there had been "no consultation with them, because there is no interference intended here with their rights." Bartlett agreed with that, but noted that their attitude toward the proposal should be considered. Apparently he did not feel strongly enough about it to take action, as there is no record of his committee or the Interior Department having contacted or received input from any residents of the area.[6]

The final hearing was held on 22 April 1960 in Washington. Intended to clarify specific legal details of the bill and identify management provisions of the proposed range, it was a four-hour pointed questioning of Leffler and Stevens by Bartlett.

Range proponents were well aware that Congress would be more sympathetic to Bartlett and Gruening's position if most of the Alaskans who testified were against the range. A month before the hearings, John Buckley wrote Sigurd Olson, expressing concern about Bartlett's "extremely anti-establishment" stance and warning that his anticipated "attack" could "cut the ground out from under" the Arctic Range. With both the state's senators adamantly opposed, he warned, there was little hope for it "unless the testimony at the hearings forces them to moderate their opposition."[7]

Seeking to encourage Alaskan sportsmen to testify, Ross Leffler sent Bud Boddy a letter to be printed in the Alaska Sportsmen's Council newsletter. Appealing to members' long-term vision, Leffler noted that like the Arctic

Range, establishment of Yellowstone National Park had faced the strong opposition of those "unable to foresee how much the area would mean to Americans of the future." But fortunately, far-sighted people succeeded in preserving it "before expanding civilization destroyed its unique character."

Reminding readers of the opposition that Secretary Seward had faced when he purchased Alaska, Leffler added that "today's critics should pause and heed the lesson of history." Only after emphasizing that the area would become "one of the important wilderness show places of the North American continent" did he mention a benefit related to the primary purpose of the sportsmen's organization. "It also will be," he added, "a last northern frontier for hunting and fishing of a type available nowhere else in the United States." Leffler's letter concluded with a schedule of hearings and an editor's note urging readers to "get out and voice their approval for this Bill."[8]

In another example of lobbying, Leffler wrote a letter marked PERSONAL AND CONFIDENTIAL to Sigurd Olson urging him to "see to it that your friends in Alaska appear and voice their unqualified approval of the bill at these hearings."[9]

On 7 October 1959, two weeks before the Alaska hearings, Olaus wrote to Leffler stating that he had been urging Alaskans to appear at the hearings and to write letters. "This seems to be the time for Alaskans to speak up," he wrote, adding that "they would make a stronger appearance if the villain 'Outsiders' did not show up too much."[10]

Alaskan proponents had been thinking along the same lines, and for some time. In a 1957 letter to Olaus about the Arctic Range, McKinley National Park, and other wilderness issues, Virginia Wood expressed the frustration she and other Alaskan wilderness enthusiasts felt in "trying to add our 'stubborn ounces' to the cause of trying to preserve something of the Alaska that attracted us to it in the first place." She suggested forming an Alaska conservation organization like the territory's sportsmen's clubs. "There is a definite resentment," she wrote,

> against any Outside organization that pokes its nose in Alaskan affairs even when it is for Alaska's good. Outside commercial interests are welcomed as "developers" of the Territory, but conservationists who are trying to help the Territory preserve their natural resources are looked upon as intruders. An organization that was strictly Alaskan might get further because of this.[11]

Wood's statement well reflects the reason that she, Celia Hunter, John Buckley, William Pruitt, John Thomson, and several other Fairbanks residents got together before the hearings to coordinate their testimony. That gathering led to the incorporation of the Alaska Conservation Society a few months later.[12] Headquartered in Wood's log home in the hills above Fairbanks, the society was Alaska's first conservation organization, another legacy of the Arctic campaign.

Fairbanks, it was known, would be the major source of testimony. In the week prior to the three-day hearings there, the *News-Miner* published two editorials urging residents to attend and support the range. The first, "Too Big? Too Soon? NO!," emphasized that other states and Canadian provinces had shown the "foresight and wisdom" to set aside proportionately large areas. The mere 2.5 percent of Alaska this proposal represented, the author stated, would provide lasting benefits through tourism and recreation.[13]

Three days later, "Vital Hearings Begin Oct. 29" made the paper's most forceful and emotional call for residents to get out and support the Arctic Range. "We feel more strongly than ever," the editorial stated, "that it is absolutely essential this withdrawal go through." The potential economic benefit of tourism was one reason to "set aside these 9,000,000 wilderness acres NOW." But the paper's appeal focused on the argument that "the Arctic Wildlife Range is predicated on more than concern for this generation of Americans." Contributing to that concern, it stated, was the "population explosion" going on in the United States and much of the world. "When America has three, six or nine times the population we now have," it asked, "will the Arctic Wildlife Range still be 'unspoiled and untouched'?" Again, the foresight of those who worked to set aside Yellowstone for future generations was called upon. "We think we owe some consideration to these generations and that by passing on this magnificent heritage to them unspoiled, we will be showing a recognition of that debt." After urging "ALASKANS TO SPEAK UP AND SPEAK UP IN A LOUD AND CLEAR VOICE," the editorial warned that

> unless Alaskan organizations and individuals determine to put up a strong fight to save this area—it might be lost. This would be a tragedy not only for this generation of Alaskans but for all generations to come.[14]

Presumably opposition leaders also coached and urged their followers to weigh in at the hearings. But little of their internal correspondence on the range issue seems to have made it to the archives, and no examples of how they may have rallied miners and other opponents have been located.

One hundred fifty-five people testified at the Washington and Alaska hearings. Their comments, as well as the interchanges between them and presiding officer Bartlett and other committee representatives, were recorded, transcribed, and printed by the Government Printing Office. Written statements submitted to the subcommittee were also included in the 527 pages of testimony.[15] From the complex of recorded facts, ideas, beliefs, and emotions supporting and opposing passage of S. 1899, I identified twelve categories of overlapping issues, which are summarized below.

A Federal Withdrawal, the State's Rights, and Outsiders

Representing the Juneau Chamber of Commerce, Frank Doogan's testimony centered on one point: The Chamber was "categorically opposed to the withdrawal. The basis of the opposition is that they are opposed to any withdrawals."[16] Patricia Oakes of Fairbanks summarized the sentiment underlying this attitude toward withdrawals when she told the committee that much of the opposition to establishment was "as a matter of principle resenting Federal control and authority."[17]

While proponents generally avoided the term "withdrawal," opponents used it liberally to associate the range proposal with the more resented military reservations and the specter of distant, unknowing bureaucrats unnecessarily restricting the personal freedom and opportunities that many sought in Alaska. In a post-hearing letter to Howard Zahniser, Urban Nelson summarized the anti-withdrawal sentiment that had been expressed at the hearings. "There is a psychological pattern in man's want for things denied," he said.

> The promoters and press appeal to an "outlander" who comes here to find that "reserved lands" deter him from what he thinks he wants. Alaska is badly scarred with abandoned mines, homesteads, canneries, fur farms and other human endeavors but these signs of man's failings are not read by the promoter, opportunist and the quick dollar getter.[18]

Arguments against the range, Nelson suggested, were largely an expression of opposition to withdrawals in general, and were particularly appealing to

FIGURE 46. *Fairbanks Daily News-Miner* headline for October 23, 1959, a week before the Fairbanks Senate hearing. Editor Snedden wanted to make certain that Fairbanks hunters knew that the statewide Alaska Sportsmen's Council supported the range at the Juneau hearing.

those lured to Alaska by unrealistic expectations. But proponents often mis-understood or mischaracterized the anti-withdrawal sentiment.

For several opponents, resistance was more specifically directed toward with-drawals managed by Nelson's agency, the Fish and Wildlife Service. Many would repeat Clarence Anderson's allegations that the agency had mismanaged fish stocks and other resources. Citing the agency's alleged law-enforcement abuses, Charles Purvis of Fairbanks said he was "suspicious of anything they might set up anywhere." He told the committee that "the Fish and Wildlife Service has done more to demoralize the people in the outlying villages than any other single organization."[19] State Senator Bob Logan of Cordova asked why this "wildly desolate and unquestionably beautiful piece of coun-try...should be taken away from the State." He argued that the state Fish and Game Department could do a better job than the Fish and Wildlife Service, whose history in the territory was "shocking." In testimony covering three pages, he went on to explain how the federal agency's management was "a crime against the people and has been a crime against the State since 1910."[20]

Others, in response to such statements, defended the agency's record. Probably the strongest rationale offered for Fish and Wildlife Service man-agement was that it would be less susceptible to the influence of the com-mercial fishing industry and development interests. In this regard, the Alaska Sportsmen's Council unequivocally stated, "This area should be created and maintained by the Federal Government, and thus kept unaffected by State politics and State pressure groups."[21]

Opponents were concerned that the feds, in managing for the "national interest," would be too accommodating of the interests of the much-resented "outsiders." Harold Strandberg of Anchorage spoke for many when he testified that the range was being sought "by people other than Alaskans. It is being forced on us by conservation groups in the States."[22] Expressing doubt that even one percent of those "clamoring" for the proposed range had ever been near it, Paul Palmer of Fairbanks was among the many who questioned the right of nonresidents to influence the future of the area.[23]

Criticism of federal and outsider influences was often expressed in the context of Alaska's recent statehood. Sixty-year resident Irving Reed saw the proposal as an effort by Fish and Wildlife Service officials to retain control over a large area after having lost most of their jurisdiction to the new Alaska Department of Fish and Game.[24] Dr. Helen Shenitz of Juneau probably best summarized this perspective in her closing statement:

> To the Fish and Wildlife Service and to all those sincere but overenthu-siastic proponents of preservation of wilderness at all cost, I want to say:

Thank you, we appreciate your concern, but please concentrate your efforts on learning a simple fact that we Alaskans love our wilderness no less but more than you do, and that from now on we are going to manage our own affairs ourselves.[25]

University student Anore Bucknell of Fairbanks spoke for the opposing perspective when she stated, "Let us not be provincial and become carried away by our newly acquired State's rights."[26] Regarding the principle of federal conservation withdrawals, hunting guide Marcus Jensen of Douglas told the committee "I do not believe Alaskans should continually snipe at the Federal Government on this point." Like most proponents, he believed that since Alaska was now part of the union, it had a responsibility to manage some of its area for the national good.[27] Antiprovincialism and the wilderness movement's growing emphasis on a larger, global responsibility found expression in Reggie Rausch's statement that "Alaska is more and more becoming an important, integral part of the planet."[28]

Finally, there was the issue Olaus Murie summarized in his statement: "the term 'withdrawal' has become a political cuss word, as if the Federal Government is the bad one trying to take land away from people."[29] Indeed, sometimes explicitly, more often implicitly, opponents conveyed the notion that the area would be withdrawn from Alaskans' use. But, as University of Alaska English professor Charles Keim countered, "Too many people seem to forget that the wildlife range wouldn't be physically lifted out of Alaska. The land always will be there for Alaskans as well as others to visit, utilize,

FIGURE 47. As conservation chairman of the National Council of State Garden Clubs, Paul Shepard helped broaden the base of the campaign's support in the lower-forty-eight states. He had recently completed a Ph.D. from Yale exploring American attitudes toward the environment. *Courtesy of Florence Shepard.*

and enjoy."[30] Morton Wood noted, "It would never occur to anyone that our national parks are withdrawn from the people.... The only difference in our case today is that the crowds of people aren't here yet."[31] Dixie Baade of Ketchikan expressed the larger perspective when she testified,

> The land area being withdrawn is not being taken from the people of Alaska but will, on the contrary, be preserved in its natural state for them, their descendents, and for the people of the rest of the world.[32]

Timeliness of the Proposal

Several opponents focused less on the desirability of a range than on the timeliness of the proposed action. State Senator Irene Ryan, chair of the resources committee, stated that action should be delayed for several years until the new state's government and Fish and Game Department were better established, and when "we actually have factual information to determine the value as to whether [the area] is important for fish and game or whether it is more important for another use."[33] Chairman Bartlett also emphasized the current paucity of biological information. He noted that "not a single Government official has been there all winter" and grilled supporters on "the desirability and even need to set this area aside for a wildlife range when, on the record, no studies, or very inadequate studies, have been made."[34] Opponents also noted that at that time the mineral potential of the area was hardly known.

Alaska's congressman Ralph Rivers, who assisted Bartlett in questioning Juneau witnesses, made the point that the area would not "be ravaged or despoiled" in the next five years. He suggested that proponents simply wait.[35] Helen Shenitz was one of several witnesses who cited Clarence Anderson's statement that "the only real threat to the wildlife and wilderness of the Alaska Arctic stems from activities of a handful of wilderness extremists and Federal officials." She went on to express the view of many that "there is no chance that in the foreseeable future this area will become accessible to too many people."[36]

But proponents had a more distant view of the foreseeable future. Potential developments and types and levels of public use didn't need to be imminent to be real threats. Morton Wood mentioned, as did many others, that the American West once "seemed just as limitless and remote as ... Alaska seems to us today." Yet people of the last century had the vision to create national parks. "There was no apparent need for them at the time," he said, adding, "We can never go backward and create a wilderness area, or a caribou herd once it has been destroyed."[37]

Many spoke with a sense of urgency. "Progress moves swiftly," warned Dan Rudisill, representing the Anchorage chapter of the Izaak Walton League. The range should be established, he said, "before tomorrow is yesterday."[38] Peter Bading of Anchorage, who had lived in the Central Brooks Range, summarized potential threats—inadequately controlled military, mining, oil exploration, and hunting operations—and stated that "in order to preserve something before it is even touched, we should start considering it now."[39] Citing the increasing interest in hunting and recreation and the improvements in transportation, the Alaska Sportsmen's Council emphasized that Alaska should learn from the past mistakes of the lower forty-eight states. Similarly, Dixie Baade referenced "the long list of once wild areas now lost for all time because of a lack of planning." She warned against a policy of "wait and see." "In this day of moon rockets and spacemen," she said, "it is later than we think."[40]

Appropriateness of Size

The proposal's nine-million-acre size was, as Senator Bartlett said, "a matter of lively dispute."[41] Opponents described it as ridiculously large, while proponents defended the boundaries. A few thought they should be expanded. Charles Stout of Fairbanks acknowledged that like most of Alaska, some of the nine million acres was beautiful. But, he asked the committee, "if one enjoys looking at a Mona Lisa painting, is it necessary to be surrounded by a thousand of them?"[42] On the other hand, Harry Geron of Fairbanks concluded his testimony in support of preserving "this relatively small area" with an expression of hope that "our children's children can enjoy a resource that will be then even more precious than it is today. That resource, gentlemen, is space."[43]

Bartlett himself instigated much of the testimony on acreage. He asked witnesses if they knew that 25 percent of Alaska was already tied up by federal withdrawals. (His number, he would be reminded, did not include the twenty million acres of PLO 82 that was to be restored to the public domain with the range's establishment.) Encouraging range opponents to comment, Bartlett reminded them that the proposal was larger than several states.

On the defensive, proponents pointed out that many states had a higher proportion of their total acreage set aside as conservation units. (Alaska's 25 percent of withdrawn land included large military reservations and PLO lands.) Kim Clark, of the Kodiak Outdoorsmen, noted that with the Arctic proposal, Alaska would have 65,000 square miles of parks, monuments, forests, and refuges—but that was just one third of the proportion of land California had dedicated to similar conservation areas. "We get that comparison everywhere we go," Bartlett grumbled.[44] Among those emphasizing percentages, Gerald

Vogelsang of Fairbanks told the committee that the range would constitute only 2.4 percent of Alaska's total acreage, and only four-tenths of one percent of the nation's total.[45] Mardy Murie asked if Alaska and the nation are "so niggardly, so poor ... that we cannot save this one and one half percent of Alaska's land as God made it."[46]

Another number questioned in testimony was the actual proportion of the range that could be considered a "withdrawal." Proponents pointed out that the portion of the proposal north of the crest of the Brooks Range—some five million acres—was already withdrawn by PLO 82. They argued that, contrary to the claims of opponents, including Bartlett, only four million acres would be "lost" from the existing public domain. Further, it was argued that with the Interior Department's plan to restore twenty million acres of the PLO land, establishment of the range should be viewed as enabling sixteen million acres to be made available for state selection and economic development.

William Pruitt provided the most detailed biological justification for the size of the range, emphasizing the home-range requirements of wolves, caribou, and other wilderness-dependent animals.[47] Olaus Murie told Bartlett that in terms of size, the range "is in a class by itself.... This area, Bob, is not even as big as it should be, ecologically speaking." Murie also offered an experiential rationale for the proposal's vastness: "And human beings in the far north," he said, "need space to travel in, and to let the imagination roam."[48]

Wildlife and Game Management

Wildlife was the most frequently mentioned consideration at the hearings, and perhaps the most contentious. In general, proponents lauded the value of the area's wildlife and argued that it needed the protection afforded by a federal reserve. Opponents tended to focus on game species that they believed were neither particularly abundant in northeast Alaska nor threatened by actions or developments that a range would limit or preclude.

Coming more from the traditional conservation-of-useful-resources perspective, opponents often pointed out—correctly—that the density of huntable species was less in the range area than in more southerly areas of the state. Among them, Warren Taylor, speaker of the State House of Representatives, had prospected in the region and testified that "the game population was very skimpy."[49] Miner Charles Stout, who had also traveled in the area, had "never seen any part of Alaska more devoid of game."[50] In response to Bartlett's strategic questions, Senator Gruening made the case that "game is far more abundant elsewhere," and that "there are much better hunting areas that are far more accessible." This fact, he said, contradicted the proposal's purpose because "this is not to be a refuge. This is to be a game range."[51]

But like Gruening, most opponents knew that while proponents had conceded to a wildlife (not game) range, they continued to view the area more as a wilderness. For that reason, they were justifiably concerned that active game "management," and particularly wolf control, would be precluded. As Irving Reed testified, "I feel sure the Arctic Wildlife Range would become a refuge and breeding ground for wolves which would continue to decimate the caribou and, to a less extent, the moose herds, on both sides of the Brooks Range."[52] Some opponents spoke to the potential impracticality of cooperative federal/state management of the area's wildlife as proposed by the Interior Department. James Brooks, of the Alaska Department of Fish and Game, addressed potential conflicts in the matter of predator control, and in doing so, predicted (correctly) that the Fish and Wildlife Service would reverse its position on wolf control in the area. "We very well might find," he testified, that "one agency [state Fish and Game] would seek to remove wolves which were preying on the herd of caribou, and the other agency [Fish and Wildlife Service] would want to protect wolves, because it felt that the influence of the wolves on the caribou was beneficial."[53]

Sheenjek expedition member Brina Kessel was one who spoke to the area's value as habitat for the lesser-known, nongame species. She mentioned lemmings, voles, and the possibility of reintroducing the extirpated musk ox. Kessel listed many songbirds that used the area, including Asiatic migrants, such as the yellow wagtail, the Arctic warbler, and the bluethroat. But in reference to the committee members' utilitarian focus, she added, "I guess these birds don't mean much to you people, probably."[54]

Many argued that the proposal represented an opportunity to avoid mistakes made in the past or in the lower forty-eight states. William Cairns was a hunter concerned that "wildlife in their natural state will be a thing of the past in the next 50 years." Citing "some 400 animals and birds that have disappeared from the earth," he said he was "afraid that my grandchildren will find slim pickings if something isn't done, and soon."[55] Although caribou were by far the most often mentioned species, many proponents were more concerned with the polar bear's need for the area as a sanctuary. Both Leffler and Pruitt told the committee that the proposal encompassed the animal's only denning area under United States jurisdiction. Pruitt went so far as to say that because "the demand for polar bear trophies has increased ... the polar bear is well on the way to becoming an endangered species."[56] Tanana Valley Sportsmens Association president James Lake expressed worry that the use of airplanes for hunting was "going to result in depletion of our polar bears before very many years have gone by." [57] Buck Harris of Anchorage, who represented no interest except "the thousands of people who have never heard of the Brooks Range," stated that "unless we have this [range] there is a chance that the white bear is going to pass into limbo, like the Arctic musk ox." He was among those who, concerned with extinction, testified that the wildlife range could be used to reestablish the musk ox. [58]

Representing the Izaak Walton League, Joseph Penfold testified, "We need only mention such wildlife species as the eastern elk, the Great Plains bison, the passenger pigeon, to illustrate resources which could have been preserved for today and for generations to come had we been foresighted rather than oversighted." [59] For many proponents, the bison/caribou analogy symbolized the foresight needed. "Our western frontier of the last century had a similar situation," Anore Bucknell stated; "its bison herds were comparable then to Alaska's great caribou herds of today. Time is irreversible and, once the habitats of these herds are destroyed, nothing can bring the animals back." [60]

Fabian Carey was among those who did not think mistakes of the last century were applicable to the decision at hand. "Alaskans cannot and should not be held accountable for the passing of the buffalo, the sage hen, the passenger pigeon, the great auk, and the dodo," he protested. While a wildlife

FIGURE 48. Two of hunting guide Charles Gray's clients on the sea ice offshore from the range proposal, late 1950s. *Courtesy of Charles Gray.*

range "may have eye appeal on office maps," he argued, it was unnecessary for proper conservation. Proponents were well intended, he conceded, but "they let sentiment overwhelm their reason."[61]

Proponents such as Frank Griffin, who had prospected in the area, argued for maintenance of "a normal balance of animals in a natural habitat." Countering Clarence Anderson's often-repeated argument that maintaining a natural system would leave herds of big game to die of starvation, disease, or predation, he argued for continuation of these processes. "Then the mercies of nature, starvation, disease, and depredations, which have left us this abundance of wildlife, can continue as they have for time before man."[62]

Toward the end of the hearings, Bartlett addressed Leffler. "This is a repetitive question," he admitted, "but nevertheless, I will ask it again: Is this considered to be a great game region within Alaska?" Leffler referred the question to his scientific advisor, John Buckley, who responded that it is not, but

> [t]here is one word which is the key to it, as far as we are concerned, and that is it is unique. We have within this area conditions that range from the truly arctic to the subarctic, and the animals, birds, mammals, fishes that go with this . . . and nowhere else in any reserve within the United States do we have this same kind of diversification. . . . Nowhere else in Alaska is there an area of this size with such a complete cross section of typical plants and animals of this northern region.[63]

Ecological and Scientific Values

The ecological and scientific values that Buckley believed would make the reserve unique among the nation's conservation units were expounded upon by the many biologists and ecologists who testified. With the exception of the committee chairman, opponents offered little rebuttal to this argument for establishment. Bartlett, who admitted, "I have trouble handling this word 'ecology,'" stated that he "would be appalled if I thought that if this range was created it was going to provide only another excuse for scads of government people to go up there and investigate."[64] While Bartlett, like most people, had some difficulty understanding scientific ecology, his problem with the word was more related to the fact that by 1959, ecology was becoming more and more associated with calls for restraint, limitation, and restrictions on development.

But many stated that this would be the ideal area in which to investigate the then rather esoteric concepts of "ecological integrity," "biological self-sufficiency," "bio-equilibrium," "reservoir of genetic material," and "evolution." Plant ecologist Leslie Viereck was among those who argued that the area's "great scientific value" lay in its function "as a basis for understanding changes that take place in other areas disturbed by man."[65] Biologist-turned-lobbyist Stewart Brandborg highlighted the area's value for the "scientific study of nature as it can be seen in a setting free of man's dominating influence."[66] Francis Williamson stressed the vulnerability of this scientific value. "The delicate biological equilibrium," he said, "is quickly and easily disturbed, and the arctic landscape irreparably defaced by only a minimum of uncontrolled activity."[67] Ornithologist Brina Kessel was the single witness who foresaw the value for what today has become a significant research focus in the area with global implications. This might be an area, she predicted, where "evidence of past and present climatic changes can be gained."[68]

Laurence Irving, one of the many U.S. Public Health Service biologists to testify in support of the proposal, was the only one to take a long-term evolutionary perspective on the role of humans, including Natives, in the region. Of particular importance, he testified, was the fact that "the present life and undisturbed terrain of that country bear the only large-scale picture of unaltered imprints of the ancient movements of man, beast, and vegetation as they developed together during the changing natural conditions of ancient times."

The current residents, he believed, enhanced the scientific possibilities of the area. From them, he stated,

> we occasional visitors can learn about natural processes as they have been observed during many years and by many generations. ... They see the natural situation ... as it appeared to their ancestors and as they hope it will be for their children.[69]

Recognizing the value of "preserving certain areas of our earth from the influences of man," many nonscientists, such as Anore Bucknell, spoke to the research value of preserving "the virgin ecological balance of this land."[70] Perhaps the scientific argument was most succinctly encapsulated by Virginia Wood, who stated the area was "of the highest importance to science as a standard of reference—a natural laboratory where biologists of today and the future can find answers to the recurring question: What was the natural order before man changed it?"[71]

Recreation

The idealism of the campaign found recurring expression in proponents' descriptions of the area's experiential opportunities, often spoken of in term of contrast to, or escape from, the conditions of postwar society. Opponents countered that the area was too inaccessible or not sufficiently appealing to attract many visitors.

Emery Tobin, former publisher of *The Alaska Sportsman* magazine, described the area's great attraction for people who wanted "to get away from civilization and go back home, so to speak, to a natural area of great wilderness beauty."[72] Alice Stuart was an adventurer who said she lived in Fairbanks because it was the jumping-off place for the Arctic. She read some of Robert Service and Rudyard Kipling's poetry and cited encroaching civilization, the increasing population, and technological advances as reasons for keeping such an area "unimpaired, undeveloped, and unspoiled for the enjoyment and enrichment and refreshment of all our people." Her plea that the area remain "a true, primeval arctic wilderness for posterity" was rooted in the belief that

> [t]he call of the wild is part of man's instinctive longing to get away from it all, to be free of the humdrum monotony and the material things of his everyday life, to be captivated by fresh wilderness and beauty, to see for himself, firsthand, what he has seen pictured in Walt Disney's beautiful nature movies.[73]

Bob Marshall's enthusiasm for Brooks Range adventure and his commitment to preserving opportunities to experience it were well represented at the hearings. In support of what he referred to as "the proposed wilderness bill," John Thomson read a section from Marshall's *Arctic Wilderness*. In response to a question from Bartlett, he acknowledged that he had never met his inspirer, but he felt that he knew Marshall from his books, and went on to opine that were he alive today, Marshall would be there testifying. Bartlett, who had known and liked Marshall, added, "I assure you...he would have been at every hearing in Alaska and in Washington." Bartlett promised to add Marshall's other Alaska book, *Arctic Village*, to the committee's reading list.[74]

In one of the most lengthy and spirited statements, the National Wildlife Federation's Stewart Brandborg explained why the area should become "a great jewel in the crown" of Alaska's recreational assets. Referencing "our modern aversion...to anything that separates us from our easy chairs, the television screens, and the other things we now consider 'necessities' for comfort and easy living," he emphasized the value of such an area to physical, emotional, and spiritual health. The federation's members, he said, were increasingly coming to value "the chance to get out where there aren't roads, there aren't all the signs of civilization, where they can get right with themselves."[75]

Celia Hunter quoted from Aldo Leopold's *A Sand County Almanac* to emphasize the importance of true wilderness-type recreation to modern

Americans: "Recreation is valuable in proportion to the intensity of its experiences, and to the degree to which it differs from and contrasts with workaday life."[76] Virginia Wood, Hunter's partner in Camp Denali, the state's earliest "ecotourism" business, spoke of the unique experience the area would offer. She told the committee of "a changing trend in values for a Nation that is finding material goals and higher standards of living are not the whole answer to the quest for the good life." She said visitors were not drawn to Alaska by its accommodations or even its scenery. "It's the psychological lift the visitor gets," Wood said, "knowing that beyond that ridge, across the valley, behind that mountain peak, there are no roads, power lines, or people, just moose, caribou, bears, and virgin country."[77]

Because of these varied benefits, and the postwar trends economist Richard Cooley and others testified to—population growth and increased buying power, leisure time, and mobility of the new "affluent society"—proponents predicted the area would experience a substantial increase in recreational use and tourism.[78]

Opponents who addressed recreation primarily argued that the projected increase in visitation was improbable because the area was too remote and inaccessible. A few characterized as selfish those who would restrict the presumed great economic benefits of mining in order to preserve recreational opportunities for a few. Iver Johnson testified that "there probably wouldn't be 10 people a year visit the place to be chewed on by mosquitoes."[79] While some understated use, visits to the region were, in fact, very few. Bartlett asked witnesses how many people visited the area. He used the occasion to enter into the record a Fish and Wildlife Service estimate that only seventy-some people had visited in 1958. Bartlett also used rhetorical questions about the number of visitors to place his preferred alternative to the range proposal into the record. Wouldn't it be better, he asked, to establish one or two 100,000-acre ranges more accessible to Anchorage and Fairbanks, "so that thousands of Alaskans living in those places could reach, at small expense and ready accessibility, Nature in its primeval state?"[80]

Ted Mathews argued that to be useful, a wilderness area has to be economically accessible by car. He provided figures on the cost for airfare from the lower forty-eight states to the area and concluded that "very, very few people" could afford to visit the area. From his experience, Mathews believed that once there, a person couldn't practically traverse the area without roads or a helicopter. "The spongy, wet moss and niggerheads make foot travel so difficult," he averred, "that hiking for pleasure is out of the question."[81] Mining engineer Charles Herbert also doubted the potential for public use of such a remote, underdeveloped area. "A tourist attraction without access roads or

FIGURE 49. Celia Hunter, mid-1950s. *Photo by Virginia Wood.*

airfields is like the mathematical expression of the square root of minus one," he stated; "it exists but no one can see it."[82]

Hunting

Although the Tanana Valley Sportsmens Association, the Alaska Sportsmen's Council, and other hunting-oriented organizations were well represented at the hearings, there was surprisingly little testimony specific to hunting. Hunters generally commented on wildlife and wilderness values. This reflected their broader interests and the fact that they had no need to be defensive; no witnesses testified against continuation of hunting, or even trapping, in the area. Certainly some among those who continued to use the word *inviolate* preferred that sport hunting be prohibited, but recognizing the sportsmen's crucial role, they remained silent on the subject.

While the question of whether hunting should be allowed was a nonissue at the hearings, some opponents expressed doubt that the secretary of the interior, for unspecified reasons, would actually allow it. Several witnesses, whose concerns seemed to be focused on the federal versus state authority principle, stated that hunting would not be as good with the Fish and Wildlife Service managing wildlife. Their principal justification was that in a range established for wilderness purposes, the feds would discontinue predator control and prevent the state from conducting it. Representative of that view was Irving

FIGURE 50. Successful grizzly bear hunter, Junjik River area.
Courtesy of Charles Gray.

Reed's warning that "if wolves are not controlled, then their kill, combined with man's increasing hunting pressure, will sooner or later lead to game extermination." He also represented the view, most often expressed by hunters like him with mining interests, that without roads the range "will become the hunting preserve of rich men who can afford private or chartered airplanes to transport them into the area."[83]

While some opponents argued that hunting opportunities would be limited in a federally managed wilderness-type range, others testified that it would have a beneficial effect on hunting quality. Charles Gray stated, "It is my assumption hunting can and would be more closely regulated in the northeast withdrawal...much as it is in the wilderness areas, than the public will ever allow it to be elsewhere in the State." He talked about how, with the advent of airplane hunting, some hunters "fly out and land practically on top of the game." He described how that interfered with the opportunity "for a genuine old fashioned hunting trip." Considering current trends, and in anticipation of future developments, Gray told the committee,

> I only hope that by the time helicopters are used in numbers, which is not far off, there will be an area in northeast Alaska where all aircraft will be restricted to certain designated areas, and where I can go and pack in or float down one of the fast rivers to a spot where I can hunt, unmolested by other hunters, the way we used to do way back in the days before 1950.[84]

Olaus Murie's often-stated concern for maintaining the venerable tradition of hunting in the face of current trends had been central to his success in recruiting sportsmen's organizations. Predictably, that concern was expressed in his testimony. "We are now developing everywhere the practice of mass hunting, along roads," he stated, "and incidentally promoting ease and laziness, which is degrading mankind." The Arctic Range, he suggested, would serve as an antidote to that trend.[85]

Mining

As noted, Senate Bill 1899 allowed for mining in the proposed range, but without allowance for surface patent and "under such regulations as may be issued by the Secretary of Interior." The possibility that these provisions might severely restrict or practicably preclude most mining was the focus of opposing testimony. Having accepted the political reality that dictated the mining compromise, range proponents did not oppose the mining allowance per se, but many advocated for its strict regulation. Their testimony heightened miners' opposition.

Mining engineer James Crawford of Fairbanks summarized the main concern underlying the industry's angst. The mining provision of S. 1899, he testified,

> is an empty provision incapable of fulfillment because of the very nature and purpose of the proposed wildlife range. The underlying purpose for the proposed range is to preserve in its original wilderness form an area roughly one-half the size of the State of Texas, with hardly a road, landing field, or tractor track on it, for theoretical benefits in the future.... When the wilderness idea was being promoted as a forerunner to the introduction to this bill, it repeatedly came out that one of the principal matters of concern to wilderness enthusiasts was the disturbance of wilderness conditions.[86]

Phil Holdsworth, whom Governor William Egan had promoted from territorial commissioner of mines to commissioner of natural resources immediately after statehood, asked the committee: "Just what is a wilderness area?" Not needing an answer, he went on to recite the definition found in S. 1123, the latest version of the wilderness legislation being debated in Congress: "'An area where the earth and its community of life are untrammeled by man, where man himself is a visitor who does not remain.'... This wilderness concept, and the expressed intent of the [mining] provisions of S. 1899," he declared, "are in direct conflict with each other."[87]

Arthur Hayr, who reminded the committee that Olaus Murie "was seeking an inviolate wilderness area," was among those who pointed out proponents' inconsistent statements regarding mining. He read two statements from the most recent *News-Miner* editorial: "The wildlife range will preserve in a primeval state one of the last untouched areas of the North American Continent," and "Development of areas within the range for mining petroleum will be allowed to proceed." Then he went on to tell the committee, "If those two statements are compatible, then you gentlemen in Congress, if you can make that effective, you will have accomplished a very excellent job."[88]

Several witnesses, such as Leo Anthony of Manley, doubted that congressional intent would be followed because the "single purpose agency" Fish and Wildlife Service "will not allow the disturbance of the regional ecology."[89] Similarly, miner Charles Herbert expected that if the range were established, the Fish and Wildlife Service "would live up to the spirit in which it was originally proposed, which is to protect it in its primitive splendor."[90]

Bartlett shared this concern, and in questioning solicitor Ted Stevens, he asked what would happen if a miner proposed a hydraulic operation that was "utterly, positively, and absolutely destructive of the surface." Stevens responded that "some range manager is going to lose his mind," but the miner could "probably take it to court and get permission to take his mineral out, if the manager refuses him."[91]

Over and over, mining advocates gave examples in which the federal bureaucracy had allegedly thwarted mining where it had been authorized by statute. John Boswell of Fairbanks was among those who cited a litany of restrictions on mining in Glacier Bay National Monument and in Mount McKinley National Park that effectively prevented most mining that was legally authorized—restrictions on firearms, airplanes, helicopters, roads, surface transportation, tree cutting, and "defacement of scenic beauty" among them. Should the secretary of the interior wish to liberalize the regulations, Boswell said, he would be "immediately subjected to tremendous pressure to refrain from doing so by the conservation lobbies."[92]

"Permits for this, permits for that, mountains of slow-moving red tape, exclusion of all forms of modern transportation, regulations that seem to be made up on the spot"—that was how Alaska Miners Association representative Carl Parker explained his belief that the supposed provision for mining would be "a clause of empty words." Like most miners, he was convinced that "we have had enough of wilderness."[93]

Many opponents made the point that those who believed the mining restrictions at Mount McKinley Park and Glacier Bay were reasonable were thinking in terms of traditional pick-and-shovel operations. But as Earl Beistline, dean of the University of Alaska's School of Mines, pointed out, "The old-time backpacking prospector is still very much needed, but his work must be supplemented by modern equipment and transportation facilities such as airplanes, helicopters, and track vehicles." Regulations that allowed mining but precluded these means, he said, "seem to resemble giving a baby a bottle of milk with no hole in the nipple."[94]

Nevertheless, many range proponents testified that whatever regulations would be promulgated would be reasonable or would specify only the minimum restrictions necessary to protect the values of their concern. Citing the "generous compromise" offered them, Celia Hunter asked, "What do the mining interests want?" Her answer represented the view of many: "Apparently only the absence of any restraint what-so-ever on their activities will satisfy them."[95] "What the miners are apparently objecting to is any control measures whatever," Morton Wood stated. "They want unrestricted carte blanche to exploit the area."[96]

Fred Dean, head of the University of Alaska's wildlife management department, acknowledged that at the current time, mining probably would not be profitable under the regulations necessary to protect the area's surface features. He said that development should wait until technology improved and mineral prices rose to a point where mining could be done with adequate environmental safeguards. Like many, Dean believed the worth of the area for recreation was greater "than it can ever be from the one-shot use of the mineral resources."[97]

Stewart Brandborg stated that relative to mining, "every safeguard must be carried out to preserve the primitive and unspoiled character of this wildlife range." In response, many miners argued that the area's aesthetic value was relative and from the larger perspective, not jeopardized by their activities.[98] Considering the proportion of the area that might be impacted, Charles Stout said that even in the unlikely event there were a hundred mines, "they would be so many pinpricks in the 9 million acres."[99] Several stated that scars would be only temporary. Miner and vocal critic Joe Vogler was among those who said that disturbed areas would recover. Besides, he said, some disturbances look like natural occurrences; mining tailing piles, for example, look like glacial deposits. "[T]he conservationists don't seem to mind taking pictures of a glacier and its tailing pile," he said, "yet they will squawk about a dredge's workings."[100]

Toward the end of the last hearing held in Washington, Bartlett read portions of five proponents' testimonies that dealt with mining. They provided evidence for a conclusion he had drawn and wished to have placed into the record:

> that proponents envision a certain thing, which would have mining very severely limited by regulations promulgated by the Interior Department. They don't want the land to be scarred by weasel trails, or by bulldozers … they all endorsed the [mining] provisions of the bill, but I left the hearing with the feeling that they believed and certainly hoped that there would be very little commercial activity within the range.[101]

Economic Consequences

An oft-expressed concern of opponents was that there would be little or no commercial activity in the reserve, and that would have a detrimental effect on the economy of the new state and, to some degree, the nation. While opponents argued that a range would result in a significant loss of mining revenue and federal highway funds, some proponents questioned their figures and argued that tourism would provide a more sustainable basis for economic growth.

University of Alaska dean Earl Beistline summarized opponents' economic argument with his statement that if the range were established, the ensuing rules and regulations "will practically eliminate development of mineral and other natural resources and hence keep an area that may prove economically important to Alaska in continued deep freeze."[102]

Although the likelihood of onerous regulations was speculative, as was the prospect of there being economically recoverable minerals, many opponents were certain a range would foreclose profitable mining operations. Some opponents, such as Denny Breaid of Fairbanks, were more concerned with the statewide precedent that establishment would set than with the potential loss of revenue from this particular area. "The creation of a wilderness area in any part of Alaska," he testified, "would stymie and prevent the economic development of Alaska by bottling up one of the last remaining known mineralized areas in the United States.... I say, let us slay the monster now before we have to live with it."[103]

Just as many conservationists urged consideration of the area's future from a national perspective, many mining advocates argued that developing the area's presumed mineral resources should be considered in the national interest. Beistline represented the views of many when he testified that

> the importance of the mineral industry is so great...that the United States would not be a world leader economically, politically, and militarily if it were not for the bountiful supply of minerals and metals.... Certainly our world's highest standard of living would not exist.[104]

Ted Mathews argued that "from the standpoint of the national interest, one must conclude that those who advocate the withdrawal...are selfish, because they would deny the people the wealth which lies in our usable resources."[105]

Celia Hunter argued that "mining interests are no longer in a position to dominate this State's thinking." She cited a survey showing that in 1957, state revenue from tourism equaled that of mining, and in subsequent years it had increased substantially. She entered into the record the recent *News-Miner* editorial predicting that tourism in the Arctic Range would bring millions of dollars into Alaska each year.[106] John Thomson offered figures showing that the value of the Alaska tourism industry had increased ten-fold since 1952. "Tourism offers immediate opportunities for the economic stabilization and betterment of Alaska," he asserted.[107] But opponents argued that the area was too remote and, without roads or airports, it would be too inaccessible to support much tourism. Wenzel Raith argued that tourists want areas with amusements and developments, "they don't want wilderness."[108]

The most immediate potential economic impact of the Arctic proposal was summarized by Senator Gruening in his testimony. "One of the serious effects of this 9-million acre withdrawal," he said, "is to deprive the State of Alaska of some $600,000 [annually] in Federal funds under formulas by which our road appropriations under the Federal aid highway legislation are calculated."[109] He referred to the new state's inclusion in the Federal Highway Program, under which the federal contribution to highway construction funding was proportionate to the percentage of a state's unappropriated and unreserved lands. Each conservation unit removed from the public domain now reduced the state's appropriation. The formula was complicated and the potential for legislation that would change Alaska's contribution requirement made the exact cost of this withdrawal difficult to determine. While many opponents cited Gruening's figure, others, including Congressman Rivers, testified that the range would instead cost Alaska $275,000. Regardless of the exact figure, state Commissioner of Public Works Richard Dowing well represented opponents' view when he told the committee that "the State faces an impossible situation of overburdening her taxpayers to continue meeting the contributions required to take full advantage of the Federal-aid alloca-tions so essential to develop an area one-half the size of the United States."[110] Representing many was Fairbanks businessman Darrell Kniffen, who com-mented that "the one thing our newborn State needs most of all, to enable us to forge ahead, is roads."[111]

Representing the opposing view, Martin Vorys said, "The estimated loss to the State of $275,000 in Federal matching funds would be a small price to pay for such a permanent range. The long-term values of this proposed range to tourists, native Alaskans, scientists everywhere, and conservation-ists would far outreach any short-term monetary loss to the State."[112] Juneau Garden Club secretary Veryl Gunderson spoke to the range's value as "an unusual tourist attraction" and said that "if the State doesn't have to build roads in the area, Alaska should not get credit for the acreage in the highway aid formula."[113]

While most proponents avoided the economic issue, others, like Virginia Wood, resisted the idea of considering the area in terms of cost-benefit ratios. "The esthetic, spiritual, recreational, and educational values of such an area," she said, "are those one cannot put a price tag on any more than one can on a sunset, a piece of poetry, a symphony, or a friendship."[114]

The Last Frontier

Both sides in the dispute called upon the notion of Alaska as "the Last Frontier" to convey how their desire for the area's future might best perpetuate the state's venerated self-image. While each side revered the frontier identity, they fundamentally disagreed about whether pioneering, in its original sense of freedom of action and opportunity, could be sustained here, and whether an authentic frontier could exist under the restraints that would inevitably be imposed by wilderness-type management.

Proponents, who drew upon frontierism more often, argued that Alaskans should learn from history and avoid the mistakes that were made in the western states. Anore Bucknell warned, "All too soon the apparently endless Alaskan frontier will take its place in history along with the previous frontiers," which, she added, "seemed as extensive and inexhaustible as do Alaska's frontiers today."[115] "We call Alaska America's last frontier," Morton Wood stated, "yet we do little to preserve a remnant of this much talked about frontier. Can't we see at a glance what has happened to all the other frontiers we had?"[116]

But lessons of the past were read differently by opponents such as Wenzel Raith, who came to the Fairbanks hearing "defending this land of opportunity in its hour of need." He cited the writings of Thomas Jefferson and Thomas Paine and the example of the old frontiersmen as evidence of the incompatibility between government control and the American dream he sought in Alaska.[117]

Joe Vogler didn't want Alaska to become like Texas, where too many restrictions caused him to suffer claustrophobia and leave. In Alaska, he enjoyed the old-time liberty, freedom, and "the right to go anywhere I wanted to." But now, he complained, "they're gradually closing it up." To Vogler, the withdrawal represented a loss of the nation's historic freedom. He remarked, "I just hope there's no more Americans born with the courage to get out and look at something over the hill."[118]

Raith had also come to Alaska "looking for the other side of the mountain." Unlike the "molly-coddles, the frothy sentimentalists who seem to favor this proposal," he also feared that the freedom, rugged individualism, and self-reliance that characterized the trailblazers and sourdoughs were being lost from the nation's character.[119]

But for proponents, the formative influence upon American character most at risk was wilderness. As Brandborg testified, wilderness "is a source of much of the vigor, self-reliance, initiative, and physical stamina of our people." In losing wilderness, he said, "we rob ourselves of the experiences and conditioning that have contributed so much to the inner strength of our people and the achievements of our Nation."[120]

Virginia Wood testified that America had always had new frontiers to push into. But now, she said, "we have come to the end of the line."

We Alaskans must reconcile our pioneering philosophy and move on to the realization that the wild country that lies now in Alaska is all there is left under our flag.

Those who see the wildlife range as a threat to their individual rights refuse to face the fact that unless we preserve some of our wild land and wild animals now, the Alaska of the tundra expanses, silent forests, and nameless peaks inhabited only by caribou, moose, bear, sheep, wolf, and other wilderness creatures can become a myth found only in books, movies, and small boys' imaginations as the Wild West is now. And I regret as much as anyone that the frontier, by its very definition, can only be a transitory thing.

The wilderness that we have conquered and squandered in our conquest of new lands has produced the traditions of the pioneer that we want to think still prevail: freedom, opportunity, adventure, and resourceful, rugged individuals. These qualities can still be nurtured in generations of the future if we are farsighted and wise enough to set aside this wild country immediately and spare it from the exploitations of a few for the lasting benefit of the many.

With that conclusion, Bartlett gave Wood the best compliment any proponent would receive. "That," he said, "was an exceptionally well prepared and well presented paper."[121]

Future Generations

Although concern for the future was implicit in both sides' arguments over which frontier legacy should prevail, specific references to the area as a bequest to future generations were almost exclusively those of proponents. Their expressions reflect the campaign's idealism and the notion, central to the wilderness legislation being debated in Congress, that wilderness should be a timeless benefit and an enduring bequest. Opponents generally expressed a short-term view of the future that in most cases did not appear to be multigenerational.

An exception was sourdough miner John Haydukovich of Delta. He stated that proponents, if successful, "will be depriving the people of Alaska, the present and future generations, of the great wealth in minerals that is lying there for them." He said the withdrawal area was "the key to our future arctic highway," and he resented their effort to "close the Arctic forever to the people of Alaska, and keep the key."[122]

Alice Stuart was among those who argued that future generations would appreciate being left "a true, primeval arctic wilderness for posterity." "What one of you," she asked committee members, "would deny your grandchildren and future generations the privilege of venturing into a small portion of unspoiled, true Arctic?"[123] Photographer Charles Ott invoked the Almighty. "It is our duty to think of future generations—not just ourselves and our petty wants. Future generations will also want to see some of the country as God created it."[124] Bud Boddy, representing both the Alaska Sportsmen's Council and the Territorial Sportsmen, spoke of the range in terms of "our moral obligation to future generations," adding, "We are really only custodians of these lands for our lifetimes."[125]

Lafayette Huffman of Paxon Lake also considered his generation to be more the area's steward than its owner. Its preservation, he said, "will give us an opportunity to be trustees over the natural resources contained therein so that future generations will enjoy and appreciate a heritage that God has bestowed upon us.... Let those of the future choose."[126]

Mardy Murie said that given present trends, future Americans "will need, and crave and benefit from wilderness experience." She also emphasized that a range would provide more options for future generations. "Do we not have some obligation to save some untouched areas, while we still have them ... so those of the future may have the choice to keep, or to use up?"[127]

Buck Moore began his testimony by stating, "I don't expect to get any benefit out of establishment of an Arctic Wildlife Range." His concern was with "leaving legacies to our children." Citing the "taxes and bonds and bonded indebtedness" they would inherit, he said this opportunity was "a good chance to leave them something that costs us nothing, and will cost them nothing."[128] Harry Geron cited a prediction that the national population would double by the twenty-first century. "Few of us will be around at that time," he said, "but those who are will pass judgment upon our actions, and I for one prefer to have their favorable opinion."[129]

Intangible and Symbolic Values

The first witness at the first hearing held in Washington was Senator Gruening, who went to considerable length to demonstrate both that he was "an all-out conservationist" and that the proposal represented a "misapplication of conservation." He was not among those conservationists who "think we should conserve the species for the species themselves" and who "go to great lengths to impose their theories and lose sight of the human stake involved." He concluded his lengthy testimony by declaring,

This gigantic reservation proposed is a fantasy, which would be set aside not for the benefit of human beings, but to satisfy some theoretical conceptions of distant men unfamiliar with Alaska.[130]

The intangible and symbolic conceptions to which the senator referred had been prominent in the popular writings of leading proponents, particularly during the early stages of the campaign. But because they represented values that Bartlett and his committee would be least receptive to, and perhaps because they were difficult to express, proponents made few direct references to them at the hearings.

Olaus Murie's statement, offered later that day, was one exception. As he often had, Murie placed the area's preservation in the context of "something that has a mental, a spiritual impact on us. This idealism, more than anything else, will set us apart as a nation striving for something worthwhile in the universe."

Unhappy with legislators' reluctance to pass the pending Wilderness Bill and other conservation legislation, he concluded that "Congress could add something bright to its record" by passing S. 1899.[131]

While several proponents argued that wilderness symbolized America's heritage and the conditions that made its citizens what they were, Wenzel Raith linked it to being "mastered about by some paternal bureaucracy" and politicians who would "swaddle us in red tape." He felt the proposal violated "the dream of America." "It is a symbol," he said, "But we cloud the dream, we fence the rainbow to preserve it for people."[132] For others testifying, people would not be the sole or even the primary beneficiaries of the range. "The main point of my appeal is moralistic," University of Alaska physicist Marjorie Rees said. "I believe that man has a responsibility to the world of nature: To be his brother's keeper, if you wish."[133]

In response to arguments that few people did or would visit the area, some witnesses, such as anthropologist Frederick Hadleigh-West, spoke to the value of "the mere presence of the area." The "esthetic and spiritual values of this proposal," he said, were as important as the more tangible aspects.[134] Richard Cooley compared the potential range to Mount McKinley. "There are not too many people who actually go to the top of the mountain," he said, "but we wouldn't necessarily want to see it removed."[135]

The final hearing, held in Washington five months after the Alaska hearings, was not a public hearing, but a four-hour questioning of Assistant Secretary Leffler and his assistants by Senator Bartlett for the stated purpose of clarifying the senator's remaining questions regarding S. 1899 and its potential effects.

In response to questions about mining directed to him, solicitor Stevens referenced an aspect of the proposal's history that continued to trouble opponents:

> When we originally started talking about this area, we were not talking
> about a range. We were not talking about a refuge. We were talking
> about a wilderness area, which would have been absolutely sacrosanct.
> There would have been no mining and no mineral leasing in it.[136]

Stevens and other department witnesses sought to assure Bartlett that
S. 1899 was a "reasonable compromise" that would practicably allow these
activities, but the senator used the occasion to enter into the record doubts
about whether an area originally intended to remain sacrosanct would in fact
be open to any resource development.

Bartlett concluded the final hearing by stating that he had not intended
to include any oral or written testimony from witnesses other than Interior
Department officials. However, he said he had just received a letter from Olaus
Murie, a plea for passage of S. 1899. "The letter is of sufficient importance, in
my opinion," Bartlett said, "to be included in the record."[137]

In his letter, Murie discussed spiritual welfare, human ecology, making a
living, and making living mean something. He talked about keeping parts
of the earth worth living on, chasing the dollar downhill, and climbing the
mountains of the Brooks Range, "to get us all on a higher level." His final
words, the last of 527 pages of testimony, encapsulated the idealism that had
stimulated and sustained the campaign.

> Alaska has a unique opportunity in the world.... Let us not fill too
> much of it with the rubbish of industrialization. The Arctic Wildlife
> Range can be a symbol of what Alaska, at its best, can do.[138]

8

House Passage, Senate Inaction, Executive Action

Many proponents want not a wildlife range,

but a true wilderness.

—Senator E. L. Bartlett[1]

The Secretary's Dilemma

Although Murie had been given the last word, proponents considered the 1959 hearings unfair. In a letter to Howard Zahniser, Urban Nelson conveyed supporters' perception that Bartlett had "solicited the points made by opponents' testimony and at times ridiculed those in favor of the Range." But in fairness to the senator, he added, it should be recognized that, given his position, "it would be virtually impossible for him to refrain from having his own strong feelings expressed."[2]

Nevertheless, the hearings had not gone well for Bartlett. Although opponents, sometimes with his assistance, were successful in entering a number of

---

◄ FIGURE 51. Caribou crossing the Kongakut River. *Photo by Wilbur Mills.*

objections into the record, those in favor of the range were in the majority. At the seven Alaska hearings, 141 people testified before or submitted statements to the hearing committee. Of these, seventy-two were for the proposal, fifty-five were against it, and fourteen expressed conditional support or opposition or were unclear as to their position.[3] In Washington, eleven organizations and members of the public testified in support of the proposal and only one was opposed. In addition, Assistant Secretary Leffler spoke in support, while Senator Gruening and Governor Egan were opposed.

Things were not going well for Bartlett on the House side either. Congressman Rivers made several attempts to prevent H.B. 7045 from leaving the Committee on Merchant Marine and Fisheries. But as he later testified, "The proponents were so ardent in their advocacy that they convinced the committee on the House side to vote unanimously to report out the bill."[4] Lobbying of committee members by Brandborg and others had paid off.

Bartlett's next move was to try to convince Secretary Seaton to support amendments that would weaken the pending bills. On 31 December 1959, the *News-Miner* ran the story "Wildlife Range Waiting Bartlett–Seaton Talks: Alaska Senator 'Disturbed' by Federal Sanctuary Plan." It suggested Bartlett would settle on a range half the size of that proposed if legislation included more favorable mining provisions.[5]

Any inclination Seaton may have had to compromise was lessened on 15 February 1960 when the full House passed H.R. 7045.[6] Two weeks later he was in Fairbanks speaking to a large gathering at the university. When asked about compromising, he said that boundary changes would be considered as long as the area could be administered "in keeping with the spirit and purpose of the original proposal." Seaton took advantage of the occasion to restate his alternative should the Senate fail to pass S. 1899. "I could withdraw the wildlife range administratively this afternoon if I choose to do so," he was quoted as saying, adding that he preferred legislation that would allow mining. Alaska Conservation Society president Leslie Viereck responded by urging Seaton to so act if Bartlett should keep the bill from going to a Senate vote as he had threatened to do. His statement was "greeted with spontaneous applause" according to the society's newsletter.[7]

On June 29, Bartlett issued a press release stating that the 86th Congress would take no further action to establish the range. With Gruening's support, he had successfully used his committee position to block transmittal of S. 1899 to the full Senate for a vote. His lengthy explanation for the action cited information gathered at the hearings. Interior Department officials, he stated, had only provided vague information about the area's game and were "hazy" about their administration plans. "The only reason many Alaskans favored statehood," Bartlett said, "was so the Federal Government would be removed from resource control." Conceding to the withdrawal, he said, would be admitting that the Interior Department had a good record of resource management in Alaska. "This most assuredly it does not," he said, offering federal management of salmon as "proof of the Federal Government's massive failure as a conservator." Of course, he pointed out the unacceptability of the bill's mining provisions as well. One of Bartlett's main points, related to all of his objections, was that "many proponents want not a wildlife range, but a true wilderness."[8]

By now it was clear to all but the most optimistic proponents that Bartlett would block consideration of S. 1899 in the next Congress as well. One of those hopeful few was Olaus Murie; he hadn't given up on his old friend. In response to the press release, he wrote two lengthy personal appeals to Bartlett. In a July letter Murie told Bartlett why he disagreed with his criticism of the federal role in Alaska, but he focused on bringing the senator to the "human angle that is so much overlooked." Alaska had a great opportunity, he said, to preserve those "intangible values that have meant so much to pioneer people, and that can mean so much to people in the future." Speaking to a lack of ethics in politics, he asked Bartlett: "Are such intangible resources, which are so hard to put into material language, but which can mean so much to the inspiration and cultural progress of people, to be entirely ignored by government?"[9] The Arctic Range issue, he said, represented progress in America's recognition of nonmaterial values.

Murie soon wrote again, reminding Bartlett that the bill he had not allowed to reach the Senate floor addressed a more embracing question: "It involves the real problem," Murie said, "of what the human species is to do with this earth."[10]

Murie's effort to connect the range issue to the notion that Americans' well-being was dependent on the well-being of the natural world surrounding them had little effect on the senator, if his subsequent statements and actions are any indication. Murie's appeal may have only succeeded in reinforcing Bartlett's concern that much of the Arctic proposal's original idealism remained, and that if established, the range would be administered as a wilderness preserve.

Proponents now shifted their efforts to appealing for administrative establishment. Sigurd Olson, who was best connected to Seaton, wrote telling him of his recent trip to that area and urging use of an executive order. "It would be a tragedy if the range failed to materialize in the way you envisioned it," he said.[11] Bud Boddy concluded his recitation of the usual arguments, including "our moral obligation to future generations," with a plea: "Therefore, I beseech you,

Mr. Secretary, to proceed with the original proposal."[12] John Thomson took a different tack, reminding Seaton of the legacy he could leave. He said American history shows "that there are times when statesmanship is vitally needed in place of the immediate pressures of expediency and party politics." By using an executive order, he said, "you could prove yourself a statesman and one who can act … for the best interests of our people for ages to come."[13]

The final attempt to block establishment came from the governor's office. Under the terms of the statehood act, Alaska was entitled to select 104 million acres of unreserved and unappropriated federal land. With Bartlett and Gruening's concurrence, Governor Egan wrote Seaton requesting approval for the state to select the area withdrawn for an Arctic Range for the surprising purpose of establishing a state wildlife management area. "It is my conviction," Egan announced in a September 26 news release, "that conservation needs of the Nation and the State for an unspoiled Arctic Wildlife management area can only be achieved under State management." Not surprisingly, the area would be open for mining, but "with such safeguards as will keep the area unspoiled and will not permit the destruction of wildlife and wild values."[14]

Proponents were unconvinced. Leslie Viereck, president of the newly formed Alaska Conservation Society, immediately responded to Egan. Obviously disturbed by the announcement, he insisted that the Arctic Range must be "free of any local pressures that might be exerted against it by the state." Citing Egan's assurance of safeguards to protect wild values, Viereck asked, "What safeguards? Whose values?"[15] Seaton was also unconvinced and he did not respond to the governor's proposal, furthering Egan's resentment.[16]

In November 1960, John F. Kennedy won the presidential election. With Democrats soon to control the executive branch, Seaton had less than two months to take action. In a letter to George L. Collins, Sigurd Olson described a meeting he had with Seaton in early December. The secretary was packing up his office, and still debating what to do with the Arctic. The threat that Democrats might make establishment a national election issue had passed. But an eleventh-hour executive establishment, Seaton knew, would be bitterly resented by Alaska politicians and the mining industry, and might well be overturned by the next administration. Olson told Collins that he and others convinced Seaton to take affirmative action. "I remember his last remark," Olson said, "'What will the Alaskans think?'" Olson said he assured the secretary that "they would fall into line."[17] Likely his personal assurance followed the lines of his recent letter to Seaton. "I am confident," Olson had stated, "that in a short time all Alaskans would embrace the Arctic Wildlife Range with enthusiastic support."[18]

C. R. Gutermuth of the Wildlife Management Institute was impatient with Alaskans and not so tactful. According to David Brower, Gutermuth "came into the secretary's office like a major storm from the Gulf of Alaska." Exasperated by Seaton's reluctance to act on his promise, he asked the secretary, "Are you just sweet-talking us, or are we going to get this damned wildlife range proclaimed by the president?"[19]

Which others sought to sway Seaton during those final days is unknown, but Justice William O. Douglas was probably among them. Both Mercedes Eicholz, Douglas's wife at the time of his Sheenjek visit, and Cathy Stone Douglas, his widow, believe it is highly likely that he did.[20] Both reported that when Douglas cared as deeply about an issue as he did about the Arctic proposal, he was not reluctant to make contacts that, as a Supreme Court justice, he would rather not have documented.

On December 7, 1960, the Department of Interior Information Service issued a press release: "SECRETARY SEATON ESTABLISHES NEW ARCTIC NATIONAL WILDLIFE RANGE." In it, Seaton referenced the opposition of Alaskan officials and the fact that Bartlett had killed S. 1899. "In these circumstances," he said,

> I felt it my duty, in the public interest, to move as promptly as possible to take the steps administratively which would assure protection and preservation of the priceless resource values contained in the proposed Arctic National Wildlife Range area.[21]

Seaton expressed hope that the next Congress would pass the bill the House had approved. His statement also acknowledged that his action, Public Land Order 2214, could be undone, "even though I cannot believe that such action would be taken in view of the unparalleled wildlife, wilderness, and scenic values involved in the new range."

That same day, president-elect Kennedy announced that Seaton would be replaced by Stewart Udall. No one could predict what that might mean for the new range. Although Udall was considered a conservationist, as a congressman he had opposed the wilderness community in the recent Dinosaur Monument fight.

As Seaton had warned, the establishing order did not provide for mineral entry. But opponents' displeasure was tempered by the fact that he did restore to the public domain twenty million acres of northern Alaska previously withdrawn by PLO 82.[22] Under its headline that day, "ALASKA GETS WILDLIFE RANGES," the *Fairbanks Daily News-Miner* happily announced that these lands "now are entirely open to public entry under public land laws."[23]

FIGURE 50. On December 6, 1960, Secretary Seaton signed the executive order establishing
the Arctic Wildlife Range and the smaller Izembek and Kuskokwim ranges. Unrelated,
president-elect Kennedy announced Seaton's replacement by Stewart Udall that day.

Three years later, the state selected a portion of the released area forty-five
miles west of the northwest boundary line that Collins had hesitantly drawn
for the range. Had range action not made the obscure coastal plain around
Prudhoe Bay available to the state, the development and revenue from North
America's largest oil field may well have remained under the control of the
federal government.

Seaton issued two other press releases that day. They announced the executive establishment of the 415,000-acre Izembek National Wildlife Range on
the Alaska Peninsula and the 1.8-million-acre Kuskokwim National Wildlife
Range in southwestern Alaska, which would later be renamed in honor of
Clarence Rhode.

What involvement did the president have in establishing the Arctic Range
and the other new refuges? Neither the Interior Department's press releases
nor its previous or subsequent announcements contain any mention of
Eisenhower's perspective or role. Eisenhower's "Public Papers of the President"
and his 1961 budget address each include only brief references to the range.
But none of the White House Central Files or the papers of the White House
staff housed in the Eisenhower library reference a position on the subject.[24]
Clearly, the president sought no credit for the controversial action, which
resulted in what many believe to be his administration's greatest conservation
achievement. Eisenhower must have approved the order. Whether his silence
reflects disinterest or a wish to distance himself from it is unknown.

Howard Zahniser tried to contact Olaus and Mardy the day of the press
release, but they were in Idaho testifying against a proposal to dam the Snake
River. The next day they received his telegram (their Wyoming ranch had no
phone). "We both wept," Mardy soon wrote Fairfield Osborn,

and I think then we began to realize what a long and complicated battle it had been. ... Sometimes it's good to have a little victory, isn't it? Even though we know also that there still has to be watchfulness, thinking, and persuasion—to keep the area natural, not "developed"—a treasure for the sensitive ones, the vigorous ones, the searchers for knowledge, for all the years to come. Surely there should be a few such places on this plundered planet![25]

Also the following day, Virginia Wood and Celia Hunter wrote to the Muries to "share the joy" in the announcement and express the much-needed encouragement the victory provided. "Conservation gets so many setbacks," they said, "it is easy to get discouraged and feel that individuals or small groups are impotent in the machinations of 'bigness' that plagues the modern world." They also recognized that the previous day's action would not end their efforts to defend the area. "There is so much to be done," they added, "and even this decision by Seaton might be reversed if some of our politicians have their way about it and we must work to secure our gains."[26]

Lois Crisler wrote that the action gave "heart and hope" to the American people. While the new range was "so little measured against our need to be un-tame in order to be human," she said, it also represented "so much measured against our greed."[27] William Pruitt immediately wrote to Olaus, and after brief congratulatory comments asked, "When do we start attempts to get it reclassified as a true wilderness area?"[28]

Not surprisingly, a News-Miner editorial approved establishment of the area it foresaw "will become the Yellowstone National Park of Alaska."[29] But surprisingly, even the Anchorage Daily Times editorial concluded that "the net result is good—not bad."[30]

Bud Boddy wrote Olaus about this "greatest step in conservation which we have witnessed during the history of our country." Emphasizing Wood and Hunter's concern, he said that state officials "are not too happy ... they do not intend to let this go by the board."[31]

Indeed, state officials and some of their constituents expressed their ire with an intensity that paralleled proponents' emotion. Like his adversaries, prospector George Widich brought a historic perspective to the action. "This Wild Life Range is the most ridiculous happening of the century," he wrote Bartlett. "How in the world can a minority put first wild animals before the betterment of the human race?"[32]

Egan's immediate response to this "bitter pill" was to criticize Seaton for not showing him the courtesy of responding to his alternative proposal for a state multiple-use wildlife area. "Alaskans may once again thank the present national administration for retarding local control and development of Alaska's resources," Egan said. "I plan to strongly protest this maneuver."[33]

The most bitter condemnation came from Senator Gruening. Seaton's "outrageous" action, his press release stated, "shows a total disregard for and usurpation of the rights of the State of Alaska." He was appalled that the lame-duck administration gave the area to the Fish and Wildlife Service, whose record in Alaska "is one of tragic failure."[34] On December 11, he sent a telegram to secretary of interior-designate Udall complaining about Seaton's action. "I urge that, as soon as you take office," he said, "you order immediate review of these withdrawals."[35] Shortly thereafter, Egan, Bartlett, Gruening, and Rivers sent Udall a telegram urging him to rescind Seaton's action.

During his final days in office, Seaton made a last attempt at legislative establishment. On January 13 he transmitted to Senate president Richard Nixon a new bill to "confirm the [administrative] establishment of the Arctic National Wildlife Range." Three days later he submitted H.R. 3155 to the House. The bill was similar to the previous Senate and House versions. However, whereas the earlier bills specified that "the Secretary *shall* administer and manage the wildlife range in a manner he finds to be in the public interest" (emphasis added), the new bill replaced the word *shall* with *may*. This weakened version also incorporated some suggestions made by the Alaska Miners Association, including language specifically guaranteeing "the right to ingress and egress from this range" for mining purposes.[36]

Predictably, proponents opposed the new bill because, as the National Wildlife Federation's newsletter reported, it "would allow activities that could destroy the very values which are intended to be preserved in the area."[37] Apparently, Alaska's congressional delegation did not care for the bill either, as the record does not reveal any indication of support, or that its members made any attempt to have either body of Congress act on it.

In March, Bartlett, Gruening, and Rivers's new focus was conveyed in a long, coauthored letter to Udall. They urged "with all possible emphasis" that he cancel Seaton's "thirteenth-hour" action and make the area available for state selection "for wildlife purposes."[38] On June 27, the three had a long meeting with Udall "to air all our grievances." In a letter to Egan that day, Gruening reported that, with difficulty, they had made some progress. "Udall is willing to consider turning back the Arctic Wildlife Range to the State," he reported, "provided the State presents a good case for it." He also suggested that Udall was concerned that in doing so, he would come "under a great barrage from the conservationists."[39]

However, a few days later Egan received a letter from Bartlett marked PERSONAL AND CONFIDENTIAL and with instructions to "tear it up and throw it away" after reading. Bartlett told Egan that his understanding was that Udall had only committed to considering a study of their proposed state takeover of the range. Bartlett was learning that, like Seaton, Secretary Udall would be their greatest obstacle. "My own guess is that he not only fears what the conservationists would do to him were he to restore the Range to the public domain," Bartlett said, "but that he is one of them himself!"[40]

Udall was, in fact, more than a conservationist, as his subsequent support of wilderness legislation and the Alaska National Interest Lands Act of 1980 would prove. Although David Brower believed the new secretary was inclined to reverse the controversial decision, Udall proved to be sympathetic to the many appeals he was receiving from advocates, such as that from Fairfield Osborn, who urged him to "courageously withstand these pressures" and defend "our last really wild frontier."[41]

Nevertheless, in August Egan sent Udall a detailed proposal for what was described as "State Administration of the Arctic Wildlife Range." Endorsed by the delegation, this last attempt to seek revocation of the range borrowed rhetoric from their opponents to convince Udall that the state fully appreciated its "wilderness assets and the invaluable flora and fauna that characterizes its unspoiled lands and waters." The state range would be "dedicated in the national interest" and "every effort would be made to preserve its wild and natural aspect … within the framework of modern, multiple use principles."[42]

Udall never acted on the proposal.

After Establishment

Even before the permanence of its new range was certain, the Fish and Wildlife Service requested a 1962 start-up budget of $180,000. Of that, $53,000 was identified for construction of two "patrol headquarters," which, ironically, were slated to be located at the places most associated with development of the early wilderness proposals—the Peters–Schrader Lakes area and the upper Sheenjek River. Also, $50,000 of the request was earmarked for the construction of a landing strip capable of accommodating large DC-3-type aircraft. Upon hearing a rumor of the proposed developments, a disgruntled Olaus Murie wrote the agency. "The less 'administration' the better," he said, "and if we wanted 'mass recreation' there, we would have worked to have it be a national park."[43] Pruitt also wrote, admonishing the agency to "make doubly certain that nothing is done in the immediate future that may jeopardize the future re-classification and upgrading of the status of the region to that of full wilderness area."[44]

But in the end it wasn't Murie and the wilderness enthusiasts who saved the area from what could have become a wilderness-eroding precedent. It was Bob Bartlett. In a lengthy, critical discussion of the appropriation request placed in the Congressional Record, he cited Clarence Anderson's statement that the area had been removed from state control to protect its wilderness character and to prevent development. But, he declared, "We now find that the initial and primary threat to these wilderness qualities stems directly from the desire of a Federal bureau to develop the area."[45]

The Record leaves no doubt that it was Bartlett's anger over the area's establishment, not wilderness concerns, that led him to submit a request to the House Committee on Appropriations that it withhold all funding for the range, which it did.[46]

Virginia Wood, who shared Murie's "the less administration the better" philosophy, vividly recalls her response and that of her conservationist friends: "Goody, goody, goody. ... Not one cent! We thought that was great!"[47]

Bartlett and Gruening successfully blocked appropriations for the range until 1969, when, a year after Bartlett's death, Gruening lost his bid for reelection. That year the Fish and Wildlife Service hired the first manager, Averill Thayer, who had been an Alaska game agent for seventeen years. As a boy, "Ave" had been enthralled by Ernest Thompson Seton's nature books and he validated opponents' fears by bringing the founders' wilderness philosophy to the task of developing a stewardship approach for the area.

State officials gave up trying to have the establishment order revoked, and the Arctic National Wildlife Range designation protected the northeast corner of Alaska until December 2, 1980. On that day, the Alaska National Interest Lands Conservation Act, bitterly opposed by Alaska officials, including now Senator Ted Stevens, provided the legislative confirmation early proponents had hoped for. And it did so without a mining compromise. The act more than doubled the area's size to 19.3 million acres and designated all but the northern coastal plain of the original range as wilderness, conferring upon it

FIGURE 53. Averill Thayer, first manager of the Arctic National Wildlife Range, with Mardy Murie at the U.S. Fish and Wildlife Service hanger in 1975. Thayer, a pilot, had just taken Mardy and Celia Hunter on a flight across lands adjacent to the wildlife range, which the ANILCA would include in the renamed Arctic National Wildlife Refuge.
Photo by Red James; courtesy of the Murie Center.

the statutory protection Zahniser had worked to place in law. The act designated three wild rivers—the Wind, the Ivishak, and the Muries' Sheenjek. It renamed the range as the Arctic National Wildlife *Refuge*, a title better suited to conveying its original purpose.

Although George Collins continued work on it for three decades after his retirement, his vision for an international reserve was not entirely realized. But today, adjacent to the area that he and Lowell Sumner intended to be a "Last Great Wilderness," lies Canada's Ivvavik and Vuntut National Parks, and to the south, the Yukon Flats National Wildlife Refuge—together comprising one of the largest blocks of nationally protected wildlands in the world.

9

A Symbol of Wilderness

This idealism, more than anything else, will set us apart as
a nation striving for something worthwhile in the universe.

—Olaus Murie[1]

The Legacy

From its origin in Bob Marshall's wild vision for a permanent wilderness frontier across northern Alaska, the Arctic campaign succeeded in establishing the nation's first vast, ecosystem-scale conservation unit and, in doing so, placed boundaries of unequaled dimension on our exploitation and domestication of nature. Campaign leaders, pioneers of the postwar shift toward ecological thinking, infused the effort with idealism. Supporters' sense that they were achieving something visionary and unprecedented energized the effort. The belief that nowhere else and never again would the

---

◀ FIGURE 54. Mount Chamberlin and Peters–Schrader lakes valley. *Photo by Wilbur Mills.*

nation have a wilderness preservation opportunity of this magnitude gave the Arctic campaign its vital force.

For the Fish and Wildlife Service, the distinctive purposes of its new charge expanded thinking about the role of predators and what a national wildlife refuge could be. At a time when sufficient political support to pass Howard Zahniser's wilderness bill seemed doubtful, the campaign's success demonstrated the power of wilderness values to overcome strong opposition and become established in law. As intended, the Arctic Range exemplified the values that its advocates soon succeeded in enshrining in the Wilderness Act of 1964. Their victory represented a milestone in the evolution of the nation's conservation ethic, set precedents for future preservation efforts, and established an area in northeast Alaska as an enduring symbol of wilderness.

In Alaska, the signing of Public Land Order 2214 in 1960 represented the power of wildlife, ecological, scientific, recreational, heritage, and bequest values to motivate its citizens and influence public policy in the new state. While nonresidents initiated the proposal and political pressure was directed toward Washington where the decision was to be made, most of the campaign action took place in Alaska. Opponents' framing of the issue as one of outsiders versus residents galvanized Alaskan conservationists and led directly to the establishment of the state's first conservation organization, the Alaska Conservation Society. The range issue established Alaskan conservationists as a political force to be reckoned with in the new state. The state's other national wildlife refuges, parks, and forests had been established with little, if any, involvement of Alaskans. The Arctic campaign was a landmark in that it was not only the first major land-allocation conflict that played out in Alaska, but also the first in which Alaskans had an influential if not decisive role in the outcome. The Arctic campaign instigated a pattern of conflict between the dominant political forces in Alaska and the residents and nonresidents who sought to protect the "national interest" by designating federal conservation units. Its success laid the groundwork for what stands as the most expansive preservation action in world history, the Alaska National Interest Lands Conservation Act of 1980 (ANILCA).

Broad-based and active public support was critical to the campaign's success. Alaskan members of national conservation organizations were joined by resident sportsmen, scientists, and members of civic, garden, and women's clubs. The effort incorporated supporters with diverse interests because its politically astute leaders portrayed the area in terms of a wide range of values—both tangible and intangible. Those values appealed to Alaskans and non-Alaskans alike, not only to those few who might visit, but also to the many more who would find satisfaction, inspiration, even hope in just knowing that such a place existed. Further motivating the diverse segments of the public to write, speak, and testify was the excitement and sense of mission that campaign leaders conveyed. Regardless of which values most attracted them, supporters felt they were involved in something unprecedented, a cause as imaginative and visionary as establishment of Yellowstone National Park had been. Not until passage of the Wilderness Act four years later would areas be designated to serve similar purposes, and not until ANILCA would such values be protected in conservation units that matched the sheer scale of the Arctic Range.

Founding Values

Doubled in size by ANILCA, the renamed Arctic Refuge embodies these founding values, as is evident in the voluminous body of literature that followed its establishment. Innumerable magazine and newspaper features and more than a dozen books—travelogues, natural histories, and glossy photo essays—describe the meanings this place holds for today's environmentalists. Many were written in response to the threat of oil development that came with ANILCA in 1980 and describe the area's values in terms of their vulnerability. These accounts reveal that the values most often cited in the campaign continue in the perception, experience, and valuation of the Arctic Refuge.

The following set of five "founding values" was synthesized through a content analysis of campaign writings and testimonies. Like any such categorization, this one is necessarily subjective and somewhat artificial—such values do not exist in the mind as discrete elements. Rather, they function as a gestalt, interrelated and perceived in the context of each other. Nevertheless, abstracting from context and folding together related expressions of value provide a framework for characterizing the variety of functions the range was seen to serve by campaign supporters. The reflections of refuge visitors who were interviewed in the course of previous research lend insight into how these values are experienced on-site today.

Wildlife and Its Ecological Context

The campaign's central concept, wilderness, has always been inseparable from wildlife. The etymology of wilderness can be traced to the Teutonic word "wil-deor": *deor* referring to animals and *wil* referring to their being wild and uncontrolled by humans. Wilderness was originally conceived of as a place of wild beasts.[2] And from the Arctic campaign's beginnings in 1951, even before political considerations necessitated a shift in advocacy from a wilderness area to a wildlife range, its leaders featured the area as a sanctuary for large mammals. Species not tolerant of, or tolerated by, civilization were a primary focus.

Accounts regularly highlighted grizzly and polar bears, Dall sheep, wolverine, the symbolic wolf, and—evocative of the vanquished buffalo—the migratory caribou. Appealing to the widest segment of the public, these animals continue to serve as highly visible representatives of the wildlife value for which the Arctic Refuge is renowned.

But for those who initiated and led the campaign, and many who joined the effort, these species were significant only partly because they were favored for viewing or hunting. More important was their emblematic status as representatives of what Aldo Leopold had termed the "community of life." Thus, Olaus Murie wrote that more important than an animal's size was its membership in "the whole assemblage of living things which go to make up the rich life of that piece of country." He emphasized the interrelatedness of all of the area's life forms, "the diverse manifestations of its life."[3]

Campaign writings and discussions first brought many conservationists to think of wildlife in an ecological context, orienting them toward a new rationale for protecting wilderness: preservation of the large-scale natural processes in which wildlife are embedded. While for many the idea of protecting all life forms—the unnoticed creatures and predatory wolves included—was new thinking, the notion of maintaining an area to perpetuate unseen processes was an entirely new dimension of conservation.

The antiquity and continuity of the area's various species and their ecological systems was a recurring theme that some leaders placed within the all-encompassing context of evolution. Northeast Alaska was to be a place, Lowell Sumner wrote, that would perpetuate "the majestic story of evolution...where its native creatures can still have freedom to pursue their future, so distant and mysterious."[4] Similarly, Olaus Murie stressed that one of the great values of the area lay in "the opportunity to study the interrelationships of plants and animals, to see how Nature proceeds with evolutionary process."[5]

Never before had the principle of maintaining ecological systems and processes been a significant factor in deciding Alaska land use and allocation. Indeed, the Arctic campaign brought the vocabulary of ecology to popular awareness in Alaska. It set national precedent as well. Bill Reffalt, historian of the national wildlife refuge system, declared that the Arctic Range "was the first conservation unit in the country to encapsulate the total ecological realm." "In that sense," he says, "it was the nation's first real wilderness, and model for what we sought to do in ANILCA."[6]

The experience of Frank Keim, a recent visitor, helps illustrate the significance of natural processes. He compares a trip made in the refuge with one he made in the Forty-Mile River area the same summer. Both provided scenery, adventure, and wildlife sightings, but an unseen presence substantially differentiated his experiences. As part of a predator-control program to increase the number of caribou in the Forty-Mile area, wolves had been captured, sterilized, and released. Wolves still inhabited the area, but, Keim said, "knowing this part of the natural order had been manipulated for human ends bothered me. I never could forget it." There may have been more caribou to see, he said, but their appeal was lessened. Keim came to realize that "the refuge is real wilderness because the wildlife is really wild...they're left alone to interact and live and die as nature intended."[7]

In the 1950s, when maintenance of ecological integrity was just beginning to be recognized as a means of protecting habitat for preferred species, the Arctic campaign was a milestone in establishing both ecological and evolutionary processes as landscape entities of intrinsic value. The Fish and Wildlife Service terminated its predator-control program in the new range and now recognizes the ecological and symbolic role of the wolves it once vilified. Soon after becoming its first manager, Averill Thayer succeeded in convincing the state game department to discontinue issuing permits for aerial wolf shooting.

Scientific Value

Aldo Leopold's writings first brought the American conservation community to an awareness of the scientific value of wilderness—"a base datum of normality," he had written, "a picture of how healthy land maintains itself as an organism." The most perfect norm, he concluded, is wilderness.[8] Leopold's son Starker and other Arctic proponents forwarded this function as one of the unique values of the area, arguing that this was the nation's best opportunity to establish a benchmark of naturalness on such a vast scale, a "scientific field laboratory," in the words of George Collins.

As predicted, the area did attract many biologists—and botanists, geophysicists, and climatologists—to study the natural order, both as it functions naturally, and as it responds to large-scale anthropogenic change. In a major project that recognizes "the distinctive function" founders of the refuge thought the area should serve, the Fish and Wildlife Service established a series of long-term ecological monitoring sites in the refuge. As Brina Kessel predicted, the refuge has become an important site for studying the effects of global climate change. Keith Echelmeyer continues a half-century-long study of the McCall Glacier's response to climate change. He describes it as the longest-term and perhaps most important such site in the American Arctic. "It's the refuge's wilderness status," he said, "that assures its continued value for research."[9]

In 2005 the scientific community made a rare, perhaps unprecedented, expression of advocacy on behalf of the Arctic Refuge. Nearly one thousand scientists joined Harvard professor Edward O. Wilson in signing a letter to President George W. Bush and the Congress describing the refuge's unique value for research and urging protection of its biological diversity and ecosystem integrity from oil development.[10]

Recreational Value

Recreation arguments supporting establishment reflect the continuing influence of the earliest wilderness precept—the notion that unaltered nature serves fundamental human needs unmet by civilization. Just as the ecological effects of environmental modification could best be understood by comparing altered areas to unaltered ones, it was believed that the psychological effects of living in an urban, industrial, and materialistic society were most apprehensible when one is immersed in areas free of such influences. In the transcendental tradition, the Arctic proposal was portrayed as a place of escape, where people could go to connect—or reconnect—to the natural world and experience it much as their distant ancestors had.

While rooted in century-old concerns regarding what was being lost to modernization, recreation arguments also reflected concerns that became more prominent in the postwar years. Among them was the development of roads and recreational infrastructure in parks and other natural areas that accompanied the rapid growth of automobile-based and convenience-oriented tourism. Opportunities to experience naturalness and solitude were threatened, and the formative and character-enhancing experiences Bob Marshall had espoused—opportunities for adventure, self-reliance, exploration, and discovery—were also at risk.

The Arctic Refuge was among the first conservation units for which provision for such challenging experiences was a significant factor in its establishment. It is the first in which a vast expanse was reserved and administered in order to enable extended journeys with maximum isolation from the influences of modern society.

A commitment to this purpose continues to guide the area's stewardship. The now 19.3-million-acre Arctic Refuge remains a place "where the wild has not been taken out of the wilderness," as the agency's letter to prospective visitors reads. "Perhaps more than anywhere in America," it asserts, the refuge "is a place where the sense of the unknown, of horizons unexplored, of nameless valleys remains alive."[11]

The refuge's entire expanse remains roadless and free of recreational improvements. There are no trails, and no signs point the way. The Fish and Wildlife Service realizes that for every management action that would diminish uncertainty and self-reliance or make the experience more convenient, predictable, and safe, something of the original purpose of this place would be lost. So visitors arrive—often with Bob Marshall's or Mardy Murie's books in their backpacks—seeking the "ultimate" wilderness experience extolled by the early proponents.

George Wuerthner chronicles the value of immersion in an area where the elemental forces of weather, wildlife, and the land present the explorer with decisions that have consequences. The self-reliance required in the Arctic Refuge, with the possibility that one could become lost or even die, he says, "is a freedom worth preserving as much as the wildlife and the wild landscape that must also be saved."[12]

Sandy Jamieson is among those who appreciate the refuge's wildness through hunting. "The refuge is like a museum," he says, "an experience that can transport you back in time." During a caribou hunt, he recalls, "I felt like I was part of that primal force that moves the caribou. For those few days of my life, I was part of the natural order of things."[13]

Campaign leaders believed that providing for these types of recreational experiences was an important reason for establishing the area. But even toward the end of the campaign, visitation was only seventy-some people a year. Given the area's remoteness, they probably would not have predicted many more than today's fifteen hundred annual visitors. Understated was what many, such as George L. Collins, considered the area's higher purpose, simply "to be preserved as it was. For no other reason but there it was, as it had always been."[14]

One of the thirteen books written about the refuge, *Nameless Valleys, Shining Mountains*, describes how on a long trek across its mountainous divide, ecologist and author John Milton came to believe that the area "should be left alone to continue its age-old cycles of life and season." The inspiration Milton found was heightened by his acceptance of the ultimate purpose Collins articulated. "And if this wilderness can also be an incidental reservoir for restoring man's spirit, then fine. But that is not the purpose of this place," he concluded. "Its purpose is to be. Man's role should be … let it be."[15]

Heritage Value

One of the associations evoked by proponents' frequent use of the word *primeval* was that of a remnant of wild, unaltered nature serving as a museum of our ancestral heritage, a repository of the Paleolithic conditions that shaped us as a species. Howard Zahniser summarized this connection to a distant past as the opportunity "to relive the lives of ancestors."[16] This function was forwarded as—and for many, has become—an element of the recreational experience available in the refuge.

Another heritage element harkens back to Frederick Jackson Turner's frontier thesis and Aldo Leopold's subsequent argument that protecting some areas as wilderness could serve to perpetuate opportunities for the type of rugged experiences believed to have shaped our national character. This cultural heritage function, an early precept of the wilderness movement, was employed by Bob Marshall in the 1930s to link preservation of the Brooks Range to perpetuation of the venerated American frontier.[17] George L. Collins began the "Last Great Wilderness" article that launched the Arctic campaign by citing Marshall's belief that "northern Alaska belonged to all the people of the nation as a frontier."[18]

Although few would consider it a motivation for visiting, many people arrive with imaginings of the history and folklore of the nineteenth-century western movement. A glimpse of "what it must have been like for the early explorers" came to Debbie Miller on a trip across the refuge. Among those who had been enthralled by stories of Daniel Boone and the journals of Lewis and Clark, she recalled thinking, "This is the sense of isolation, the vastness, self-reliance and feeling of exploration they must have known."[19] Former President Jimmy Carter, a visitor and staunch defender of the refuge, recently raised the area's cultural heritage association as a reason for opposing oil development. The Arctic Refuge, he said, "is a symbol of our natural heritage, a remnant of frontier America that our first settlers once called wilderness."[20]

Bequest Value

Responsibility to future generations was a repeated concern in the early literature and testimony on the refuge. Wildlife and recreational values in particular were frequently discussed in terms of "posterity," "leaving legacies to our children," and "our moral obligation to future generations." Proponents routinely framed the conflict as a contest between temporary benefits versus a timeless legacy. As Virginia Wood testified regarding the area's potential for perpetuating formative and character-enhancing experiences, "These qualities can still be nurtured in generations of the future if we are farsighted and wise enough to set aside this wild country immediately, and spare it from the exploitations of a few for the lasting benefit of the many."[21]

Of course, similar rhetoric had been used in previous conservation conflicts, but postwar developments lent a new sense of urgency. Not only were proponents seeing unprecedented rates of landscape alteration and environmental degradation, but they also lived with the atomic bomb and its psychological fallout. Of the first generation to seriously question whether their descendants would inherit the same Earth, they were stirred by ominous possibilities inconceivable before their time.

"There are going to be increasing numbers of young people, and older ones," Mardy Murie repeatedly wrote, "who will need and crave and benefit from the experience of travel in far places, untouched places." Present trends, she warned, could result in "turning the children of the near future into robots and automatons and weaklings."[22] She and others warned that while the need for wild places was increasing, fewer of them would be available to future generations.

But the campaign was also about passing on a legacy of hope and encouragement. As intended, it demonstrated that despite powerful opposition, those who believe that progress can include preserving remnants of our natural heritage can prevail in the political process. Stewart Brandborg, an influential figure in both the establishment of the Arctic Range and the passage of ANILCA twenty years later, recalls that the victory was "an awakening to those of us in the national wilderness movement to Alaska's potential for leaving to future generations what we denied them down here." The "big thinking" that characterized the Arctic conflict, he says, "inspired and prepared the following generation for the ANILCA battle."[23]

With language reminiscent of Mardy Murie, who inspired her career, bestselling author Terry Tempest Williams reminds Americans that the Arctic Refuge represents a promise made by the past generation to those of the future. In *Seasons of Life and Land*, a book opposing oil development, she pleads for an "act of restraint by the United States Congress in the name of the Arctic National Wildlife Refuge." "The eyes of the future are looking back at us," she says, "and they are praying for us to see beyond our own time."[24]

A Compromise

Wildlife and ecology, science, recreation, heritage, and bequest: these values inspired leaders of the Arctic campaign, captured the public imagination, galvanized political support, and continue in contemporary literary descriptions and experiential accounts of the Arctic Refuge. But there was more to the creation of the Arctic Range than the triumph of wilderness values in the political process. That these values inspired the necessary public support should certainly be granted. But as with Yellowstone Park, its standard of comparison throughout the campaign, the range's founding purposes do not tell the whole story of its origin.

Arctic proponents regularly argued that Alaskans should be guided by the vision and altruism that inspired the establishment of America's first national park. They referred to what historians now call the Yellowstone "creation myth"—the story of a group of early explorers sitting around a campfire, recounting the area's wondrous features, and committing themselves to its preservation. Whether or not the event occurred as told, the story omits the fact that lobbying by the Northern Pacific Railroad, not conservationists, was the most influential factor in the passage of the Yellowstone Park Act.[25]

Nor did the Arctic Range have the virgin birth many accounts suggest. The victory was in part the product of a political quid pro quo—a tradeoff. In return for its designation, the national conservation community quietly withdrew its opposition to revocation of Public Land Order 82, which had effectively protected most of arctic Alaska from individual, corporate, and state appropriation. *News-Miner* publisher Bill Snedden, who had penned effusive and influential editorials espousing preservation of the region "as God had made it," was in fact more motivated by the prospect of oil wealth believed to lie beneath the twenty million acres that, concurrent with the range's establishment, were finally released for potential development. Had that release not occurred, the federal government, not the new state, may well have controlled the revenue flowing from discovery of the giant Prudhoe Bay oil field, and Alaska today would be a far different place. One can speculate that the new state, becoming more aware of the oil potential, might have later successfully lobbied for acquisition of the area as part of its statehood entitlement. However, the fact remains—though seldom recognized by either side—that the myriad consequences of state ownership of the Prudhoe Bay complex are also a legacy of the Arctic campaign.

A Symbol

The opposing positions that played out in the range controversy can be traced to the late-nineteenth-century emergence of conservation as an element of federal policy, the consequent establishment of national forest, park, and wildlife refuge systems, and the conflict between utilitarian conservation and nature preservation that emerged as management philosophies were developed for those systems. Through the 1950s these two approaches further diverged, becoming opposing environmental paradigms, each with a set of shared values, assumptions, and beliefs prescribing humans' appropriate relationship to the environment and responsibility to future generations. Social theorists describe these paradigms as the "dominant Western worldview" and the contrasting "new ecological paradigm."[26]

Underlying opposition to the Arctic Range, the dominant Western worldview placed emphasis on a belief in human separateness from and right to dominate nature; a confidence that progress, growth, and prosperity will continue and that resources will continue to be abundant; a commitment to laissez-faire government, private property rights, and the individual's right to exploit natural resources; and the assumption that science and technology can solve any environmental problems incidental to progress.

The assumptions underlying this worldview had changed little since colonial times and had served the developing nation well. Of course, Thoreau, Muir, and others had warned of consequences. But it was not until the postwar period that the necessary preconditions were present—sufficient degrees of urbanization, industrialization, landscape degradation, and public education among them—to concern a significant number of people and stimulate a broad-based response.

The "new ecological paradigm" incorporated Aldo Leopold's fusion of modern science with the transcendental/romantic notion of humans as interdependent and obligate members of a community of life. This perspective gave primacy to the belief that our species, like all others, must live within ecological constraints. It emphasized the finite nature of many resources and held that the concept of sustainability should guide government resource policy. This paradigm assumed that science and technology are limited in their capacity to prevent potentially disastrous consequences if humans do not accept the need to live within the natural limits of the biosphere. Inherently holistic, this emerging perspective linked all environmental issues to the broad concern that led Leopold to ask "whether a still higher 'standard of living' is worth its cost in things natural, wild, and free."[27]

True, not all who worked for the area's establishment expressed the leaders' idealism, referenced ecological thinking, or sought to challenge the dominant notion of progress. Many were just motivated by utilitarian conservation concerns. For them, the withdrawal would simply protect the area's most interesting wildlife, its scenic condition, and opportunities for hunting, recreation, and tourism. Campaign leaders spoke convincingly to these pragmatic interests, which they shared, and in doing so, broadened the campaign's base of support.

But when Olaus Murie stated, in what became the final sentence of 527 pages of Senate hearing testimony, that the "Arctic Wildlife Range can be a symbol of what Alaska, at its best, can do," he alluded to their undeclared motivation. The campaign to preserve this place and its wildness was part of a larger struggle to expand thinking about conservation and reorient it toward the new order of threat. Its success was a small step in the effort to advance the emerging ecological paradigm and to further the accompanying shift that historian Daniel Philippon aptly describes as expanding the focus from "preserving the pieces" of nature to "protecting the planet."[28]

Eloquently encapsulating the founders' more encompassing, even global, hope is the often-cited essay Lowell Sumner wrote for the twenty-fifth anniversary celebration of the range's establishment. It begins with "The Statue of Liberty...symbol of our American dream and a democracy that is 209 years old." In the far north, he continued, is another American symbol:

> the handiwork of millions of years of patient evolution...and this one too, symbolizes freedom: freedom from the crowding and pollution of our cities, freedom to continue, unhindered and forever if we are willing, the particular story of Planet Earth unfolding here—freedom for us as well who need to come to the few out-of-the-way places still remaining where we can breathe freely, be inspired, and understand a little of the majestic story of evolution, but also where we can learn to appreciate and respect the intricate and inscrutable unfolding of the Earth's destiny—when free from meddling human concerns and the urge to take possession of and use up what we so imperfectly understand.[29]

Herein Sumner telescopes the emerging ecological and evolutionary thinking, postwar environmental concerns, and transcendental insight of the campaign's origin into an analogy linking an established icon with a new one. His comparison reminds us that the Arctic Refuge is much more than a remnant of unaltered nature, just as the Statue of Liberty is more than an aesthetic piece of sculpture. While the statue is a human construction, revered by Americans because it represents national ideals, this place, as a last great wilderness, is a human construct, revered by its devotees because its preservation represents the aspirations and ideals embodied by wilderness. The refuge, like the statue, is an aesthetic entity and it too is a symbolic artifact, created by the timeless human act of conferring meaning to a place.

Indeed, since Collins and Sumner sat on the edge of Last Lake and sketched its boundary lines, this landscape was meant to represent a vision for the future that transcended its boundaries. While the early hope that it would become "a place set apart" from the inventions and conventions that dominate our relationship with the natural world was not fully realized, its establishment did serve as an encouraging demonstration of Americans' capacity to draw upon what David Brower declared their "least exploited resource, Restraint." Although the cultural, spiritual, and ecological values proponents spoke to were not explicitly recognized in the area's establishing order, they are implicit in its central statutory purpose—to preserve wilderness values. And the hope that a place embodying those values might remind distracted Americans, as Howard Zahniser said, of their "membership in the whole community of life" and of their "dependence and interdependence, indebtedness and responsibility" continues to find expression in contemporary refuge writings.[30]

In his recent essay, "It's a R-E-F-U-G-E," Charles Konigsburg observes that "we are all made better, more human, even if it's just in knowing that such a special place is held inviolate for our fellow creatures—and for us as well." The understandings that emerge from the existence of the Arctic Refuge, he says, "help us to appreciate our inseparable relationship with all species, our proper place among all forms of life within this incredibly beautiful world we jointly inhabit."[31]

The desire to preserve a remote corner of Alaska that might carry such meaning can be attributed to the clash between two ideological value systems. But the campaign's roots precede the 1950s and the divergent perspectives regarding the exploitation, conservation, and ecology of nature represented by the dominant and challenging environmental paradigms.

Ultimately the struggle originated in conflicting views of our role in the larger scheme of things that remain deeply ingrained in American culture and, perhaps more deeply, in the human psyche. Most of the arguments that played out in the Arctic controversy had, in various forms, been debated for centuries. But the postwar order confronted the nation with a question that was all but unimaginable to previous generations. Controversy over this area's future became—and remains—emblematic of "the real problem," as Olaus Murie characterized it, "of what the human species is to do with this earth."[32]

Epilogue

George L. Collins retired from the National Park Service in late 1960 and continued to work for the protection of wildlands through the nonprofit organization he established, Conservation Associates. Until the final months of his ninety-seventh year, his Remington typewriter clanked out letters opposing oil drilling on the refuge's coastal plain.

Lowell Sumner transferred to Washington, D.C., in 1960, where he continued to expand ecological thinking as the National Park Service's chief research biologist. In 1967, he retired to his New Mexico homestead, where he wrote science sections for *Encyclopedia Britannica* and worked on local conservation issues until his death in 1989.

Olaus and Mardy Murie made a last trip to the Sheenjek—their "place of enchantment"—in 1961. Olaus continued to lead the Wilderness Society until ill health forced his retirement in 1962. He died of cancer the following year at age seventy-five. After his death, Mardy moved from the background to the foreground of the wilderness movement and received a great many awards and honors, including the Presidential Medal of Freedom in 1998. She died in 2003 at their ranch, now the Murie Center in Moose, Wyoming, at age 101.

Brina Kessel retired from the University of Alaska Fairbanks in 1999, where she is curator of ornithology emerita. She is currently coauthoring a major reference work on the birds of Alaska.

Bob Krear retired in 1984 as a biology professor at Michigan Technological University. Now eighty-three, he is finishing a book on his lifetime of fieldwork.

◄ FIGURE 55. Caribou on Lobo Lake, an Olaus Murie drawing from *Two in the Far North.*

George Schaller is now vice president of the Wildlife Conservation Society and author of fifteen books based on his wildlife studies throughout the world. Constantly traveling, he is involved in conservation and research projects in Laos, Mongolia, Iran, and Tajikistan.

After the 1960 presidential election, Fred Seaton returned to his family's newspaper business in Hastings, Nebraska. He unsuccessfully ran for governor in 1962, then served as publisher of the *Hastings Tribune* until his death in 1974.

Howard Zahniser succeeded Olaus Murie as the Wilderness Society's executive director and worked tirelessly for enactment of the wilderness bill. In May of 1964, after overseeing sixty-five rewrites and testifying before nineteen congressional hearings on the bill, he suffered a fatal heart attack, four months before President Johnson signed the Wilderness Act into law.

Stewart Brandborg succeeded his mentor, Howard Zahniser, as head of the Wilderness Society and devoted the next twelve years to expanding the new wilderness system and lobbying for what became the Alaska National Interest Lands Conservation Act (ANILCA). He left the society in 1976 and, now eighty-two, serves on the board of Wilderness Watch.

Celia Hunter succeeded Brandborg as interim director of the Wilderness Society, the first woman to head a national environmental organization. In December 2001, after working late into the night writing letters urging congressional representatives to oppose oil drilling on the Arctic Refuge's coastal plain, the eighty-two-year-old Hunter died in her Fairbanks home.

William Pruitt was fired from the University of Alaska in 1962 because of his courageous opposition to an Atomic Energy Commission plan, endorsed by the university, to use nuclear explosives to blast a harbor in northwest Alaska. He then joined the faculty of the University of Manitoba. Now retired, the eighty-three-year-old Pruitt continues to advise researchers and introduce students to Ernest Thompson Seton's ideas.

Virginia Wood is now eighty-eight and the matriarch of Alaska conservation. From her log home in the wooded hills north of Fairbanks, she continues to garden, split firewood, write and prepare testimony in defense of Alaska's wildlands, and carry forward the spirit that infused the Arctic campaign.

Notes

The following abbreviations are used within citations of frequently referenced archival sources:

ACS   Alaska Conservation Society Papers (APR)

ANWR   Arctic National Wildlife Refuge files, U.S. Fish and Wildlife Service, Fairbanks

APR   Archives, Alaska and Polar Regions Department, University of Alaska Fairbanks

MMP   Margaret Murie Papers (APR)

NCTC   National Conservation and Training Center, Shepherdstown, WV

OMP   Olaus Murie Papers (APR)

RKP   Roger Kaye Papers (author's personal collection; some of the materials in this collection will be deposited at APR)

INTRODUCTION

1. Olaus Murie, statement submitted to U.S. Congress, Senate, Committee on Interstate and Foreign Commerce, Subcommittee on Merchant Marine and Fisheries, Hearings, S. 1899, A Bill to Authorize the Establishment of the Arctic Wildlife Range, Alaska, 86th Congress, 1st session, Part 1, 30 June 1959 (Washington, DC: GPO, 1960), 58–59. The 1959 Senate hearings on the Range proposal are hereafter referred to as AWR Hearings. Part 1 of the hearings was held in Washington, DC, on 30 June 1959. Part 2 of the hearings was held in seven Alaska communities (20–31 October 1959) and in Washington, DC (April 22, 1959).

2. Collins and Sumner, "Northeast Arctic," 13–26.

3. Those interviews that were taped and transcribed are listed at the end of the references. The majority of the interviews were not taped.

4. Tall, "Our Last Wilderness," 154.

5. Olaus J. Murie to Hon. E. L. Bartlett, 17 August 1960, MMP, Box 2, Folder 18.

6. In facilitating understanding of the concepts that have and continue to underlie efforts to protect this area's wilderness character, this study recognizes that some wilderness qualities receive less than fair consideration because the measurement, description, and comparison of such costs and benefits are carried out within a management paradigm historically insensitive to many core wilderness values. Better represented are the benefits of developments, economic opportunities, and, in some cases, the individual's freedom from regulation that jeopardize the founding wilderness values.

7. Recognizing the potential for bias inherent in such research, I began this effort with the process of "bracketing" my perspectives on the two major subjects of concern, the Arctic Refuge and wilderness. Bracketing is a mental exercise in which the researcher identifies, then sets aside taken-for-granted assumptions, preconceptions, and paradigmatic commitments, making them less likely to influence interpretation of the data.

8. Response of Interior Department Solicitor Ted Stevens to questioning by Alaska Senator Bob Bartlett during AWR Hearings, Part 2, 434.

9. Public Land Order 2214, 1960.

10. References to the agency proposed, then selected, to administer the Arctic proposal are confusing because it was variously referred to as the Fish and Wildlife Service, Bureau of Biological Survey, or the Bureau of Sport Fisheries and Wildlife. In 1940 the Bureau of Biological Survey and the Bureau of Fisheries merged to form the Fish and Wildlife Service. Each bureau maintained a separate identity. The Fish and Wildlife Act of 1956 officially established the Fish and Wildlife Service, comprised of two new bureaus: the Bureau of Sport Fisheries and Wildlife and the Bureau of Commercial Fisheries. Although correspondence and statements prior to the 1956 Act occasionally refer to the Bureau of Biological Survey, and those after the Act occasionally refer to the Bureau of Sport Fisheries and Wildlife, employees and programs within these bureaus were part of the Fish and Wildlife Service throughout the Arctic campaign years, 1951–1960. Thus, to avoid confusion, they will be consistently referred to as Fish and Wildlife Service throughout this text.

11. Urban Nelson, acting regional director, Bureau of Sport Fisheries and Wildlife, to Forbes L. Baker, 12 August 1959, Roger Kaye Papers, hereafter referred to as RKP. Located at the Alaska and Polar Regions Department, Rasmuson Library, University of Alaska Fairbanks. This archive is hereafter referred to as APR.

12. This statement was taken from a copy of the speech Nelson sent to Frederick C. Dean, 22 November 1961, RKP. Dean was editor of the biological papers found in *Science in Alaska,* ed. G. Dahlgren Jr., 1961 (College: Alaska Division, American Association for the Advancement of Science. Nelson's edited speech was printed as "The Bureau of Sport Fisheries and Wildlife's Position on the Arctic National Wildlife Range," 69–76.

13. The Arctic National Wildlife Range established in 1960 was expanded from 8.9 million acres to 19.3 million acres and redesignated the Arctic National Wildlife Refuge by the Alaska National Interest Lands Conservation Act of 1980 (ANILCA), Public Law 96–487 in U.S. *Statutes at Large* 94, 2371. As discussed in Chapter 5, the terms *range* and *refuge* were nearly synonymous in the 1950s, with ranges having been more associated with large mammals and big game hunting.

CHAPTER 1: GENESIS OF THE CAMPAIGN

1.   Murie, *Journeys to the Far North*, 242.

2.   U.S. Congress, *Alaska: Its Resources and Development*, 213. Although Marshall's contribution was the most preservation-oriented, the report generally emphasized caution in the development of Alaska's resources and expressed a need to avoid mistakes made in the lower forty-eight states.

3.   Nash, "Tourism, Parks, and the Wilderness Idea," 17.

4.   Representative of the angry response of many Alaskans was the *Fairbanks Daily News-Miner* editorial facetiously titled "Let's Keep Alaska a Wilderness, Oh, Yeah." It was published on 16 January 1939, shortly after the report was released.

5.   Olaus Murie's initial reaction to Marshall's proposal, and his change in thinking about it during the Arctic campaign, was provided by Margaret Murie in an interview with the author, 27 March 1992.

6.   The Wilderness Act of 1964, Public Law 88–577 in U.S. *Statutes at Large*, 78. The definition of wilderness was crafted by Howard Zahniser. For an analysis of Zahniser's intent, and the meaning and significance of the "untrammeled" concept, see Scott, "Untrammeled," "Wilderness Character," 72–79.

7.   This discussion occurred on 18 September 2000. Echelmeyer is a professor at the University of Alaska's Geophysical Institute.

8.   Glacken, *Traces on the Rhodian Shore*; Oelschlaeger, *The Idea of Wilderness*; Nash, *Wilderness and the American Mind*.

9.   For comprehensive treatments of these aspects of the postwar era, see Hayes, *History of Environmental Politics* and *Beauty, Health, and Permanence*. See also Gottlieb, *Forcing the Spring*.

10.   Richard Cooley, AWR Hearings, Part 2, 124–26. Cooley was citing the study by Marion Clawson of Resources for the Future, Inc., entitled "The Crisis in Outdoor Recreation." It was reprinted in the March–April 1959 issue of *American Forests*.

11.   Ibid.

12.   A summary of the growth and ideological development of the mainline conservation organizations from 1945 to 1965 is found in Fox, *The American Conservation Movement*, 251–90. Membership in the Wilderness Society was 1,673 in 1946 (Minutes of the 1948 Annual Meeting of the Council of the Wilderness Society). On 31 December 1960 it was reported to be 16,695 (Report of the Executive Secretary and Editor, 24 July 1961). Both documents are found in the Wilderness Society Collection, Conservation Collection, Denver Public Library, Denver. Citations courtesy of AnneMarie Lankard Moore.

13.   "The Wilderness Society Platform," *Living Wilderness* (September 1935), 2.

14.   As cited in McIntosh, *The Background of Ecology*, 7–8.

15.   Olaus Murie, "Wild Country as a National Asset," 27. One of the main points Murie makes in this seminal article is that wilderness should be defended for its intangible, spiritual, and recreational values. He deplores the notion that "we are so thoroughly seeped in the economic, material tradition that we subconsciously conclude that we must argue on that basis" (p. 24).

16.   Aldo Leopold, "Why the Wilderness Society," 6.

17.   Aldo Leopold, *A Sand Country Almanac*. Parts of many of the essays in the book had been previously published, so probably all campaign leaders were already familiar with Leopold's ideas. Further, many of the campaign's leaders were personal friends of

Leopold. For thorough treatments of Leopold's ideological contributions, see Meine, *Aldo Leopold*, and Flader, *Thinking Like a Mountain*.

18.   Several typologies of wilderness values or purposes have been forwarded to describe the widening range of benefits wilderness is believed to serve. The earliest was Bob Marshall's three categories: (1) physical benefits associated with exploration, exertion, and self-reliance; (2) mental benefits associated with cognitive freedom; and (3) aesthetic benefits associated with being immersed in beauty ("The Problem of the Wilderness," 31–35). Subsequent schemes go beyond his limited concern with experiential functions. See especially McCloskey, "Evolving Perspectives on Wilderness Values," 13–18. See also Michael Nelson, "Wilderness Preservation Arguments," 54–200.

19.   Virginia Wood, letter to the editor, *Fairbanks Daily News-Miner*, dated 27 January 1958.

20.   The most complete treatment of Marshall is found in Glover, *A Wilderness Original*. More specific to influences upon his philosophy is Glover's "Romance, Recreation, and Wilderness." Marshall's most definitive description of wilderness and the values it held for him is found in his "The Problem of the Wilderness." This influential article was widely reprinted. Describing Marshall's ideas about Alaska is Kaye, "Alaska and Beyond."

21.   Marshall, *Arctic Wilderness*, 2. The second edition, published in 1970, was titled *Alaska Wilderness: Exploring the Central Brooks Range*.

22.   Marshall, "The Problem of the Wilderness," 35.

23.   Marshall, *Arctic Village*, 379.

24.   Marshall, "The Problem of the Wilderness," 32, 33.

25.   Ibid., 32.

26.   Marshall, *Arctic Wilderness*, 2.

27.   Marshall, "Fallacies in Osborne's Position," 5.

28.   Robert Marshall, as cited in Zahniser, "The Need for Wilderness Areas," 38.

29.   This was how Collins described his position. His official title at this time was chief, State and Territorial Division, Region Four, National Park Service.

30.   National Park Service, "A Recreation Program for Alaska," 1955, Alaska Recreation Survey, Washington, DC.

31.   Collins, "Notes on Alaska Recreation Survey, Special Reference ANWR Proposal, as Requested in Letter of 2 November 1985 from Mrs. Debbie Miller to George L. Collins," George L. Collins Papers, APR. This fifteen-page, handwritten letter was provided to assist Miller in writing her book on the Arctic Refuge, *Midnight Wilderness*.

32.   Dedera, "A Conservationist's Search for Truth."

33.   Collins, "Consideration of the Arctic National Wildlife Range," 14.

34.   Joshua Collins interview, 11 December 2002.

35.   Collins, "Background Information," 10.

36.   Ibid., 11.

37.   "George L. Collins: *The Art and Politics of Park Planning and Preservation, 1920–1979*: An Interview," conducted by Ann Lage in 1978 and 1979, ix, 189 (emphasis added).

38.   George L. Collins interview, 28 March 1993, APR.

39.   The National Park Service Act is found in U.S. *Statutes at Large*, 39 (1916), 535.

40.   Sellars, *Preserving Nature in the National Parks*, 4–5. Sellar's study documents the historical conflict between managing parks for recreational and tourism purposes and ecological purposes.

41. Sumner, "Wildlife Management."

42. Joshua Collins interview, 11 December 2002.

43. George L. Collins interview, 28 March 1993.

44. Sumner, "Biological Research and Management," 15.

45. Joshua Collins interview, 11 December 2002.

46. Hendee, Stankey, and Lucas, *Wilderness Management*, 18. Pages 18–23 of this standard wilderness management textbook contain perhaps the best summary of these management approaches.

47. For an insightful analysis of Aldo Leopold's land aesthetic, see Callicott, *In Defense of the Land Ethic*, 239–47.

48. Marietta Sumner et al., "Remembering Lowell Sumner," 36.

49. Sumner, "Arctic National Wildlife Refuge Address." Unable to attend the twenty-fifth anniversary celebration of the Arctic Refuge held in Fairbanks, Alaska, Sumner sent this two-page statement to be read at the gathering. RKP.

CHAPTER 2: TO NORTHEAST ALASKA

1. Sumner and Collins, "Arctic Wilderness," in *Living Wilderness*, then a publication of the Wilderness Society.

2. Lowell Sumner to Olaus Murie, 5 October 1951, Margaret Murie Papers, hereafter referred to as MMP, Box 2, Folder 18, APR. Sumner cites his report in this letter.

3. The Fish and Wildlife Service extended its predator control to Alaska in 1948. In 1953 it became a cooperative program with the Territory of Alaska, and in 1959, with the new state. The wolf shooting and poisoning program on the north slope was a response to what was widely believed to be a substantial decline in caribou numbers in the 1940s.

4. Lowell Sumner travel journal, 20 April 1951 entry, United States Department of the Interior, National Park Service, George Collins Papers, File No. 207-10.

5. George L. Collins travel journal, 15 April 1951, 24 April 1951, and 15 August 1952 entries, United States Department of the Interior, National Park Service, George L. Collins Papers, File No. 207-10, APR.

6. Alaska Game Commission, *Twelfth Annual Report*, 1 July 1950–30 June 1951, 20–21.

7. Richard Carroll interview, 14 September 2002.

8. Meyers, "He Wrestled a Wolf," 15–16.

9. Alaska Game Commission, *19th Annual Report*, 1 July 1957–30 June 1958, 32, 34.

10. Gruening to Rhode, 11 March 1950, Alaska State Archives, Juneau, Record Group 101, File 25, 470–75.

11. George L. Collins travel journal, 24 April 1951 entry.

12. Ibid.

13. Collins, *The Art and Politics of Park Planning and Preservation*, 198.

14. Lowell Sumner to Olaus Murie, 5 October 1951, MMP, Box 2, Folder 18.

15. Wilderness Society to Oscar Chapman, undated, MMP, Box 2, Folder 18.

16. Collins, *The Art and Politics of Park Planning and Preservation*, 199, 192.

17. Aldo Leopold, *A Sand County Almanac*, 269. For a discussion of the role of "monumentalism" in early preservation efforts, see Runte, *National Parks*.

18. Aldo Leopold, *A Sand County Almanac*, 291.

19. George L. Collins interview, 30 January 1999.

20. Alaska Game Commission, *Thirteenth Annual Report*, 1 July 1951–30 June 1952. Two books describe Operation Umiat and the aerial shooting and poisoning of wolves: Jim Rearden's biography of predator control agent Frank Glaser, *Alaska's Wolf Man*, and Fish and Wildlife Service agent Ray Tremblay's *On Patrol*.

21. As cited in Rawson, *Changing Tracks*, 187.

22. Ibid., 246.

23. Description of this development and the quotations draws upon Rawson, *Changing Tracks*, 244–45, and Virginia Wood interview, 9 March 2005.

24. David Brower, *For Earth's Sake*, 486.

25. Brower discusses Darling and other campaign leaders in *For Earth's Sake*, 486; Leopold and Darling, *Wildlife in Alaska*, vi, 4.

26. Collins describes the group's discussion of "protective custody" for the area in his "Notes on Alaska Recreation Survey." See also interviews with Collins by Lage, 1978 and 1979, and Kaye, 1993.

27. Collins, *The Art and Politics of Park Planning and Preservation*, 192.

28. George L. Collins interview, 28 March 1993.

29. George L. Collins to Louis Giddings Jr. in Appendix B, "Genesis of the Arctic International Wildlife Range Idea, 1952," in Collins, *The Art and Politics of Park Planning and Preservation*, 345.

30. Collins, *The Art and Politics of Park Planning and Preservation*, 191–92.

31. Ibid., 192.

32. Collins and Sumner, "Arctic Research Laboratory, Progress Report," 1, 2.

33. Aldo Leopold, *A Sand County Almanac*, 274.

34. MacKaye, "Dam Site *vs.* Norm Site," 243.

35. Collins and Sumner, "Arctic Research Laboratory, Progress Report."

36. As cited in Sutter, "Driven Wild," 421.

37. "The Types of Wilderness Recognized," 2.

38. Harvey, *A Symbol of Wilderness*.

39. Richard Leonard to Oscar L. Chapman, 12 September 1952, MMP, Box 2, Folder 18.

40. Federation of Western Outdoor Clubs, "Resolution: Arctic Wilderness Preserve," undated. On 22 October 1953, Edgar Wayburn sent Olaus Murie and Howard Zahniser copies of the resolution. MMP, Box 2, Folder 18.

41. Collins and Sumner, "A Proposed Arctic Wilderness International Park," 20.

42. Collins, *The Art and Politics of Park Planning and Preservation*, 194.

43. Collins and Sumner, "A Proposed Arctic Wilderness International Park," 2, 32.

CHAPTER 3: A LAST GREAT WILDERNESS

1. Sumner and Collins, "Arctic Wilderness," 14.

2. George L. Collins to Olaus Murie, 21 June 1953, MMP, Box 2, Folder 18.

3. "Mission 66" would result in 1,197 miles of new roads, 1,502 new parking areas, 575 new campgrounds, 535 new water systems, 218 new utility buildings, 221 new administrative buildings, 1,239 new employee housing units, and 114 new visitor centers, as well as many reconstructed or rehabilitated facilities. Sellars, *Preserving Nature in the National Parks*, 184. See also Wirth, *Parks, Politics, and the People*, 262–67.

4.   Adolph Murie, "Comments on Mission 66 Plans, and on Policies Pertaining to Mount McKinley NP," 8 November 1956, as cited in Brown, *Denali*, 201.

5.   Adolph Murie, "Field Studies in Mount McKinley National Park, 1953," RKP.

6.   George L. Collins interview, 28 March 1993.

7.   Collins, *The Art and Politics of Park Planning and Preservation*, 198.

8.   Opposition to the Arctic proposal was closely related to opposition to what was perceived by many as colonial treatment by the federal government. For a definitive description of the social, economic, and political forces behind the statehood movement, see Naske, *An Interpretive History of Alaska Statehood*.

9.   U.S. Congress, House Committee on Public Lands, *Statehood for Alaska*, 80th Congress, 1st session, April 1947, 280.

10.   Gruening described his conservation philosophy and role in the eagle bounty issue in AWR Hearings, Part 1, 3–7.

11.   As cited in Coates, *The Trans-Alaska Pipeline Controversy*, 89.

12.   Ibid., 87.

13.   As cited in John Whitehead, "The Governor Who Opposed Statehood: The Legacy of Jay Hammond," in Haycox and Mangusso, eds., *An Alaskan Anthology*, 371.

14.   George L. Collins travel journal, 23 March 1951 entry, George L. Collins Papers, File No. 207-10, APR.

15.   As cited in Doherty, "The Arctic National Wildlife Refuge," 38.

16.   Carnes, *A Preliminary Geographical Survey*, 1.

17.   Ibid., 38.

18.   However, Everglades National Park, dedicated in 1947, was nearly a million acres in size. In terms of purpose it was precedential in that its enabling act specified maintenance of wilderness and ecological conditions. The act specified that developments to provide visitor access must not interfere with primitive conditions, but it did not preclude them. Unlike the Arctic Refuge, the Everglades would see development of some roads, trails, and other public-use facilities. Nevertheless, establishment of a large national park emphasizing maintenance of natural conditions over public use set a precedent Arctic proponents undoubtedly profited from. See Runte, *National Parks*, especially pages 128–40.

19.   Runte, *National Parks*, 2.

20.   Collins and Sumner, "Northeast Arctic."

21.   George L. Collins interview, 18 March 1992.

22.   Dufresne, *Alaska's Animals and Fishes*, 3. Dufresne was among the first Alaskans to warn of the territory's vulnerability to frontier treatment of its natural resources.

23.   Collins and Sumner, "Northeast Arctic," 13, 26.

24.   "Dr. Murie Reports on Wilderness Study of Impressive Brooks Range," *Fairbanks Daily News-Miner*, undated clipping, Olaus Murie Papers, APR, hereafter referred to as OMP. Murie believed that maintaining some vestige of the frontier was important to residents as well as non-Alaskans. He went on to say that "there are many other individuals up here [in Alaska] who have declared to me their deep feeling for Alaska and especially the original frontier aspects that mean so much to many Americans."

25.   Turner, "The Significance of the Frontier in American History."

26.   Alice Stuart, AWR Hearings, Part 2, 412.

27.   Hackett, "Alaska's Vanishing Frontier," 1.

28. Wenzel Raith, AWR Hearings, Part 2, 360–65.

29. For detailed treatment on the cultural heritage and identity function of national parks, see Runte, *National Parks*.

30. Sumner, "A Letter from the Arctic." The letter was addressed to Richard Leonard of the Sierra Club.

31. Sumner and Collins, "Arctic Wilderness," 14, 8.

32. Ibid., 14.

33. Al Anderson, Alaska Development Board to George L. Collins, 28 September 1953, MMP, Box 2, Folder 18.

34. Al Anderson to George L. Collins, 12 October 1953, MMP Box 2, Folder 18.

35. George L. Collins to Governor Frank Heintzleman, 22 October 1953, MMP, Box 2, Folder 18.

36. George L. Collins to Harold E. Anthony, 18 November 1953, MMP Box 2, Folder 18.

37. A. Starker Leopold to Col. W. Winston Mair, Canadian Wildlife Service, 1 December 1953, MMP, Box 2, Folder 18.

38. Col. W. Winston Mair to A. Starker Leopold, 23 November 1953, MMP, Box 2, Folder 18.

39. "Would Set Aside Wilderness Area in Northeast Alaska," *Fairbanks Daily News-Miner*, 27 January 1954, 1.

40. Charles Gray, letter to the editor, *Fairbanks Daily News-Miner*, 29 January 1954.

41. Charles Gray interview, 30 October 2003, APR.

42. Sven Gustav Norder, letter to the editor, *Fairbanks Daily News-Miner*, 2 February 1954.

43. Carl E. Wilson, letter to the editor, *Fairbanks Daily News-Miner*, 23 February 1954.

44. James S. Couch, letter to the editor, *Fairbanks Daily News-Miner*, 30 January 1954.

45. William O. Pruitt Jr., letter to the editor, *Fairbanks Daily News-Miner*, 4 February 1954.

46. William Pruitt interview, 20 May 2003.

47. Ibid.

48. Seton, *The Arctic Prairies*, 269.

49. Charles Gray, letter to the editor, *Fairbanks Daily News-Miner*, 4 February 1954.

50. William O. Pruitt Jr., letter to the editor, *Fairbanks Daily News-Miner*, 15 February 1954.

51. Virginia Wood, letter to the editor, *Fairbanks Daily News-Miner*, 18 February 1954.

52. Virginia Wood interview, 10 November 2002, APR.

53. Virginia Wood, AWR Hearings, Part 2, 335–39.

54. John L. Buckley to George L. Collins, 12 January 1954, MMP, Box 2, Folder 18.

55. William O. Pruitt Jr. to George L. Collins, 11 March 1954, MMP, Box 2, Folder 18.

56. Paul Shepard to Starker Leopold, 1 November 1954, MMP, Box 2, Folder 18. Although Shepard would not personally visit the area until thirty-four years later, his motivations for working to protect it can be gleaned from the thirteen books he later wrote exploring the psychological consequences of the postwar order and loss of the natural conditions of our evolutionary heritage. This analysis of Paul Shepard's motivation was provided by his widow Florence Shepard, interview, 23 January 2003.

57. George L. Collins to Dr. Harold E. Anthony, 18 November 1953, MMP, Box 2, Folder 18.

58. Lowell Sumner to Sally Carrighar, 10 March 1954, MMP, Box 2, Folder 18.

59. George L. Collins interview, 28 March 1993.

60. Joshua Collins interview, 11 December 2002.

61. George L. Collins interview, 28 March 1993.

62. Lawrence C. Merriam to Director, National Park Service, 8 December 1953, MMP, Box 2, Folder 18.

63. George L. Collins to Olaus Murie, 11 January 1954, MMP, Box 2, Folder 18.

64. Following the death of Wilderness Society director Robert Sterling Yard in 1945, Olaus Murie quit his job with the Fish and Wildlife Service to become the organization's half-time director, working out of his home in Jackson, Wyoming. At that time Howard Zahniser assumed the role of executive secretary, handling the organization's Washington, DC, affairs. Murie held the title of director from 1945 until 1962 and served as president from 1950 to 1957. Zahniser was the society's executive secretary from 1945 to 1962, and was also referred to as the executive director from 1962 until his death in 1964. Murie and Zahniser functioned, and were often described, as co-directors.

65. Fox, *The American Conservation Movement*, 269.

66. Ed Zahniser (Howard's son) interview. Howard Zahniser was president of the Thoreau Society in 1956 and 1957.

67. The Wilderness Act of 1964, Public Law 88-577 in U.S. *Statutes at Large*, 78.

68. Howard Zahniser to C. Edward Graves, 25 April 1959, Wilderness Society Files.

69. Howard Zahniser, "The Need for Wilderness Areas," 40. During early hearings on the Wilderness Act, this influential paper was inserted into the *Congressional Record* by Senator Hubert Humphrey. A sidebar to this article (p. 37) states that this paper "introduced a chain of circumstances that...led finally to introduction of the Wilderness Bill by Senator Humphrey and others."

70. Several of Murie's writings reference Seton. In "Seton's Influence Renewed," Murie described Seton's "dominant influence," his contribution toward cultivating "a charitable attitude toward wild animals," and his association of spiritual values with wild nature.

71. Murie's research was reported in the often-cited report "Alaska-Yukon Caribou."

72. Although for purposes of authorship she used "Margaret E. Murie," she is best known and preferred to be referred to as "Mardy."

73. Dunlap, *Saving America's Wildlife*.

74. Olaus Murie to E. W. Nelson, 10 July 1923, as cited in Glover, "Thinking Like a Wolverine."

75. Olaus Murie to Mr. Redington, 30 April 1929, Murie Center Files, Moose, WY.

76. Olaus Murie to Clifford C. Pressnall, 7 December 1952, Murie Center Files. Pressnall was in charge of the agency's Predator Control Branch.

77. Olaus Murie to Daniel Janzen, 6 April 1957, Murie Center Files.

78. Olaus J. Murie, "Wilderness Philosophy," 67, 65, 67, 61.

79. Olaus J. Murie, "Wilderness Conference on Yellowstone Lake," 15.

80. Olaus J. Murie, "Wilderness Philosophy," 59.

81. Olaus J. Murie, "Seton's Influence Renewed," 22.

82. Olaus J. Murie, "What Does Wilderness Mean to Us?," 18.

83. Olaus J. Murie, AWR Hearings, Part 1, 58–59.

84. Olaus J. Murie, "Plan for Exploration."

85. Harvey, *A Symbol of Wilderness*, 130.

86. Olaus J. Murie to Samuel H. Ordway Jr., 15 April 1954, MMP, Box 2, Folder 18. Ordway was vice president of the Conservation Foundation, the major sponsor of the expedition.

87. Howard Zahniser to Olaus J. Murie, 19 April 1954, MMP, Box 2, Folder 18.

88. Olaus J. Murie to Darrell Watt, 13 February 1963, MMP Box 2, Folder 18. Murie is responding to a request by UAF graduate student Watt for information on the effort leading to establishment of the Range. Sheenjek expedition member Robert Krear later recalled an evening discussion on the river during which the group agreed that the Fish and Wildlife Service was the agency most likely to leave the area "unencumbered" by recreational improvements. Given its tradition of providing visitor conveniences, they were "not certain we could expect that of the National Park Service" (Krear, "The Olaus Murie Brooks Range Expedition").

89. Olaus J. Murie, "Ethics and Predators," 20, 19. This is an uncomplimentary book review of *Alaska's Fish and Wildlife* by Clarence J. Rhode and Will Barker (Washington, DC: Government Printing Office, 1953).

90. Olaus J. Murie, "Ethics in Wildlife Management," 293.

91. Samuel Ordway Jr. to Olaus J. Murie, 9 April 1954, Director's Office, New York Zoological Park, Wildlife Conservation Society Archives, Alaska Folder.

92. Osborn, *Our Plundered Planet*, 201. Mardy Murie would use the book's title as a phrase in some of her Arctic proposal writings, presumably to associate the proposal with the book's apocalyptic message.

93. William O. Douglas, *My Wilderness: East to Katahdin*, 289.

94. William O. Douglas, *A Wilderness Bill of Rights*, 86. For insight into Douglas's environmental philosophy, see his semiautobiographical book, *Of Men and Mountains*. See also Murphy, *Wild Bill*.

95. George L. Collins to Olaus Murie, 4 May 1954, MMP, Box 2, Folder 18.

96. Fairfield Osborn to Olaus and Marty [Mardy], 30 April 1954; John L. Buckley to Dr. Fairfield Osborn, 31 December 1954; Fairfield Osborn to Dr. Buckley, 10 January 1955, Director's Office, New York Zoological Park, Wildlife Conservation Society Archives, Alaska Folder.

97. Collins, *The Art and Politics of Park Planning and Preservation*, 201.

98. Olaus Murie to Mr. Redington, 30 April 1929, RKP.

99. Olaus J. Murie, "Alaska with O. J. Murie," 29. Murie used this phrase in several publications at the time. His thoughts about the appropriateness and role of hunting are detailed in "How Shall We Hunt?" and "Ethics in Wildlife Management."

100. Joel Smith to Olaus J. Murie, 8 July 1955, MMP, Box 2, Folder 18.

101. Nash, *Wilderness and the American Mind*, 219, 200.

102. Harvey, *A Symbol of Wilderness*, 55, 279, 290.

CHAPTER 4: THE 1956 SHEENJEK EXPEDITION

1. Olaus J. Murie, "Wilderness Philosophy," 66.

2. Keith Herrington interview, 17 November 2004.

3. Olaus J. Murie, "A Brief Report," OMP, Box 8.

4. Brina Kessel interview, 22 January 2003.

5. Robert Krear interview, 22 January 2003.

6. Schaller, "Arctic Legacy," 62, 63–64.

7.   Margaret E. Murie, *Two in the Far North*, 289.

8.   Schaller, "New Area for Hunters." The title was not one the author suggested.

9.   "Arctic Wildlife Range Film," *News Bulletin of the Alaska Conservation Society*, no. 1, March 1960. This was the first issue of the *News Bulletin*, edited by Ginny (Virginia) Hill Wood. As will be explained in Chapter 7, the Alaska Conservation Society was formed around the Arctic range issue. The films have been restored and are available through the NCTC, Shepardstown, WV. Production information provided by Robert Krear, telephone interview, 17 May 2004.

10. Fox, *The American Conservation Movement*, 239.

11. Collins, *The Art and Politics of Park Planning and Preservation*, 190.

12. William O. Douglas, *My Wilderness: The Pacific West*.

13. Olaus J. Murie, "Alaska-Yukon Caribou"; *The Elk of North America*; and *A Field Guide to Animal Tracks*.

14. Margaret E. Murie, *Two in the Far North*, 315.

15. Schaller, *Arctic Valley*, 4–5.

16. George B. Schaller interview, 11 December 2002.

17. Olaus J. Murie, "Nature in the Arctic," 30.

18. Schaller, "Arctic Legacy," 65.

19. Olaus J. Murie, "Arctic Wilderness," 10, 11. The article appeared in *Outdoor America*, a publication of the Izaak Walton League, for which Murie had served on the board of directors.

20. Olaus J. Murie, "The Grizzly Bear and the Wilderness," 73.

21. Aldo Leopold, *A Sand County Almanac*, 103.

22. Olaus J. Murie, "Ethics in Wildlife Management," 293.

23. Olaus J. Murie, "Wilderness Philosophy," 63.

24. Margaret E. Murie, *Two in the Far North*, 297.

25. Schaller, "Arctic Legacy," 65.

26. Margaret E. Murie, "A Live River in the Arctic," 13. In February 1960, this article was reprinted in *Alaska Sportsman* magazine as "We Explore the Sheenjek."

27. Olaus J. Murie, "Wolf," 218.

28. Donald Murie interview, 14 January 2003.

29. Olaus J. Murie, "Wolf," 221, 220, 218.

30. William O. Douglas, *My Wilderness: The Pacific West*, 30.

31. Olaus J. Murie, "Wolf," 221.

32. Margaret E. Murie, *Two in the Far North*, 385.

33. Schaller, *Arctic Valley*, 206.

34 . Collins and Sumner, "Northeast Arctic," 20–21.

35. "ANWR Ecological Inventory and Monitoring Plan."

36. Schaller, *Arctic Valley*, foreword.

37. Ibid., 3, 206–7.

38. Robert Krear interview, 22 January 2003. Mardy Murie describes their expedition through the Central Brooks Range in part II of *Two in the Far North*.

39. Olaus J. Murie, "Nature in the Arctic," 31.

40. Olaus J. Murie, "Wilderness Philosophy," 67.

41. Olaus J. Murie, "Alaska," 8.

42. Olaus J. Murie, "Alaska with O. J. Murie," 29.

43. Theodore Roosevelt, as cited in Nash, *Wilderness and the American Mind*, 151.

44. Margaret E. Murie, "A Live River in the Arctic," 10.

45. Margaret E. Murie, *Two in the Far North*, 373.

46. Margaret E. Murie, AWR Hearings, Part 1, 60. She also used most of this narrative in several of her magazine articles.

47. Ibid.

48. Margaret E. Murie, *Two in the Far North*, 289.

49. Olaus J. Murie, "Wilderness Philosophy," 60. Murie was quoting an article in *Science* magazine. He made the point that scientists are increasingly recognizing the threats posed by science and considering what he called "human ecology."

50. Worster, *Nature's Economy*, 343–45.

51. As quoted in Wolf, *Son of the Wilderness*, 77.

52. Aldo Leopold, *A Sand County Almanac*, 117.

53. Zahniser, "The Need for Wilderness Areas," 40.

54. Ibid., 42.

55. Olaus J. Murie, *Journeys to the Far North*, 184.

56. Margaret E. Murie, *Two in the Far North*, 374 (emphasis in original).

57. Olaus J. Murie, "Alaska," 8.

58. Margaret E. Murie, *Two in the Far North*, 340.

59. Olaus J. Murie, "Campfire Lecture on Meanings," 27. Murie was reviewing the book by Storer. This now-classic book questioned postwar technology and whether man could find "within his heart the incentives and wisdom to use these new-found powers wisely, and with responsibility."

60. Shepard, *Coming Home to the Pleistocene*.

61. Olaus J. Murie, "Wilderness Philosophy," 58.

62. See Wilson, *Biophilia*.

63. For an account of findings in the field of exploratory behavior in the 1950s, see Fowler, *Curiosity and Exploratory Behavior*, and Anderson, *The Ulysses Factor*.

64. Olaus J. Murie, "Wilderness Philosophy," 59.

65. William O. Douglas, *My Wilderness: The Pacific West*, 10.

66. Brina Kessel interview, 22 January 2003.

67. Schaller, "Arctic Legacy," 64.

68. Olaus J. Murie, *Journeys to the Far North*, 225–26.

69. Olaus J. Murie, "Wilderness Philosophy," 59.

70. Margaret E. Murie, "A Live River in the Arctic," 10.

71. Ibid.

72. Robert Krear, "The Olaus Murie Brooks Range Expedition."

73. Olaus J. Murie, "Wilderness Philosophy," 61–62. Murie is citing a statement by Dr. Clayton G. Rudd in "In the Cause of Real Values," *Naturalist* (Spring 1961).

74. Schaller, "Arctic Legacy," 64.

75. William O. Douglas, *My Wilderness: The Pacific West*, 16–17.

76. Margaret E. Murie, *Two in the Far North*, 275.

77. See Csikszentmihalyi, *Flow*.

78. Margaret E. Murie, *Two in the Far North*, 321.

79. Ibid., 311.

80. Olaus J. Murie Field Notes, 2 August 1956, OMP, Box 8, Folder 43.

81. Olaus J. Murie, AWR Hearings, Part 1, 59.

82. The American concept of wilderness began with transcendentalists such as Ralph Waldo Emerson, Henry David Thoreau, and later romantic naturalists such as John Muir whose philosophies developed from childhood Christian faiths. Although Emerson, Thoreau, and Muir later rejected religious doctrine, their vocabulary of expression remained religious in tone and voice. Their frequent reference to wilderness as a temple or cathedral echoes through the current popular literature. The inspiration they found in wilderness, and the means by which they found it, parallels the experience of the leaders and prophets of most world religions including Jesus, Elijah, Moses, Mohammed, and the Buddha. For a detailed treatment of the spiritual and religious underpinning of the American wilderness movement, see Stephen Fox's chapter "Lord Man: The Religion of Conservation," pp. 358–73 in Fox, *The American Conservation Movement*. For summaries of relevant research on the psychology of religion and spiritual experience, see Emmons, *The Psychology of Ultimate Concerns*, and McDonald et al., "The Spirit in the Wilderness." See also Martin and Carlson, "Spiritual Dimensions of Health Psychology."

83. Olaus J. Murie, "Wild Country as a National Asset," 1–2.

84. William O. Douglas, *My Wilderness: The Pacific West*, 17.

85. Olaus J. Murie, "Wild Country as a National Asset," 2. The interpretation of Olaus's spirituality presented is synthesized from his many writings, from interviews with Mardy and sons Donald and Martin, and Glover's "Thinking Like a Wolverine."

86. William O. Douglas, *My Wilderness: The Pacific West*, 17. Douglas's father was a Presbyterian minister.

87. Olaus J. Murie, "Nature in the Arctic," 30.

88. Krear, "The Olaus Murie Brooks Range Expedition."

89. Olaus J. Murie, "Alaska with O. J. Murie," 2.

90. Olaus J. Murie, "Nature in the Arctic," 30.

91. Margaret E. Murie, *Two in the Far North*, 340.

92. Sumner, "Special Report"; Sumner and Leonard, "Protecting Mountain Meadows."

93. Olaus J. Murie, "Nature in the Arctic," 30.

94. Margaret E. Murie, *Two in the Far North*, 289.

95. As early as 1936 the Muries' friend Lowell Sumner wrote a report on the impacts of recreational use in which he questioned "how large a crowd can be turned loose in a wilderness without destroying its essential qualities." Nevertheless, his warning was largely unheeded until the 1970s. Today, slightly over half of designated wilderness areas have group size limits. The Arctic Refuge now limits guided groups to seven individuals for backpacking trips and ten for float trips.

96. Olaus J. Murie, *Journeys to the Far North*, 188.

97. Margaret E. Murie, AWR Hearings, Part 1, 60.

98. Margaret E. Murie, *Two in the Far North*, 374.

99. Olaus Murie, AWR Hearings, Part 1, 59.

100. Robert Marshall, *Arctic Wilderness*, ix, 2.

101. William O. Douglas, "For Every Man and Woman Who Loves the Wilderness," 23–24.

102. Olaus J. Murie to Walt Disney, 16 December 1956, RKP.

103. Darling, *Pelican in the Wilderness*, 333.

104. Olaus J. Murie Field Notes, 24 June 1956, OMP, Box 8, Folder 43.

105. For a more thorough treatment of primitivism, see Nash, *Wilderness and the American Mind*, and Oelschlaeger, *The Idea of Wilderness*.

106. Seton, *Boy Scouts of America*, 1, 2, quoted in Nash, *Wilderness and the American Mind*, 148.

107. Olaus J. Murie, "Boyhood Wilderness," 30. See also Murie's "Seton's Influence Renewed"; Murie's son Donald, in his interview with the author, affirms Seton's influence and the significance of *Two Little Savages*.

108. Zahniser, "The Need for Wilderness Areas," 41; Aldo Leopold, *A Sand County Almanac*, 274.

109. Olaus J. Murie, *Journeys to the Far North*, 242.

110. The Indians' perspective was provided by Peter Tritt during the course of numerous informal discussions with the author in Arctic Village during the late 1980s and early 1990s; Margaret E. Murie, *Two in the Far North*, 315.

111. Olaus J. Murie Field Notes, 15 July 1956, OMP, Box 8, Folder 43.

112. Olaus J. Murie Field Notes, 24 June 1956, OMP, Box 8, Folder 43.

113. Keith Herrington interview, 17 November 2004.

114. Margaret Tritt interview, 17 October 2001.

115. Olaus J. Murie Field Notes, 15 July 1956, OMP, Box 8, Folder 43; Olaus J. Murie, "Alaska with O. J. Murie," 30. Interviews with both Schaller and Krear affirm that Murie told the Indians a wilderness reserve would not interfere with their traditional activities.

116. Richard Carroll interview, 14 September 2002.

117. Olaus J. Murie, "Alaskan Summer on the Sheenjek River."

118. Morva Hoover interview, 18 December 2003.

119. Olaus J. Murie to George L. Collins, 29 November 1956, MMP, Box 2, Folder 18.

120. Arthur Hayr, AWR Hearings, Part 2, 365–68.

121. Charles Gray interview, 30 October 2003.

122. As reported in Nelson, *Northern Landscapes*, 45.

123. Olaus J. Murie to George L. Collins, 29 November 1956, MMP, Box 2, Folder 18.

124. Olaus J. Murie, "Alaska with O. J. Murie," 30.

125. Olaus J. Murie to Bishop William Gordon, 2 October 1957, MMP, Box 2, Folder 18.

126. Sigurd Olson Jr. to Olaus Murie, 29 February 1956, MMP, Box 2, Folder 18.

127. Lois Crisler to Olaus Murie, 24 October (no year), MMP, Box 2, Folder 18.

128. Ibid.

129. Olaus J. Murie to Fairfield Osborn, 4 November 1956, MMP, Box 2, Folder 18. In this letter Murie also discusses confusion regarding many aspects of the still-unnamed Arctic proposal. However, he definitively states that "there should be no prohibition of hunting as such."

130. The road had been cut by a military contractor in support of the cold-war buildup of coastal defense sites.

131. Lowell Sumner, "Your Stake in Alaska's Wildlife and Wilderness," 66. This often-cited article was inserted into the Senate hearing record by Bartlett at the request of Virginia Wood. AWR Hearings, Part 2, 337.

132. Ibid., 68–69.

133. Crisler, "Where Wilderness Is Complete," 4.

134. Ibid.

135. The Leopold quote was taken from the foreword to *A Sand County Almanac*, xix.

CHAPTER 5: WILDERNESS, WILDLIFE RANGE, OR BOTH?

1. Virginia Wood, letter to the editor, *Fairbanks Daily News-Miner*, 27 January 1958.

2. Buck Moore, AWR Hearings, Part 2, 140.

3. Jim King interview, 24 November 2003; Interior Department Solicitor Ted Stevens responds to Alaska Senator Bob Bartlett's questions regarding the effect an executive order would have on mining in AWR Hearings, Part 2, 434–36.

4. Olaus J. Murie to Fairfield Osborn, 18 February 1957, MMP. Box 2, Folder 18.

5. Phil Holdsworth, AWR Hearings, Part 2, 115–20. Holdsworth was formerly commissioner of mines.

6. Sumner, "The Pressures of Civilization," 5–6.

7. A. Starker Leopold, "Wilderness and Culture," 6–7.

8. Fifth Biennial Wilderness Conference, 3.

9. Olaus J. Murie to Fairfield Osborn, 18 February 1957, MMP, Box 2, Folder 18.

10. Olson, "The Spiritual Aspects of Wilderness," 140; "The Spiritual Need," 215.

11. Olson, *The Singing Wilderness*, 130; the definitive biography of Olson is David Backes, *A Wilderness Within*.

12. Collins, *The Art and Politics of Park Planning and Preservation*, 199.

13. Fifth Biennial Wilderness Conference, 13, 15.

14. For a discussion on these points between Interior Department Solicitor Ted Stevens and Alaska Senator Bob Bartlett, see AWR Hearings, Part 2, 428–29. This reasoning is also consistent with Jim King's recollection. Jim King interview, 24 November 2003.

15. George L. Collins, "Notes on Alaska Recreation Survey."

16. William O. Pruitt Jr. to Alaska Representative Ralph Rivers, 6 March 1959, MMP, Box 2, Folder 18.

17. Collins, "Notes on Alaska Recreation Survey."

18. Collins, *The Art and Politics of Park Planning and Preservation*, 199; George L. Collins interview, 28 March 1993.

19. As cited in Jim Rearden, letter to author, 2 December 2003, RKP.

20. Alaska Game Commission, 19th Annual Report.

21. Olaus J. Murie, "Shall We Destroy or Enjoy?," 2; Murie made a similar statement in "Prey of Poison."

22. Clarence J. Rhode to Olaus Murie, 21 May 1957, MMP, Box 2, Folder 18.

23. Margaret E. Murie, *Two in the Far North*, 357.

24. Olaus J. Murie, "Brief Account of a Journey to Alaska."

25. The Tanana Valley Sportsmens Association was an outgrowth of the Tanana Valley Game Protective and Propagation Association, and considered itself the first conservation organization in the Territory of Alaska. At the time it had about five hundred members.

26. The Tanana Valley Sportsmens Association's resolution of 14 May 1957, and the organization's supporting letters were included in the record of the AWR Hearings, Part 2, 293–95.

27. Ibid., 295–96.

28. At the Fairbanks AWR Hearings, Tanana Valley Sportsmens Association representative Glenn De Spain told Senator Bartlett the association had prepared the suggested plan. AWR Hearings, Part 2, 294.

29. George Marshall to Olaus Murie, 13 June 1957, MMP, Box 2, Folder 18. Marshall was mainly arguing against use of airplanes in wilderness.

30. Nelson, *Northern Landscapes.*

31. Joe Vogler interview, 1991.

32. Joe Vogler, AWR Hearings, Part 2, 228–34.

33. Ivan Thorall interview, 6 February 2004. Thorall's concern was in part validated in 1980 when ANILCA more than doubled the size of the original range.

34. Dr. John Buckley, AWR Hearings, Part 2, 395.

35. Mrs. Earl Cook, AWR Hearings, Part 2, 418–19.

36. Vernon E. Haik Sr. to Clarence J. Rhode, 1 June 1957, RKP.

37. Fox, *The American Conservation Movement,* 283.

38. Olaus J. Murie to Mrs. Paul Haggland, 2 October 1957, MMP, Box 2, Folder 18. Haggland was president of the Fairbanks Garden Club. Murie made similar statements in his many other solicitations of support.

39. Bryan P. Glass to Olaus Murie, 27 July 1957, MMP, Box 2, Folder 18.

40. Ira N. Gabrielson to Ross Leffler, 24 September 1957, RKP.

41. Richard E. Warner to Secretary Frederick A. Seaton, 2 December 1957, RKP.

42. Richard W. Westwood to Secretary Fred Seaton, 20 September 1957, RKP.

43. Philip H. Moore to Ross L. Leffler, 8 November 1957, RKP.

44. Miss Mary H. Harris to Area Administrator, Bureau of Land Management, 3 September 1957, RKP.

45. Clarence J. Rhode to Olaus J. Murie, 8 November 1957, MMP, Box 2, Folder 18.

46. Stewart Brandborg interview, 13 March 2003.

47. Stewart Brandborg, AWR Hearings, Part 1, 49.

48. "Statement of Alaska Sportsmens Council on Establishment of Arctic Wildlife Range, as Proposed by Senate Bill 1899 and House Bill 7045," AWR Hearings, Part 2, 422–23; A. W. "Bud" Boddy, AWR Hearings, Part 2, 92.

49. "Bud" Boddy, AWR Hearings, Part 2, 92.

50. As reported in *News Bulletin of the Alaska Conservation Society* 1, 3 (August 1960): 2. Virginia Wood was the editor.

51. "Arctic Wildlife Area Is Proposed," *Fairbanks Daily News-Miner,* 13 July 1957. The "national wilderness area system" to which Leffler referred existed only as a proposal in the Wilderness Bill Zahniser had drafted.

52. Dick Whittaker to Dr. and Mrs. Murie, 22 July 1957, MMP, Box 2, Folder 18.

53.   Memorandum from director, Bureau of Sport Fisheries and Wildlife to secretary of the interior, undated, RKP.

54.   Memorandum from director, Bureau of Sport Fisheries and Wildlife to Director, Bureau of Land Management, Subject: Establishment of Arctic Wildlife Range, 7 November 1957, RKP. This statement appeared in Sumner and Collins, "Arctic Wilderness," 14. Protection of wildlife, wilderness, and frontier values are the rationale for the action provided in the "Narrative Report of the U.S. Fish and Wildlife Service for period ending January 1, 1958, a memo from: Assistant Secretary for Fish and Wildlife to Members of Senate Committee on Interstate and Foreign Commerce and Members of House Committee on Merchant Marine and Fisheries," Sigurd F. Olson Papers, Box 80, Arctic Range Folder, Minnesota Historical Society.

55.   "Minutes of the Second Meeting of the Advisory Committee of Fish and Wildlife: Department of the Interior, November 14 and 15, 1957," Sigurd F. Olson Papers, Box 80, Arctic Range Folder.

56.   "Statement by Secretary Fred A. Seaton on Steps to Open Twenty Million Acres in Northern Alaska to Mining and Mineral Leasing," MMP, Box 2, Folder 18.

57.   Bob Bartlett, AWR Hearings, Part 2, 174; Ted Stevens, AWR Hearings, Part 2, 434.

58.   Ted Stevens, AWR Hearings, Part 2, 34; Martin Vorys, AWR Hearings, Part 2, 172.

59.   Bob Bartlett, AWR Hearings, Part 1, 48, and Part 2, 194.

60.   Robert Rausch, AWR Hearings, Part 2, 164–70.

61.   Robert and Reggie Rausch interview, 19 January 2005, RKP.

62.   "Alaska…The Great Land," *Fairbanks Daily News-Miner*, 20 November 1957.

63.   Michael Carey, "Fred Seaton of Nebraska and His Friend in Alaska," unpublished manuscript, RKP.

64.   Fairbanks Chamber of Commerce to BLM (Anchorage), 30 January 1958, ACS Papers, APR, Box 57, BLM File; "Game Range Backed by Chamber," *Fairbanks Daily News-Miner*, March 1958.

65.   Mrs. Mae N. Morris to Mr. Fred Seaton, 21 November 1957, RKP.

66.   George Schaller to Olaus and Mardy Murie, 23 November 1957, MMP, Box 2, Folder 18.

67.   Fairfield Osborn to Olaus, 16 December 1957, MMP, Box 2, Folder 18.

68.   George L. Collins to Olaus Murie, 29 November 1957, MMP, Box 2, Folder 18.

69.   Lowell Sumner to Olaus and Mardy Murie, 21 November 1957, MMP, Box 2, Folder 18.

70.   Olaus J. Murie to Lowell Sumner, 3 December 1957, MMP, Box 2, Folder 18.

71.   Thomson, "Ascent of Mount Michelson." R. E. (Pete) Isto published a similar account, "Mount Michelson, Brooks Range," in the *American Alpine Journal*.

72.   John P. Thomson interview.

73.   *Federal Register*, 21 January 1958, Doc. 58-456, 364.

74.   The optimism of miners and industry officials is illustrated throughout their testimony in the AWR Hearings, Part 2. The Geological Survey's incomplete information and speculation is noted in a memo from its director to the Interior Department's legislative counsel. Tho B. Nolan to legislative counsel, 14 March 1960, RKP. Owens's opinions are found in J. E. Owens to Senator O'Mahony, 19 November 1959, and J. E. Owens to Secretary of Interior, 14 September 1960, RKP.

75.   James A. Williams to Hon. E. L. "Bob" Bartlett, 22 December 1959, printed in AWR Hearings, Part 2, 133–34.

76.   Douglas B. Colp, AWR Hearings, Part 2, 256–57.

77.   Harold Strandberg, AWR Hearings, Part 2, 175–80.

78.   "That Arctic Wildlife Range" (editorial), *Fairbanks Daily News-Miner*, 29 January 1958. It should be noted that Clifford Cernick was the paper's editor; Snedden was president and publisher. According to Charles Gray, who would succeed Snedden, Snedden either wrote the Arctic Range editorials or approved any that Cernick wrote.

79.   Ben F. Potter to Honorable Fred Seaton, 1 April 1958, ACS Papers, Box 57, Folder 625.

80.   Memorandum from BLM Operations Supervisor, Fairbanks to the Area Administrator, BSF&W, 20 March 1958, RKP. The main category of opposition was that the commenter "objects to mining restrictions or oil and gas development."

81.   Ernest Wolff to Hon. Mr. Fred A. Seaton, 6 March 1958, ACS Papers, Box 57, Folder 626.

82.   Eskil Anderson, letter to the editor, *Jessen's Weekly*, 3 March 1958. *Jessen's Weekly* was published in Fairbanks.

83.   For Boddy, see A. W. "Bud" Boddy to All Conservationists, 17 April 1958, RKP. The supporting comments are found in the MMP, ACS, and Bartlett Papers, and RKP.

84.   Virginia Hill Wood, Celia M. Hunter, and Morton S. Wood to Director, Bureau of Land Management, 30 March 1958, ACS Papers, Box 57, Folder 625.

85.   James M. Lake to Director, Bureau of Land Management, 2 April 1958, ACS Papers, Box 57, Folder 625.

86.   George B. Schaller to Director, Bureau of Land Management, 5 April 1958, ACS Papers, Box 57, Folder 625.

87.   Rosella McCune to Mr. Edward Woozley, 13 April 1958, ACS Papers, Box 57, Folder 625.

88.   Herb and Lois Crisler to the Secretary of the Interior, Mr. Seaton, 14 May 1958, RKP. A response by Assistant Secretary Ross Leffler acknowledged that Crisler's letter "discusses a fundamental problem which is a matter of grave concern to the Department of the Interior." However, Leffler's mention that mining, hunting, and trapping would be allowed indicates that the department did not share the Crislers' deeper philosophical concern (Ross Leffler to Mr. and Mrs. Crisler, 29 May 1958, RKP).

89.   "Our Public Lands" (editorial), *Fairbanks Daily News-Miner*, 21 March 1958.

90.   "Holdsworth Blasts Wildlife Reserve," *Juneau Daily Empire*, 5 March 1958, RKP.

91.   "that 9,000,000-acre withdrawal" appeared in the *Bulletin*, a publication of the Territory of Alaska Department of Mines, based in Juneau. Although the article was unsigned, the *Fairbanks Daily News-Miner* attributed it to Commissioner Holdsworth. So did the Associated Press in "Holdsworth Blasts Wildlife Reserve."

92.   "Where Are the Mines?," *Fairbanks Daily News-Miner*, 7 March 1958.

93.   "That 9 Million Acre Withdrawal," *Fairbanks Daily News-Miner*, 14 March 1958, 4. In response to reader interest and allegations that the editorial did not fairly represent the points Holdsworth made, the *News-Miner* published his entire article. See "Article by Mines Commissioner Opposes Arctic Wildlife Range in N. E. Alaska," 17 March 1958, 6.

94.   H. Francis, letter to the editor, *Fairbanks Daily News-Miner*, 19 March 1958.

95.   Joe Vogler, letter to the editor, *Fairbanks Daily News-Miner*, 21 March 1958.

96.   Alfred W. Withrow, letter to the editor, *Fairbanks Daily News-Miner*, 11 March 1958.

97. C. M. Kinyon, letter to the editor, *Fairbanks Daily News-Miner*, 13 March 1958.

98. Fabian Carey, letter to the editor, *Fairbanks Daily News-Miner*, 13 March 1958.

99. Stanley Samuelson, letter to the editor, *Fairbanks Daily News-Miner*, 11 March 1958.

100. "Article by Mines Commissioner Opposes Arctic Wildlife Range in N. E. Alaska," *Fairbanks Daily News-Miner*, 7 March 1958.

101. "The Mischief Good Men Do" (editorial), *Fairbanks Daily News-Miner*, 17 March 1958.

102. Charles Gray interview, 6 February 2004.

103. As reported in "Seaton Opens Alaskan Area," *Washington Post* and *Times Herald*, 21 November 1957, A-2.

104. "Wildlife Group Throws Block in Alaska Statehood Hearing," *Fairbanks Daily News-Miner*, 16 March 1957. At issue was a territorial bill that would have set up a single commission to administer both commercial and sports fisheries as well as wildlife. Bud Boddy, president of the Alaska Sportsmens Council was cited as stating the commission would be "dominated by commercial fishing interests" at the expense of programs for the conservation of other resources.

105. Clarence J. Rhode to Phil R. Holdsworth, 6 March 1958, RKP.

106. Virginia Wood, letter to the editor, *Fairbanks Daily News-Miner*, 27 January 1958.

107. David R. Brower, "Mathematics for the Billions," 12.

108. Seaton, "America's Largest Wildlife Area," 119, 120, 119. The region's indigenous residents were not listed among those who would benefit from the area's preservation. Although authorship was attributed to Seaton, who had little background as an outdoorsman and no history of using such parlance, it was more likely written by Ted Swem or Olaus Murie and arranged for publication by Seaton's friend Sigurd Olson, who was president of the magazine's parent organization, the National Parks Association.

109. Howard Zahniser, AWR Hearings, Part 1, 56.

110. Dr. William O. Pruitt Jr., AWR Hearings, Part 2, 327.

111. Memorandum, Director, National Park Service to Secretary of the Interior, 24 January 1958, RKP. The statement limiting Natives' hunting and trapping to that "for their own needs" would have precluded their commercial trapping and bounty hunting of wolves, which were among their primary uses of the area.

112. Memorandum, Regional Director, Bureau of Sport Fish and Wildlife to Director, Bureau of Sport Fish and Wildlife, 7 February 1958, RKP.

113. Minutes of March 4, 1958, MMP, Box 2, Folder 18. For Brower's account of his role in the campaign, see his autobiography, *For Earth's Sake*, especially pages 486–87.

114. J. C. Boswell to Olaus Murie, 7 March 1958, MMP, Box 2, Folder 18.

115. Olaus J. Murie to John Boswell, 12 March 1958, MMP, Box 2, Folder 18.

116. Krear, "The Olaus Murie Brooks Range Expedition."

117. Olaus J. Murie to Fairfield Osborn, 15 March 1958, MMP, Box 2, Folder 18.

118. Jim King interview, 24 November 2003. King was a Fish and Wildlife Service game agent pilot and participated in the search for Rhode. Checking hunters would have been the responsibility of enforcement agent Stanley Fredericksen, who was in charge of wildlife law enforcement for the Brooks Range District. Rhode probably intended to stop to do some sheep hunting with his son Jack, who would soon leave for his final semester at the University of Washington. In the 1950s it was not uncommon for Fish and Wildlife Service pilots and others to hunt while conducting law-enforcement patrols.

119. Niilo Koponen, letter to the editor, *Fairbanks Daily News-Miner*, 20 August 1958. Regarding federal control of fish and wildlife, the main concern of Koponen and others was the use of fish traps in Alaska waters by Washington State fishermen and processors and their political influence on federal fisheries management.

120. Jack De Yonge, "Sportsman Denies Any Maneuver," *Fairbanks Daily News-Miner*, 20 August 1958.

121. "Secretary Sees Surge of Activity," *Fairbanks Daily News-Miner*, 25 August 1958.

122. "FWS Men Overdue on Flight," *Fairbanks Daily News-Miner*, 25 August 1958.

123. "Rhode, Fredericksen Unreported for Days," *Fairbanks Daily News-Miner*, 26 August 1958.

124. Jack De Yonge, "Relatives Join Hunt for Plane: Reporter Tells of Massive Arctic Search," *Fairbanks Daily News-Miner*, 29 August 1958.

125. As cited in Rearden, "Clarence Rhode." Rearden was a friend of Rhode's and was guiding hunters in the area at the time.

126. Fairbanks residents Debbie Miller and Sidney Stephens discovered the wreckage. For a detailed account of the discovery, see Miller, *Midnight Wilderness*, 137–60. Miller's account of the adventurous, challenging, and exploratory aspects of their trip that led to the discovery exemplifies the type of recreational experience many Arctic proponents hoped would be available here.

CHAPTER 6: FINALLY, LEGISLATION INTRODUCED

1. For a discussion of the psychological concept of "outcroppings," see Neuman, *Social Research Methods*, 438–39.

2. Ernest Gruening to Hon. Fred A. Seaton, 27 April 1959, RKP.

3. Allston Jenkens to Hon. Fred A. Seaton, 22 April 1959, RKP.

4. H. Robert Krear to Hon. Fred A. Seaton, 14 April 1959, RKP. Contributing to the interpretation were Robert Krear's interviews with the author.

5. Wilbur L. Libby to Dr. Fred A. Seaton, 14 May 1959, RKP.

6. Martin Murie interview, 16 December 2002, APR.

7. Margaret E. Murie to Mr. J. O. Kimartin, 31 March 1965, RKP.

8. Isto, "Alaskan Geographic Names," 77–84. Isto ended his presentation to the Alaskan scientists in attendance at the Twelfth Alaska Science Conference with a statement that epitomized what Murie opposed: "Many of you listening to me might some day give your name to a mountain or river now lying unknown and unnamed. By living and working here, and gaining some prominence in public-spirited service, your name may be preserved and remembered in the geographic record of Alaska" (p. 84). In 1966, following Isto's death, the mountain believed at the time to be the highest in the Brooks Range was renamed Isto. It had been formerly called Mount Leffingwell.

9. Gerald FitzGerald to Olaus J. Murie, 5 December 1956, RKP.

10. Olaus J. Murie to Hon. Fred A. Seaton, 8 December 1959, RKP. Murie may well have gone into greater detail in a subsequent telephone call.

11. Olaus J. Murie to Richard W. Westwood, 8 June 1959, RKP.

12. Fred A. Seaton to Mr. Jenkins, 29 April 1959, RKP. Seaton also stated in these letters that consideration was being given to renaming the Kenai Moose Range after Rhode.

13. Proclamation 4729 of 29 February 1980, *Federal Register*, Vol. 45, No. 44, Tuesday, 4 March 1980, Presidential Documents, 14003. Chuck Clusen, chairman of the Alaska

Coalition at the time, was present during the ceremony in the East Room of the White House. He recalls that the principle purpose of the ceremony was to stir up support for the pending Alaska National Interest Lands Conservation Act. Chuck Clusen interview, 27 July 2004, APR.

14.   H. Robert Krear to Mr. Jimmy Carter, 25 April 1980, RKP. As he mentioned in the letter, Krear was also involved in the effort to change the name of Mount McKinley National Park to "Denali," a Native name for the mountain.

15.   Bill Reffalt interview, 2 September 2004. In his interview with the author, Clusen also states that Douglas's name on the Arctic Refuge was "anathema" to Stevens.

16.   House Joint Memorial No. 23, in AWR Hearings, Part 1, 61.

17.   Henry Gettinger to the Honorable Fred A. Seaton, 17 March 1959, RKP.

18.   E. R. Barnes to Mr. Fred A. Seaton, 5 March 1958, Sigurd F. Olson Papers, Box 80, Arctic Range File.

19.   Douglas Ayres Jr. to Secretary of Interior Mr. Fred A. Seaton. Both Ayres's letters are dated 31 January 1959, RKP. The response Ayres received from Assistant Secretary Ross Leffler referenced "maintenance of undisturbed ecological and wilderness conditions" and the contradictory provisions for allowing mineral, oil, and gas leasing. Ross Leffler to Mr. Ayres, 26 February 1959, RKP.

20.   Martin Vorys to Fred A. Seaton, 4 June 1959, RKP.

21.   William O. Pruitt to Hon. Ralph J. Rivers, 6 March 1959, MMP, Box 2, Folder 18.

22.   Vogt, *The Road to Survival*, and Osborn, *Our Plundered Planet*.

23.   Senate Bill 4028, introduced 18 June 1958. The full text of the bill, along with detailed commentary, was printed in *Living Wilderness* (Summer–Fall 1958): 1–16.

24.   William O. Pruitt to Hon. Ralph J. Rivers, 6 March 1959, MMP, Box 2, Folder 18.

25.   This statement was part of a handwritten note by Pruitt to Olaus, written on a copy of the above correspondence. MMP, Box 2, Folder 18.

26.   Olaus J. Murie to Hon. Ralph J. Rivers, 27 March 1959, MMP. Box 2, Folder 18. During the Senate hearings Rivers expressed conceptual support for the Range and indicated that his chief concern was the loss of highway funding the withdrawal would cause (see Chapter 7). AWR Hearings, Part 2, 115.

27.   Ralph J. Rivers to Mr. Olaus J. Murie, 2 April 1959, MMP. Box 2, Folder 18.

28.   Minutes: "Arctic Wildlife Range Meeting, October 28, 1958. Department of Interior—Room 3156," RKP.

29.   Ross Leffler to Mr. Robertson, 10 March 1958, RKP.

30.   Sigurd F. Olson to Mr. Ross Leffler, 16 March 1959, RKP.

31.   Draft no. 580307, titled: "To U.S. State Dept for Secretary of External Affairs of the Dominion of Canada regarding joint action setting aside as an Arctic Game Range and Wilderness Area, the Brooks Range on either side of the Alaska-Yukon Border" (undated), RKP.

32.   Robert Rausch, "The Outlook for Conservation in Alaska." Address presented to the Sixth Biennial Wilderness Conference, San Francisco, 20–21 March 1959, RKP.

33.   Doris F. Leonard to the Secretary of the Interior, 22 March 1959, MMP, Box 2, Folder 18.

34.   "Secretary Seaton Sends Arctic Wildlife Range Bill to Congress," Department of Interior Information Service, 1 May 1959, RKP.

35. Fred A. Seaton to Hon. Richard Nixon, 30 April 1959, in AWR Hearings, Part 1, 2–3.

36. Authority for the Fish and Wildlife Service to delegate some wildlife management functions on wildlife refuges to the states was found in the Code of Federal Regulations, 1949 Edition, Title 50, Subpart C. Subsection 21.34 stated that "state cooperation may be enlisted in the regulation, management, and operation" of refuges that allow hunting. Assistant Secretary Leffler describes the federal and state roles in managing hunting on refuges and the ultimate supremacy of the federal government in his response to Senator Bartlett. AWR Hearings, Part 2, 442–44, 448–49.

37. Harold Strandberg to Hon. E. L. Bartlett, 16 May 1959, in AWR Hearings, Part 1, 62.

38. William A. Egan to Honorable Fred A. Seaton, 25 May 1959, RKP.

39. "Wildlife Range—Boon to State" (editorial), *Fairbanks Daily News-Miner*, 21 May 1959. Olaus Murie wrote Clifford Cernick, the paper's editor, thanking him for this and previous editorials, which he considered evidence of a hopeful trend toward greater recognition of Alaska's intangible values. Olaus J. Murie to Mr. Clifford Cernick, 29 May 1959, MMP, Box 2, Folder 18.

40. Charles Gray, AWR Hearings, Part 2, 389–91. See also Charles Gray interview.

41. Statement of C. R. Gutermuth, Wildlife Management Institute, to the House Committee on Merchant Marine and Fisheries, Subcommittee on Fisheries and Wildlife Conservation, Hearings, H.R. 7045, 156–63.

42. C. L. Anderson to Hon. Ernest Gruening, 21 May 1959, in AWR Hearings, Part 1, 62–63. Anderson's perspective in regard to the state vs. federal wildlife authority issue is detailed in "Statement of Clarence L. Anderson, Commissioner of the Alaska Department of Fish and Game, Juneau, Alaska." It was read at the Juneau Senate hearing by James Brooks, chief of the division of game of the Alaska Department of Fish and Game, and entered into the record by Bartlett. AWR Hearings, Part 2, 107–8.

43. Charles F. Herbert, AWR Hearings, Part 2, 184.

44. A. W. "Bud" Boddy to Mr. Ross Leffler, 30 September 1959, RKP.

45. These three resolutions were reported in the "Statement of Clarence Anderson," AWR Hearings, Part 2, 108. In later testimony the Alaska Board of Game chairman offered the opinion that all Board of Game members personally supported Governor Egan's unqualified opposition to the range. Richard Janson, AWR Hearings, Part 2, 198–200.

46. Urban C. Nelson to Forbes L. Baker, 19 October 1959, RKP.

47. Fabian Carey, letter to the editor, *Fairbanks Daily News-Miner*, 27 May 1959. The wolf refuge Carey referred to was probably the Nelchina wolf study area, temporarily closed to the taking of wolves for research purposes.

48. John P. Thomson, letter to the editor, *Fairbanks Daily News-Miner*, 26 May 1959.

49. Virginia Hill Wood, letter to the editor, *Fairbanks Daily News-Miner*, 6 June 1959.

50. Stewart Brandborg interviews, 13 March 2003, 9 November 2002. Brandborg believes the federation's efforts generated hundreds of letters to House and Senate committee members. It is doubtful that any except Alaska's single member, Bartlett, would have archived them. None of them were found in any of the relevant collections this research effort was able to locate.

51. "Main Trails and Bypaths" (editorial), *Alaska Sportsman* (July 1959), 7.

52.   Miss Nancy Camp to Mr. Fred A. Seaton, 26 June 1959, RKP. Although the editorial that prompted her to write was specific to the Arctic Range proposal, she apparently was also supporting the concurrent efforts to establish the Kuskokwim and Izembek refuges as well.

53.   Olaus J. Murie to Mr. Bob Henning, 14 July 1959, MMP. Box 2, Folder 18.

54.   Robert A. Henning to Mr. Olaus J. Murie, 20 July 1959, MMP. Box 2, Folder 18. Olaus again responded to Henning, pointing out the number of Alaskan individuals and organizations that supported the range. Olaus J. Murie to Mr. Robert A. Henning, 28 July 1959, MMP, Box 2, Folder 18.

CHAPTER 7: SENATE HEARINGS

1.   Olaus J. Murie, AWR Hearings, Part 2, 457.

2.   Attending the hearings were committee staff members Harold Baynton, Harry Huse, and Frank Barton. Congressman Morgan Moulder of Missouri participated in the Anchorage hearing and Alaska's congressman, Ralph Rivers, participated in the Juneau hearing. John Buckley, an advisor to Leffler, accompanied the committee on six Alaska hearings.

3.   Victor Fischer, *Alaska's Constitutional Convention*, 22–23. See also Claus-M. Naske, *Bob Bartlett of Alaska*.

4.   Committee on Merchant Marine and Fisheries.

5.   Sherman Noyes and Senator Bartlett, AWR Hearings, Part 2, 374.

6.   Senator Bartlett, Secretary Leffler, Mr. Stevens, and Dr. Buckley, AWR Hearings, Part 2, 451.

7.   John L. Buckley to Mr. Sigurd F. Olson, 16 September 1959, MMP, Box 2, Folder 18.

8.   Ross Leffler to Bud (Boddy), undated, MMP, Box 2, Folder 18.

9.   Ross Leffler to Mr. Sig Olson, Sigurd F. Olson Papers, Box 80, Arctic Range Folder.

10.   Olaus J. Murie to Mr. Ross Leffler, 7 October 1959, MMP, Box 2, Folder 18.

11.   Ginny Wood to Olaus, 30 April 1957, MMP, Box 2, Folder 18.

12.   For a history of the organization's founding, see *News Bulletin of the Alaska Conservation Society*, March 1960 and Summer 1961 issues. See also Celia Hunter's comments in McCloskey, *Wilderness*, 186–87. Bolstered by their success with this first major Alaska environmental conflict, the society soon thereafter came to play a leading role in blocking two subsequent environmentally destructive proposals: the use of nuclear devices to blast a harbor in northwest Alaska and the construction of a dam on the Yukon River at Rampart Canyon.

13.   "Too Big? Too Soon? NO!" (editorial), *Fairbanks Daily News-Miner*, 20 October 1959.

14.   "Vital Hearings Begin Oct. 29" (editorial), *Fairbanks Daily News-Miner*, 23 October 1959. Also that day was the front-page headline "SPORTSMEN BACK HUGE RESERVE," which reported the support of the Alaska Sportsmen's Council for the range at the Juneau hearing.

15.   AWR Hearings, Parts 1 and 2.

16.   Frank Doogan, AWR Hearings, Part 2, 90.

17.   Patricia Oakes, AWR Hearings, Part 2, 410.

18.   Urban C. Nelson to Howard Zahniser, 20 November 1959, RKP.

19. Charles Purvis, AWR Hearings, Part 2, 420.

20. Hon. B. J. Logan, AWR Hearings, Part 2, 201–6.

21. Statement of Alaska Sportsmen's Council, AWR Hearings, Part 2, 422.

22. Harold Strandberg, AWR Hearings, Part 2, 175.

23. Paul Palmer, AWR Hearings, Part 2, 311.

24. Irving Reed, AWR Hearings, Part 2, 265.

25. Dr. Helen Shenitz, AWR Hearings, Part 2, 106.

26. Anore Bucknell, AWR Hearings, Part 2, 281.

27. Marcus F. Jensen, AWR Hearings, Part 2, 95.

28. Reggie Rausch, AWR Hearings, Part 2, 145.

29. Olaus J. Murie, AWR Hearings, Part 2, 465.

30. Charles Keim, AWR Hearings, Part 2, 282.

31. Morton S. Wood, AWR Hearings, Part 2, 333.

32. Dixie Baade, AWR Hearings, Part 2, 77–78.

33. Hon. Irene Ryan, AWR Hearings, Part 2, 157.

34. Senator Bartlett, AWR Hearings, Part 2, 138.

35. Congressman Rivers, AWR Hearings, Part 2, 114.

36. Dr. Helen Shenitz, AWR Hearings, Part 2, 105–6.

37. Morton S. Wood, AWR Hearings, Part 2, 333–34.

38. Dan L. Rudisill, AWR Hearings, Part 2, 137.

39. Peter Bading, AWR Hearings, Part 2, 147–156.

40. Dixie Baade, AWR Hearings, Part 2, 78.

41. Senator Bartlett, AWR Hearings, Part 2, 452.

42. Charles E. Stout, AWR Hearings, Part 2, 360.

43. Harry Rufus Geron, AWR Hearings, Part 2, 397.

44. Senator Bartlett, AWR Hearings, Part 2, 192.

45. Gerald Vogelsang, AWR Hearings, Part 2, 358.

46. Margaret E. Murie, AWR Hearings, Part 2, 59.

47. William Pruitt, AWR Hearings, Part 2, 326.

48. Olaus J. Murie, AWR Hearings, Part 2, 457.

49. Hon. Warren Taylor, AWR Hearings, Part 2, 245.

50. Charles E. Stout, AWR Hearings, Part 2, 360.

51. Hon. Ernest Gruening, AWR Hearings, Part 1, 14.

52. Irving Reed, AWR Hearings, Part 2, 266.

53. James Brooks, AWR Hearings, Part 2, 113.

54. Brina Kessel, AWR Hearings, Part 2, 324.

55. Wm. F. Cairns Jr., AWR Hearings, Part 2, 187.

56. Dr. William O. Pruitt, AWR Hearings, Part 2, 326. Senator Bartlett shared the concern that polar bears might become extinct. AWR Hearings, Part 2, 158.

57. James M. Lake, AWR Hearings, Part 2, 396.

58. Buck Harris, AWR Hearings, Part 2, 161.

59. J. W. Penfold, AWR Hearings, Part 1, 38.

60. Anore Bucknell, AWR Hearings, Part 2, 282.
61. Fabian Carey, AWR Hearings, Part 2, 304–5.
62. Frank Griffin, AWR Hearings, Part 2, 370.
63. John Buckley, AWR Hearings, Part 2, 445–46.
64. Senator Bartlett, AWR Hearings, Part 2, 138, 99.
65. Leslie A. Viereck, AWR Hearings, Part 2, 408.
66. Stewart Brandborg, AWR Hearings, Part 1, 51.
67. Francis S. L. Williamson, AWR Hearings, Part 2, 166.
68. Brina Kessel, AWR Hearings, Part 2, 324.
69. Dr. Laurence Irving, AWR Hearings, Part 2, 141.
70. Anore Bucknell, AWR Hearings, Part 2, 281.
71. Virginia Wood, AWR Hearings, Part 2, 335.
72. Emery F. Tobin, AWR Hearings, Part 2, 81.
73. Alice Stuart, AWR Hearings, Part 2, 412–14.
74. John P. Thomson and Senator Bartlett, AWR Hearings, Part 2, 350–54.
75. Stewart Brandborg, AWR Hearings, Part 1, 49–52.
76. Celia Hunter, AWR Hearings, Part 2, 342.
77. Virginia Hill Wood, AWR Hearings, Part 2, 335–36.
78. Richard Cooley, AWR Hearings, Part 2, 125.
79. Iver Johnson, AWR Hearings, Part 2, 235.
80. Senator Bartlett, AWR Hearings, Part 2, 99, 268, 84, 117.
81. Ted C. Mathews, AWR Hearings, Part 2, 226.
82. Charles F. Herbert, AWR Hearings, Part 2, 183.
83. Irving Reed, AWR Hearings, Part 2, 265–66.
84. Charles Gray, AWR Hearings, Part 2, 390–91.
85. Olaus J. Murie, AWR Hearings, Part 2, 456.
86. James D. Crawford, AWR Hearings, Part 2, 275–76.
87. Phil Holdsworth, AWR Hearings, Part 2, 116.
88. Arthur Hayr, AWR Hearings, Part 2, 367–68. The *News-Miner* editorial Hayr cited was published the day before, on 30 October 1959.
89. Leo Anthony, AWR Hearings, Part 2, 143–44.
90. Charles F. Herbert, AWR Hearings, Part 2, 186.
91. Senator Bartlett and Ted Stevens, AWR Hearings, Part 2, 438.
92. John C. Boswell, AWR Hearings, Part 2, 375–76.
93. Carl G. Parker, AWR Hearings, Part 2, 258–59.
94. Dean Earl H. Beistline, AWR Hearings, Part 2, 249–50.
95. Celia Hunter, AWR Hearings, Part 2, 341.
96. Morton S. Wood, AWR Hearings, Part 2, 334.
97. Frederick C. Dean, AWR Hearings, Part 2, 406–7.
98. Stewart M. Brandborg, AWR Hearings, Part 1, 50.
99. Charles E. Stout, AWR Hearings, Part 2, 360.
100. Joe Vogler, AWR Hearings, Part 2, 231.

101. Senator Bartlett, AWR Hearings, Part 2, 454.

102. Dean Earl H. Beistline, AWR Hearings, Part 2, 251.

103. Denny G. Breaid, AWR Hearings, Part 2, 409.

104. Dean Earl H. Beistline, AWR Hearings, Part 2, 248.

105. Ted C. Mathews, AWR Hearings, Part 2, 227.

106. Celia Hunter, AWR Hearings, Part 2, 343.

107. John P. Thomson, AWR Hearings, Part 2, 351.

108. Wenzel Raith, AWR Hearings, Part 2, 364.

109. Hon. Ernest Gruening, AWR Hearings, Part 1, 7.

110. Richard Dowing, AWR Hearings, Part 2, 121.

111. Darrrell Kniffen, AWR Hearings, Part 2, 411.

112. Martin Vorys, AWR Hearings, Part 2, 170.

113. Veryl Gunderson, AWR Hearings, Part 2, 131.

114. Virginia Hill Wood, AWR Hearings, Part 2, 336.

115. Anore Bucknell, AWR Hearings, Part 2, 282.

116. Morton S. Wood, AWR Hearings, Part 2, 333.

117. Wenzel Raith, AWR Hearings, Part 2, 363.

118. Joe Vogler, AWR Hearings, Part 2, 232.

119. Wenzel Raith, AWR Hearings, Part 2, 362.

120. Stewart Brandborg, AWR Hearings, Part 1, 49–52.

121. Virginia Hill Wood, Senator Bartlett, AWR Hearings, Part 2, 337–38.

122. John Haydukovich, AWR Hearings, Part 2, 380–81.

123. Alice Stuart, AWR Hearings, Part 2, 413–14.

124. Charles J. Ott, AWR Hearings, Part 2, 339.

125. A. W. "Bud" Boddy, AWR Hearings, Part 2, 92.

126. Lafayette Huffman, AWR Hearings, Part 2, 288.

127. Margaret E. Murie, AWR Hearings, Part 1, 60.

128. Buck Moore, AWR Hearings, Part 2, 139–40.

129. Harry Geron, AWR Hearings, Part 2, 396.

130. Hon. Ernest Gruening, AWR Hearings, Part 1, 3–10.

131. Olaus J. Murie, AWR Hearings, Part 1, 59.

132. Wenzel Raith, AWR Hearings, Part 2, 363.

133. Marjorie Rees, AWR Hearings, Part 2, 410.

134. Frederick Hadleigh-West, AWR Hearings, Part 2, 305.

135. Richard Cooley, AWR Hearings, Part 2, 129.

136. Ted Stevens, AWR Hearings, Part 2, 434.

137. Senator Bartlett, AWR Hearings, Part 2, 456.

138. Olaus J. Murie, AWR Hearings, Part 2, 457.

CHAPTER 8: HOUSE PASSAGE, SENATE INACTION, EXECUTIVE ACTION

1. Statement by Senator E.L. (Bob) Bartlett, (D-AK), ACS Papers, Box 57, Folder 623.

2. Urban C. Nelson to Howard Zahniser, 20 November 1959, RKP.

3.   In his report, Claus-M. Naske offers a slightly different tally of Alaskans' testimony: seventy-three in support of the range, fifty-three against, and twelve whose support or opposition was conditional or unclear.

4.   Congressman Rivers, AWR Hearings, Part 2, 115. The House committee reported H.R. 7045 to the full House on 5 August 1959.

5.   *Fairbanks Daily News-Miner*, 31 December 1959.

6.   In a formal statement, Representative Rivers stated he withdrew his opposition because he believed a favorable amendment to the Federal Highway Act was forthcoming. "Statement of Representative Ralph J. Rivers, Congressman from Alaska, before the Subcommittee on Fish and Wildlife of the House Committee on Merchant Marine and Fisheries, on H. R. 7045," MMP, Box 2, Folder 18. However, Rivers was quoted in the newspaper as saying, "I wasn't making enough progress so I let it go through. I felt our Senators will oppose it in its present form and any reduction in land area can be made by them." *Fairbanks Daily News-Miner*, 14 February 1960.

7.   "Seaton Comments on the Arctic Wildlife Range," *News Bulletin of the Alaska Conservation Society* 1 (March 1960).

8.   Statement by Senator E. L. (Bob) Bartlett, (D-AK), ACS Papers, Box 57, Folder 623.

9.   Olaus J. Murie to Hon. E. L. Bartlett, 27 July 1960, MMP, Box 2, Folder 18.

10.   Olaus J. Murie to Hon. E. L. Bartlett, 17 August 1960, MMP, Box 2, Folder 18.

11.   Sigurd F. Olson to Mr. Fred Seaton, 6 October 1960, Sigurd F. Olson Papers, Box 80, Arctic Range Folder, Minnesota Historical Society.

12.   A. W. "Bud" Boddy to Mr. George W. Abbot, 12 October 1960, Sigurd F. Olson Papers, Box 20, Arctic Range Folder, Minnesota Historical Society.

13.   John P. Thomson to Hon. Fred Seaton, 10 July 1960, RKP.

14.   "Governor's Office—News Release," 26 September 1960, ACS Papers, Box 57, Folder 623.

15.   Leslie A. Viereck to Governor William A. Egan, 28 September 1960, ACS Papers, Box 57, Folder 623.

16.   Press Release, from the Office of Senator Ernest Gruening, 12 December 1960, E. L. Bartlett Papers, Box 11, Folder 113.

17.   Sigurd F. Olson to George L. Collins, 2 December 1970, Sigurd Olson Papers, Box 80, Arctic Range Folder.

18.   Sigurd F. Olson to Mr. Fred Seaton, 6 October 1960, Sigurd F. Olson Papers, Box 80, Arctic Range Folder, Minnesota Historical Society. Olson's intervention with Seaton is described in David Backes's biography of Olson, *A Wilderness Within*, 298–99.

19.   As reported by David R. Brower in *For Earth's Sake*, 486.

20.   Mercedes Eicholz interview, 15 June 2004, APR; and Cathy Stone Douglas, interview, 2 August 2004.

21.   "Secretary Seaton Establishes New Arctic National Wildlife Range," Department of the Interior Information Service, 7 December 1960, RKP.

22.   Ibid.

23.   "Alaska Gets Wildlife Ranges," *Fairbanks Daily News-Miner*, 7 December 1960.

24.   Eisenhower, "Special Message to the Congress," 393; and Valoise Armstrong, Eisenhower Library archivist, letter to author, 14 April 2005.

25. Mardy Murie to Dr. Fairfield Osborn, 7 January 1961, MMP, Box 2, Folder 18.

26. Ginny and Celia to Olaus and Mardie, 8 December, 1960, MMP, Box 2, Folder 18.

27. Crisler, *Where Wilderness Is Complete*, 36.

28. William O. Pruitt Jr. to Dr. Olaus Murie, 9 December 1960, MMP, Box 2, Folder 18.

29. "Who Should Be Embarrassed?" (editorial), *Fairbanks Daily News-Miner*, 7 December 1960.

30. "Alaska Winds Up with More Open Acres" (editorial), *Anchorage Daily Times*, 12 December 1960.

31. A. W. "Bud" Boddy to Mr. Olaus Murie, 12 December 1960, MMP, Box 2, Folder 18. Statements by Boddy, Wood, and Hunter reflect the concern of many supporters that the secretary's action might not constitute final resolution of the issue. They knew Seaton might make a final attempt at legislative establishment, which he did, unsuccessfully, a month later. They also knew that state officials would press the next administration to revoke the establishing order, which they did, also unsuccessfully. Supporters probably presumed that if state officials could not get the order revoked, they would seek a legislative resolution that would be more favorable to their interests, which they did not. Thus, the victory was somewhat tentative, and this was probably the reason why the national organizations did not celebrate or issue press releases heralding what turned out to be their final victory.

32. George Widich to Senator E. L. Bartlett, 4 April 1961, E. L. Bartlett Papers, Box 11, Folder 112, APR.

33. "Here Is Text of Egan's Statement on Land Order," *Fairbanks Daily News-Miner*, 7 December 1960.

34. Press Release: "From the Office of Senator Ernest Gruening," 12 December 1960, E. L. Bartlett Papers, Box 11, Folder 113, APR.

35. Ernest Gruening to Secretary of Interior-designate Stewart Udall, 11 December 1960, E. L. Bartlett Papers, Box 11, Folder 113, APR.

36. Fred Seaton to Hon. Richard Nixon, 13 January 1961, and "Seaton Asks Legislative Confirmation of Arctic Wildlife Range," Department of the Interior Information Service News Release, 16 January 1961. E. L. Bartlett Papers, Box 11, Folder 113, APR.

37. "Arctic Wildlife Range Legislation Requires Amendment Now," *Conservation News* (undated clipping), RKP.

38. Ernest Gruening, E. L. Bartlett, Ralph J. Rivers to Honorable Stewart L. Udall, 15 March 1961, E. L. Bartlett Papers, Box 11, Folder 112, APR.

39. Ernest Gruening to Hon. William A. Egan, 27 June 1961, E. L. Bartlett Papers, Box 11, Folder 112, APR.

40. E. L. Bartlett to Honorable William A. Egan. 29 June 1961, E. L. Bartlett Papers, Box 11, Folder 112, APR.

41. Fairfield Osborn to Hon. Stewart L. Udall, 26 April 1961, RKP.

42. "Statement Relating to State Administration of the Arctic Wildlife Range," and E. L. Bartlett, Ernest Gruening, Ralph J. Rivers to Honorable Stewart L. Udall, 11 August 1961, E. L. Bartlett papers, Box 11, Folder 112, APR.

43. Olaus J. Murie to Mr. David L. Spencer, 6 January 1961, MMP, Box 2, Folder 18.

44. William O. Pruitt Jr. to Mr. Urban C. Nelson, 14 February 1961, RKP.

45. "Arctic Wildlife," *Congressional Record—Senate*, 21 September 1961, 19362–64.

46. E. L. Bartlett to Hon. Michael J. Kirwan, 11 April 1961, E. L. Bartlett Papers, Box 11, Folder 112, APR. Kirwan was the committee chairman.

47. Virginia Wood interview, 10 November 2002.

CHAPTER 9: A SYMBOL OF WILDERNESS

1. Olaus J. Murie, AWR Hearings, Part 1, 59.

2. Nash, *Wilderness and the American Mind*, 1–3.

3. Olaus J. Murie, "Arctic Wilderness," 10; "Nature in the Arctic," 30.

4. Sumner, "Arctic National Wildlife Refuge Address."

5. Olaus J. Murie, "The Grizzly Bear and the Wilderness," 73.

6. Bill Reffalt interview, 25 January 2005.

7. Frank Keim interview, 9 July 1997.

8. Aldo Leopold, *A Sand County Almanac*, 274.

9. Keith Echelmeyer interview, 22 November 2000.

10. Arctic Refuge Science Letter Signatories to the Honorable George W. Bush, 2005; Edward O. Wilson to Colleagues, 5 January 2005, RKP.

11. U.S. Fish and Wildlife Service, letter to prospective visitors (undated). ANWR Files.

12. Wuethner, "Hiking and Floating the Arctic National Wildlife Refuge Offers a Sanctuary for the Spirit," 22.

13. Sandy Jamieson interview, 21 February 1999.

14. George L. Collins interview, 28 March 1993.

15. Milton, *Nameless Valleys, Shining Mountains*, 105.

16. Zahniser, "The Need for Wilderness Areas," 41.

17. Marshall, *Arctic Wilderness*, 1.

18. Collins and Sumner, "Northeast Alaska," 13.

19. Debbie Miller interview, 18 September 1997.

20. Jimmy Carter, "Foreword" to Banerjee, *Seasons of Life and Land*, 13. As noted, the cultural heritage for which this area would serve as a touchstone referred to the short period of Euro-American westward expansion. How preservation might serve to perpetuate the history and culture of the area's indigenous people was hardly mentioned. But by the 1960s and 1970s, the ever-evolving wilderness concept came to reflect society's changing attitudes toward Native Americans. By the late 1980s, protection of Native tradition and culture had become a prominent rationale for opposing oil development in the area and preserving its wilderness qualities. Today, no listing of Arctic Refuge values would be complete without it.

21. Virginia Hill Wood, AWR Hearings, Part 2, 338.

22. Margaret E. Murie, AWR Hearings, Part 1, 60.

23. Stewart Brandborg interview, 20 January 2005.

24. Williams, "Wild Mercy," 171.

25. The legislation was titled "An Act to set apart a certain Tract of Land lying near the Head-waters of the Yellowstone River as a public Park." For a detailed study of the role of the campfire story in Yellowstone's establishment, see Schullery and Whittlesey, *Myth and History in the Creation of Yellowstone National Park*; see also Sellars, *Preserving Nature in the National Parks*, 7–10.

26.   Dunlap and Van Liere, "The 'New Environmental Paradigm'"; "Commitment to the Dominant Social Paradigm."

27.   Aldo Leopold, *A Sand County Almanac*, xix.

28.   Philippon, *Conserving Words*, 28.

29.   Sumner, "Arctic National Wildlife Refuge Address."

30.   Zahniser, "The Need for Wilderness Areas."

31.   Charles Konigsburg, "It's a R-E-F-U-G-E," in Lentfer and Servid, *Arctic Refuge*, 31–32.

32.   Olaus J. Murie to Hon. E. L. Bartlett, 17 August 1960, MMP, Box 2, Folder 18.

References

Articles and Papers

"Arctic Wildlife Range Film." *News Bulletin of the Alaska Conservation Society* 1 (March 1960).

Brower, David R. "Mathematics for the Billions." *Sierra Club Bulletin* (January 1958): 11–13.

Carey, Michael. "Birth of a Cause." *Anchorage Press* 13 (5–11 February 2004): 5.

———. "Fred Seaton of Nebraska and His Friend in Alaska." Unpublished manuscript, RKP.

Clawson, Marion. "The Crisis in Outdoor Recreation." Reprint no. 13. Washington, DC: Resources for the Future, Inc., 1959.

Collins, George L., and Lowell Sumner. "Northeast Arctic: The Last Great Wilderness." *Sierra Club Bulletin* 38 (October 1953): 13–26.

———. "Background Information for Use in Connection with a Proposal for an Arctic International Wildlife Range." *University of British Columbia Law Review* 6(1) (June 1971): 3–11.

———. "Consideration of the Arctic National Wildlife Range in the Proposal for a Trans Alaska-Canada Gas Transmission Line." 1973. George L. Collins Papers, APR.

———. "Notes on Alaska Recreation Survey, Special Reference ANWR Proposal, as Requested in Letter of 2 November 1985 from Mrs. Debbie Miller to George L. Collins." George L. Collins Papers, APR.

The Conservation Foundation. "Alaska Program Appraisal." New York: Wildlife Conservation Society and New York Zoological Park, 1952.

Crisler, Louis. "Where Wilderness Is Complete." *Living Wilderness* 60 (Spring 1957): 1–4.

Dedera, Don. "A Conservationist's Search for Truth: Famed Naturalist George Collins Explains What It Means to Be a Conservationist." *Exxon USA* (undated). George L. Collins Papers, APR.

Doherty, Jim. "The Arctic National Wildlife Refuge: The Best of the Last Wild Places." *Smithsonian* 12 (March 1996): 32–40.

Douglas, William O. "For Every Man and Woman Who Loves the Wilderness." *Living Wilderness* 58 (Fall–Winter 1956–57): 23–24.

Dunlap, R. E., and K. D. Van Liere. "Commitment to the Dominant Social Paradigm and Concern for Environmental Quality. *Social Science Quarterly.* 65 (1984): 1013–28.

———. "The 'New Environmental Paradigm': A Proposed Measuring Instrument and Preliminary Results." *Journal of Environmental Education* 9 (Summer 1978): 10–19.

Eisenhower, Dwight D. "Special Message to the Congress on the Legislative Program," 3 May 1960. *Public Papers of the Presidents of the United States, D. D. Eisenhower, 1960–61.* Washington, DC: GPO, 1961.

Findlay, J. D. "History and Status of the Arctic National Wildlife Range." *University of British Columbia Law Review* 6(1) (1971): 15–21.

Glover, James M. "Romance, Recreation, and Wilderness: Influences on the Life and Work of Bob Marshall." *Environmental History Review* 14 (1990): 22–39.

———. "Thinking Like a Wolverine: The Ecological Evolution of Olaus Murie." *Environmental Review* 12 (Fall–Winter 1989): 29–45.

Hadleigh-West, Frederick. "Anthropology in the Arctic National Wildlife Range." In *Science in Alaska,* ed. George Dahlgren Jr., 51–53. College, AK: Alaska Division, American Association for the Advancement of Science, 1961.

Henning, Robert. "Main Trails and Bypaths" (editorial). *Alaska Sportsman* (July 1959): 7.

Isto, R. E. "Alaskan Geographic Names." In *Science in Alaska,* ed. George Dahlgren Jr., 77–84. College, AK: Alaska Division of the American Association for the Advancement of Science, 1961.

———. "Mount Michelson, Brooks Range." *American Alpine Journal* 32 (1958): 93–95.

Kaye, Roger. "Alaska and Beyond: The Wilderness Legacy of Robert Marshall." *Wild Earth* 4 (Winter 2000): 44–49.

———. "The Arctic National Wildlife Refuge: An Exploration of the Meanings Embodied in America's Last Great Wilderness." In *Wilderness Science in a Time of Change,* comps. Stephen F. McCool, David N. Cole, William T. Borrie, Jennifer O'Loughlin, vol. 2, 73–80. Ogden, UT: U.S. Department of Agriculture, Forest Service, Rocky Mountain Research Station, RMRS-P-15, 2000.

Kessel, Brina, and George B. Schaller. "Birds of the Upper Sheenjek Valley, Northeastern Alaska." *Biological Papers of the University of Alaska* 4 (May 1960).

Krear, Robert. "The Olaus Murie Brooks Range Expedition." Unpublished eighty-page manuscript comprising part three of Krear's draft book describing his career, RKP.

Laycock, George. "Our Last Arctic Wilderness—A Gift Denied?" *Audubon* (July 1976): 80–102.

Leopold, Aldo. "Why the Wilderness Society?" *Living Wilderness* 1 (September 1935): 6.

Leopold, A. Starker. "Wilderness and Culture." In *Fifth Biennial Wilderness Conference: Summary of Proceedings,* ed. George Marshall, 6–7. San Francisco, 15–16 March 1957.

MacKaye, Benton. "Dam Site vs. Norm Site." *Scientific Monthly* (October 1950): 241–47.

Madison, Mark. "Olaus Murie: A Naturalist's Life." In *Proceedings of the 2000 Symposium,* Murie Center, Moose, WY, 20–23 July 2000, 41–44.

Marshall, Robert. "Fallacies in Osborne's Position." *Living Wilderness* 1 (September 1935): 4–6.

———. "The Problem of the Wilderness." *Scientific Monthly* 2 (February 1930): 31–35.

Martin, J., and C. Carlson. "Spiritual Dimensions of Health Psychology." In *Behavior Therapy and Religion: Integrating Spiritual and Behavioral Approaches to Change*, ed. W. R. Miller and J. E. Martin. Newbury Park, CA: Sage, 1988.

Mason, R. "First Ascents in the Romanzof Mountains, Eastern Brooks Range." *American Alpine Journal* 3 (1959): 295–96.

McCloskey, Michael. "Evolving Perspectives on Wilderness Values: Putting Wilderness Values in Order." In *Preparing to Manage Wilderness in the 21st Century: Proceedings of the Conference*. General Technical Report SE-66. Asheville, NC: USDA Forest Service, 1990, 13–18.

McCloskey, Michael. "The Wilderness Act of 1964: Its Background and Meaning." *Oregon Law Review* 45 (June 1966): 288–321.

McDonald, Barbara, Richard Guldin, and G. Richard Wetherhill. "The Spirit in the Wilderness: The Use and Opportunity of Wilderness Experience for Spiritual Growth." In *Wilderness Benchmark 1988: Proceedings of the National Wilderness Colloquium Held in Tampa, Florida, January 13–14, 1988*. Asheville, NC: U.S. Southeastern Forest Experiment Station, 193–207.

Meyers, Larry. "He Wrestled a Wolf." *Alaska Sportsman* 6 (June 1952): 14–17, 40–45.

Murie, Margaret E. "A Live River in the Arctic." *Living Wilderness* 61 (Summer–Fall 1957): 7–13.

———. "Return to the Sheenjek." *Living Wilderness* 138 (July–September 1977): 4–12.

———. "Summer on the Sheenjek." *Defenders of Wildlife* 5 (September–October 1987): 34–38.

———. "A Week on Lobo." *Animal Kingdom* 1 (January–February 1957): 18–23.

———. "We Explore the Sheenjek." *Alaska Sportsman* 25(7) (February 1960): 40–46.

Murie, Olaus J. "Aircraft and Wilderness." *Living Wilderness* 12 (Autumn 1947): 2–6.

———. "Alaska." *Living Wilderness* (February 1945): 3–8.

———. "Alaska with O. J. Murie." *Living Wilderness* 58 (Winter 1956–57): 28–30.

———. "Alaskan Summer on the Sheenjek River" (undated report). MMP, Box 2, Folder 18.

———. "Arctic Wilderness." *Outdoor America* (January 1958): 10–11.

———. "Boyhood Wilderness." *Living Wilderness* (March 1942): 30–31.

———. "Brief Account of a journey to Alaska by Olaus J. Murie and Margaret E. Murie, in the interest of furthering designation of an Arctic Wildlife Range in the Brooks Range of Alaska—the trip being financed by the Conservation Foundation." 15 June 1957. MMP, Box 2, Folder 18.

———. "A Brief Report on the 1956 Brooks Range Expedition" (undated report). OMP, Box 8.

———. "Campfire Lecture on Meanings." *Living Wilderness* 47 (Winter 1953–54): 26–27.

———. "Ethics and Predators." *Living Wilderness* 50 (Autumn 1954): 19–20.

———. "Ethics in Wildlife Management." *Journal of Wildlife Management* 3 (July 1954): 289–93.

———. "The Grizzly Bear and the Wilderness." *Animal Kingdom* 3 (May–June 1957): 68–73.

———. "Nature in the Arctic." *National Parks* 132 (January–March 1958): 28–31.

———. "Once Again ... A Warning." *Living Wilderness* 23 (Winter 1947–48): 18–19.

———. "Plan for Exploration of the South Slope of the Brooks Range" (undated report). MMP, Box 2, Folder 18.

———. "Prey of Poison." *Outdoor America* (February 1959): 8–9.

———. "Seton's Influence Renewed." *Living Wilderness* 50 (Autumn 1954): 22–23.

———. "Shall We Destroy or Enjoy?" *Living Wilderness* 71 (Winter 1959–60): 1–5.

———. "What Does Wilderness Mean to Us?" *Living Wilderness* 68 (Spring 1959): 16–20.

———. "Wild Country as a National Asset." *Living Wilderness* 45 (Summer 1953): 1–12.

———. "Wilderness Conference on Yellowstone Lake." *Living Wilderness* 77 (Summer–Fall 1961): 14–18.

———. "Wilderness Philosophy, Science, and the Arctic National Wildlife Range." In *Science in Alaska*, ed. George Dahlgren Jr., 58–69. College, AK: Alaska Division of the American Association for the Advancement of Science, 1961.

———. "Wolf." *Audubon* (September–October 1957): 218–21.

Nash, Roderick. "Tourism, Parks, and the Wilderness Idea in the History of Alaska." *Alaska in Perspective* 4, 1. Anchorage: Alaska Historical Commission and the Alaska Historical Society, 1981.

Naske, Claus-M. "The Arctic National Wildlife Range." In *National Wildlife Refuges of Alaska: A Historical Perspective*, by David L. Spencer, Claus-M. Naske, and John Carnahan, 97–116. Anchorage: U.S. Fish and Wildlife Service and the Arctic Environmental Information and Data Center, 1979.

Nelson, Michael P. "An Amalgamation of Wilderness Preservation Arguments." In *The Great New Wilderness Debate*, ed. J. Baird Callicott and Michael P. Nelson, 154–200. Athens: University of Georgia Press, 1998.

Nelson, Urban C., and David L. Spencer. "The Bureau of Sport Fisheries and Wildlife's Position on the Arctic National Wildlife Range." In *Science in Alaska*, ed. George Dahlgren Jr., 69–76. College, AK: Alaska Division of the American Association for the Advancement of Science, 1961.

Olson, Sigurd. "The Spiritual Aspects of Wilderness." In *Voices for the Wilderness*, ed. William Schwartz. New York: Ballantine Books, 1969.

———. "The Spiritual Need." In *Wilderness in a Changing World*, ed. Bruce M. Kilgore. San Francisco: Sierra Club, 1966, 215.

Pruitt, William O., Jr. "Animal Ecology and the Arctic National Wildlife Range." In *Science in Alaska*, ed. George Dahlgren Jr., 44–51. College, AK: Alaska Division of the American Association for the Advancement of Science, 1961.

Rearden, Jim. "Clarence Rhode." *Alaska Magazine* (January 1980): 11–54.

Richie, Robert J., and Robert A. Childers. "Recreation, Aesthetics and Use of the Arctic National Wildlife Range and Adjacent Areas, Northeast Alaska." Unpublished preliminary report, November 1976, 240 pp. ANWR Files.

Schaller, George B. "Arctic Legacy." In *Seasons of Life and Land*, ed. Subhankar Banerjee, 62–69. Seattle: Mountaineers Books, 2003.

———. *Arctic Valley: A Report on the 1956 Murie Brooks Range, Alaska Expedition.* 1957, APR.

———. "New Area for Hunters." *Outdoor Life* (March 1958): 33–37.

Scott, Douglas W. "Untrammeled," "Wilderness Character." *Wild Earth* (Fall–Winter 2001–2002): 72–79.

Seaton, Fred A. "America's Largest Wildlife Area." *National Parks* (July–September 1958): 117–44.

Sumner, Lowell. "Alaska's Biological Wealth: Why Let History Repeat Itself?" In *Science in Alaska, 1951, Proceedings: Second Alaskan Science Conference,* 337–39, Alaska Division of the American Association for the Advancement of Science, 1951.

———. "A Letter from the Arctic." *Sierra Club Bulletin* 38 (October 1953): 27–35.

———. "Arctic National Wildlife Refuge Address, 25th Anniversary." 30 November 1985. RKP.

———. "Biological Research and Management in the National Park Service: A History." *George Wright Forum* 3, 4 (Autumn 1983): 3–25.

———. "The Pressures of Civilization." In *Fifth Biennial Wilderness Conference: Summary of Proceedings.* San Francisco, March 15–16, 1957, ed. George Marshall, 5–6.

———. "Wildlife Management." Paper presented at the National Park Service Conference, Yosemite National Park, 18 October 1950, Records of the National Park Service, National Archives, Entry 19, Record Group 79.

———. "Your Stake in Alaska's Wildlife and Wilderness." *Sierra Club Bulletin* 41 (December 1956): 63–68.

Sumner, Lowell, and George L. Collins, "Arctic Wilderness." *Living Wilderness* 47 (Winter 1953–54): 4–15.

Sumner, Lowell, and Richard M. Leonard. "Protecting Mountain Meadows." *Sierra Club Bulletin* (May 1947): 53–62.

Sumner, Marietta, George L. Collins, George Sprugel, O. L. Wallis, and Robert M. Linn. "Remembering Lowell Sumner." *George Wright Forum* 6 (4) (1990): 36–38.

Tall, Benita. "Our Last Wilderness." *Science News Letter* 76 (5 September 1959): 154.

"That 9,000,000-Acre Withdrawal." *TDM Bulletin* (Alaska Territorial Division of Mines) 6 (3) (March 1958).

Thomson, John P. "Arctic Adventure." *Alaska Conservation Society News Bulletin* 3 (August 1960): 4–5.

———. "Ascent of Mount Michelson." *Appalachia* (December 1957): 508–10.

Turner, Frederick Jackson. "The Significance of the Frontier in American History." In *Frontier and Section: Selected Essays of Frederick Jackson Turner,* ed. Ray Billington. Englewood Cliffs, NJ: Prentice Hall, 1961.

"The Types of Wilderness Recognized." *Living Wilderness* 1 (September 1935): 2.

Williams, Terry Tempest. "Wild Mercy." In *Seasons of Life and Land,* ed. Subhankar Banerjee. Seattle: Mountaineers Books, 2003, 171.

Wuerthner, George. "Hiking and Floating the Arctic National Wildlife Refuge Offers a Sanctuary for the Spirit." *Trilogy* 4(5) (September–October 1992): 13–22.

Zahniser, Howard. "The Need for Wilderness Areas." *Living Wilderness* no. 59 (Winter–Spring 1956–57): 37–43.

Books

Anderson, J. R. L. *The Ulysses Factor: The Exploring Instinct in Man.* New York: Harcourt Brace Jovanovich, 1980.

Backes, David. *A Wilderness Within: The Life of Sigurd F. Olson.* Minneapolis: University of Minnesota Press, 1997.

Banerjee, Subhankar. *Seasons of Life and Land.* Seattle: Mountaineers Books, 2003.

Brower, David R. *For Earth's Sake: The Life and Times of David Brower.* Salt Lake City: Gibbs-Smith, 1990.

Brown, William E. *Denali: Symbol of the Alaskan Wild: An Illustrated History of the Denali–Mount McKinley Region, Alaska.* Virginia Beach, VA: Donning, 1993.

Callicott, J. Baird. *In Defense of the Land Ethic: Essays in Environmental Philosophy.* New York: State University of New York Press, 1989.

Coates, Peter A. *The Trans-Alaska Pipeline Controversy.* Fairbanks: University of Alaska Press, 1993.

Cohen, Michael P. *The History of the Sierra Club, 1892–1970.* San Francisco: Sierra Club Books, 1988.

Collins, George L. *The Art and Politics of Park Planning and Preservation, 1920–1979.* Berkeley: University of California Press, 1980.

Crisler, Lois. *Arctic Wild.* New York: Harper & Row, 1958.

Csikszentmihalyi, Mihaly. *Flow: The Psychology of Optimal Experience.* New York: Harper & Row, 1990.

Darling, F. Fraser. *Pelican in the Wilderness: A Naturalist's Odyssey in North America.* London: George Allen & Unwin, 1956.

Douglas, Marjory Stoneman. *The Everglades: River of Grass.* New York: Rinehart, 1947.

Douglas, William O. *My Wilderness: East to Katahdin.* Garden City, NY: Doubleday, 1961.

———. *My Wilderness: The Pacific West.* Garden City, NY: Doubleday & Company, 1960.

———. *Of Men and Mountains.* San Francisco: Chronicle Books Edition, 1990.

———. *A Wilderness Bill of Rights.* Boston: Little, Brown and Company, 1965.

Dufresne, Frank. *Alaska's Animals and Fishes.* New York: A. S. Barnes, 1946.

Dunlap, Thomas R. *Saving America's Wildlife.* Princeton, NJ: Princeton University Press, 1988.

Emmons, Robert A. *The Psychology of Ultimate Concerns: Motivation and Spirituality in Personality.* New York: Guilford Press, 1999.

Fischer, Victor. *Alaska's Constitutional Convention.* Fairbanks: University of Alaska Press, 1975.

Flader, Susan. *Thinking Like a Mountain: Aldo Leopold and the Evolution of an Ecological Attitude Toward Deer, Wolves, and Forests.* Columbia: University of Missouri Press, 1974.

Fowler, Harry. *Curiosity and Exploratory Behavior.* New York: Macmillan, 1965.

Fox, Stephen. *The American Conservation Movement.* Madison: University of Wisconsin Press, 1981.

Glacken, Clarence J. *Traces on the Rhodian Shore.* Berkeley: University of California Press, 1973.

Glover, James M. *A Wilderness Original: The Life of Bob Marshall.* Seattle: Mountaineers Books, 1986.

Gottlieb, Robert. *Forcing the Spring: The Transformation of the American Environmental Movement.* Washington, DC: Island Press, 1993.

Harvey, Mark W. T. *A Symbol of Wilderness: Echo Park and the American Conservation Movement.* Seattle: University of Washington Press, 1994.

Haycox, Stephen W., and Mary Childers Mangusso. *An Alaskan Anthology: Interpreting the Past.* Seattle: University of Washington Press, 1996.

Hayes, Samuel P. *Beauty, Health, and Permanence.* Cambridge: Press Syndicate of the University of Cambridge, 1987.

————. *A History of Environmental Politics Since 1945*. Pittsburgh: University of Pittsburgh Press, 2000.

Hendee, John C., George H. Stankey, and Robert C. Lucas. *Wilderness Management*, 2d ed. Golden, CO: North American Press, 1990.

Kauffmann, John M. *Alaska's Brooks Range: The Ultimate Mountains*. Seattle: Mountaineers Books, 1992.

Leopold, Aldo. *A Sand County Almanac with Essays on Conservation from Round River*. New York: Ballantine Books, 1966.

Leopold, A. Starker, and F. Fraser Darling. *Wildlife in Alaska: An Ecological Reconnaissance*. New York: Ronald Press Company, 1953.

Lentfer, Hank, and Carolyn Servid, comps. *Arctic Refuge: Circle of Testimony*. Minneapolis: Milkweed Editions, 2001.

Marshall, Robert. *Arctic Village*. New York: Quinn & Boden Co., 1933.

————. *Arctic Wilderness*. Berkeley: University of California Press, 1956.

McCloskey, Maxine E., ed. *Wilderness: The Edge of Knowledge*. San Francisco: Sierra Club Books, 1970.

McIntosh, Robert P. *The Background of Ecology: Concepts and Theory*. Cambridge: Cambridge University Press, 1985.

Meine, Curt. *Aldo Leopold: His Life and Work*. Madison: University of Wisconsin Press, 1974.

Miller, Debbie. *Midnight Wilderness*. San Francisco: Sierra Club Books, 1990.

Milton, John. *Nameless Valleys, Shining Mountains*. New York: Walker and Co., 1969.

Muir, John. *A Thousand-Mile Walk to the Gulf*. Boston: Houghton Mifflin, 1916.

Murie, Adolph. *A Naturalist in Alaska*. New York: Devin-Adair, 1961.

Murie, Margaret E. *Two in the Far North*, 3d ed. Anchorage: Alaska Northwest Publishing, 1979.

Murie, Olaus J. *The Elk of North America*, 2d ed. Jackson, WY: Teton Bookshop, 1979.

————. *A Field Guide to Animal Tracks*. Boston: Houghton Mifflin, 1954.

————. *Journeys to the Far North*. Palo Alto, CA: The Wilderness Society and American West Publishers, 1973.

Murphy, Bruce Allen. *Wild Bill: The Legend and Life of William O. Douglas*. New York: Random House, 2003.

Nash, Roderick. *Wilderness and the American Mind*, 3d ed. New Haven: Yale University Press, 1982.

Naske, Claus-M. Bob Bartlett of Alaska: A Life in Politics. Fairbanks: University of Alaska Press, 1979.

————. *An Interpretive History of Alaska Statehood*. Anchorage: Alaska Northwest Publishing Company, 1973.

Nelson, Daniel. *Northern Landscapes: The Struggle for Wilderness Alaska*. Washington, DC: Resources for the Future, 2004.

Neuman, W. Lawrence. *Social Research Methods: Qualitative and Quantitative Approaches*. Needham Heights, MA: Allyn & Bacon, 1997.

Oelschlaeger, Max. *The Idea of Wilderness*. New Haven, CT: Yale University Press, 1991.

Olson, Sigurd. *The Singing Wilderness*. New York: Knopf, 1956.

Osborn, Fairfield. *Our Plundered Planet.* Boston: Little, Brown and Company, 1948.

Philippon, Daniel. *Conserving Words: How American Nature Writers Shaped the Environmental Movement.* Athens, GA: University of Georgia Press, 2004.

Rawson, Timothy. *Changing Tracks: Predators and Politics in Mt. McKinley National Park.* Fairbanks: University of Alaska Press, 2001.

Rearden, Jim. *Alaska's Wolf Man.* Missoula, MT: Pictorial Histories Publishing, 1998.

Runte, Alfred. *National Parks: The American Experience.* Lincoln: University of Nebraska Press, 1979.

Schullery, Paul, and Lee Whittlesey. *Myth and History in the Creation of Yellowstone National Park.* Lincoln: University of Nebraska Press, 2003.

Sellars, Richard West. *Preserving Nature in the National Parks: A History.* New Haven: Yale University Press, 1997.

Seton, Ernest Thompson. *The Arctic Prairies.* London: Constable, 1911.

———. *Boy Scouts of America: A Handbook of Woodcraft, Scouting, and Lifecraft.* New York, 1910.

———. *Wild Animals I Have Known.* New York: Charles Scribner's Sons, 1902.

Shepard, Paul. *Coming Home to the Pleistocene.* Washington, DC: Island Press/ Shearwater Books, 1998.

Storer, John H. *The Web of Life.* New York: Devin-Adair, 1953.

Tremblay, Ray. *On Patrol: True Stories of an Alaskan Game Warden.* Anchorage: Alaska Northwest Books, 2004.

Vogt, William. *The Road to Survival.* London: Victor Gollancz, 1947.

Wilson, E. O. *Biophilia.* Cambridge: Harvard University Press, 1984.

Wirth, Conrad L. *Parks, Politics, and the People.* Norman: University of Oklahoma Press, 1980.

Wolf, Linnie Marsh. *Son of the Wilderness: The Life of John Muir.* New York: Alfred A. Knopf, 1951.

Worster, Donald. *Nature's Economy.* San Francisco: Sierra Club Books, 1977.

Government Publications

U.S. Department of Interior

"Arctic National Wildlife Range, Alaska: Wilderness Study Report." 1973. ANWR Files.

"ANWR Ecological Inventory and Monitoring Plan." October 2000. ANWR Files.

Carnes, W., ed. *A Preliminary Geographical Survey of the Kongakut–Firth River area, Alaska-Canada.* Washington, DC: U.S. Government Printing Office, National Park Service, 1954.

Collins, George L., and Lowell Sumner. "Arctic Research Laboratory, Progress Report, July 22–Aug. 8, 1952, Biological Survey of the Mount Michelson–Kongakut River Area—the National Park Service." George L. Collins Papers, APR.

———. "A Proposed Arctic Wilderness International Park: A Preliminary Report Concerning Its Values." Alaska Recreation Survey, Preliminary Statement, Nov. 1952. Arctic Wilderness International Park, U.S. Department of the Interior, National Park Service, Region Four.

Murie, Olaus J. "Alaska-Yukon Caribou." *North American Fauna* no. 54. Washington, DC: Bureau of Biological Survey, 1935.

"A Recreation Program for Alaska." Washington, DC: National Park Service, Alaska Recreation Survey, 1955.

Rhode, Clarence J., and Will Barker. "Alaska's Fish and Wildlife." Washington, DC: Government Printing Office, 1953.

Sumner, Lowell. "Special report on a wildlife study of the High Sierra in Sequoia and Yosemite National Parks and adjacent territory." Inservice Report. Washington, DC: National Park Service Archives, 1936.

U.S. Congress, Senate

Committee on Interstate and Foreign Commerce, Subcommittee on Merchant Marine and Fisheries, Hearings, S. 1899, *A Bill to Authorize the Establishment of the Arctic Wildlife Range, Alaska, and for other purposes.* 86th Congress, 1st session. Records of the U.S. Senate. Washington, DC: Government Printing Office, 1960.

U.S. Congress, House of Representatives

Committee on Merchant Marine and Fisheries, Subcommittee on Fisheries and Wildlife Conservation, Hearings, H.R. 7045, *A Bill to Authorize the Establishment of the Arctic Wildlife Range, Alaska, and for other purposes.* July 1, 1959. 86th Congress, 1st session, Records of the U.S. House of Representatives. Washington, DC: Government Printing Office, 1959.

"Alaska: Its Resources and Development," Appendix B, National Resources Committee, House Document no. 485, 75th Congress, 3rd session. Washington, DC: Government Printing Office, 1938.

Hackett, William H. "Alaska's Vanishing Frontier: A Progress Report." House Subcommittee on Territories and Insular Possessions. Washington, DC: Government Printing Office, 1951.

House Committee on Public Lands, *Statehood for Alaska*, 80th Congress, 1st session, April 1947.

Dissertations

Sutter, Paul S. "Driven Wild: The Intellectual and Cultural Origins of Wilderness Advocacy During the Interwar Years." Ph.D. diss., University of Kansas, 1987.

Watt, Richard Darrell. "The Recreational Potential of the Arctic National Wildlife Range." M.S. thesis, University of Alaska Fairbanks, 1966.

Films

White Wilderness. Herb and Lois Crisler, co-producers. Walt Disney Films, distributed by Buena Vista Film Distribution, 1958.

Arctic Wildlife Range. Filmed by Robert Krear and produced by Thorne Films, Boulder, Colorado, 1959.

Letter from the Brooks Range. Filmed by Robert Krear and produced by the Conservation Foundation, New York, 1959.

Taped and Transcribed Interviews

Archives, Alaska and Polar Regions Department, University of Alaska Fairbanks

Stewart Brandborg interview with author, 13 March 2003

Chuck Clusen interview with author, 27 July 2004

George L. Collins interview with author, 28 March 1993

Joshua Collins interview with author, 11 December 2002

Mercedes Eicholz interview with author, 15 June 2004
Charles Gray interview with author, 30 October 2003
Keith Herrington interview with author, 17 November 2004
Anore Jones interview with author, 16 December 2002
Brina Kessel interview with author, 22 January 2003
Jim King interview with author, 24 November 2003
David Klein interview with author, 12 December 2002
Robert Krear interview with author, 22 January 2003
Donald Murie interview with author, 14 January 2003
Martin Murie interview with author, 16 December 2002
William Pruitt interview with author, 20 May 2003
Wenzel Raith interview with author, 10 October 2004
George B. Schaller interview with author, 11 December 2002
Averill Thayer interview with author, 21 November 2003
Virginia Wood interview with author, 10 November 2002

Archival Collections

Alaska State Archives, Juneau, AK

Arctic National Wildlife Refuge Files, U.S. Fish and Wildlife Service, Fairbanks, AK

Archives, Alaska and Polar Regions Department, University of Alaska Fairbanks
Alaska Conservation Society Papers
E. L. Bartlett Papers
George L. Collins Papers
Ernest Gruening Papers
Margaret Murie Papers
Olaus Murie Papers
Ralph J. Rivers Papers

Conservation Manuscripts Collection, Denver Public Library, Denver, CO
Papers of Olaus Murie

Minnesota Historical Society, St. Paul, MN
Sigurd F. Olson Papers

The Murie Center, Moose, WY

National Archives, Washington, DC
Records of the U.S. Fish and Wildlife Service
Records of the National Park Service

Index